The Wesley Breviary

John Wesley

ISBN: 9798570591738

Contents

Introduction

In 1750 John Wesley (1703-1791) published a 50-volume collection of "extracts from and abridgments of the choicest pieces of practical divinity which have been published in the English tongue," as he phrased it, in the collection's subtitle. In 1821 this collection was reprinted in 30 volumes. In this substantial collection, Wesley included a version of the Daily Office, he entitled *Devotions for Every Day in the Week, and the Great Festivals*.

The Daily Office[1] has its origins in the Apostolic tradition of praying the Lord's Prayer three times a day.[2] Over the centuries this practice developed into the Liturgy of the Hours, another name for the Daily Office. The office was prayed by English Catholics prior to the Reformation. After the Reformation, the canonical hours of prayer were retained by the Church of England. John Wesley, being an Anglican priest, was well acquainted with the tradition of praying the hours.

This version of the Daily Office can be traced back to English lawyer and Roman Catholic, John Austin (1613-1669). The original title was, *Devotions, First Part: In the Ancient Way of Offices, With Psalms, Hymns, and Prayers for every Day in the Week, and every*

---

[1] The terms Daily Office refers to the prayer tradition itself. A breviary is a book containing the canonical hours. Breviary is derived from the Latin *breviarium* ("abridgement").

[2] *Didache,* Chapter 8

Holiday in the Year. Austin published the work under the pseudonym William Barclay. Unfortunately, the original publishing date has been lost to history. In 1701, English divine George Hickes (1642-1715) published a reformed edition for Anglican use. Wesley based his own edited and abridged version on Hickes 'edition.

The ancient Christian maxim *lex orandi, lex credendi* (Latin: "the law of prayer is the law of belief.") expresses the great truth that one's prayer life is inseparable from one's theological beliefs. A tendency to dichotomize theological study and worship exists within segments of Christianity. The Liturgy of the Hours is not only theologically substantive, but it is intimately connected with the devotional treasures of the ancient Church. As Wesley said, "This book is not fitted for devotion only, but instruction also." Moreover, praying the Daily Office allows the Christian to sanctify every part of the day with prayer and God's Word.

H. J. Volk, Editor

To the Reader.

This excellent book is not fitted for devotion only, but instruction also; so as to contain in it, together with the devotional part, a complete system of the Christian doctrine, by entertaining the mind with proper considerations upon the being, nature and attributes of God; upon the mysterious economy of the ever blessed Trinity, for our creation, redemption, and sanctification; upon the original of evil, and the conduct of divine justice and mercy hereupon, in exactest harmony; upon the two covenants, and the laws and rules of each; upon the universal providence of GOD, and the various periods and revolutions belonging to it; upon the" incarnation of the SON of GOD, for the recovery of lost man, and the wonderful love of the FATHER in giving this his only SON to be a propitiation for the sins of the world; upon his holy nativity and circumcision, his subjection to the Law, and most perfect obedience, his baptism and solemn inauguration, his fasting and temptation, his agony and bloody sweat, his cross and passion, his precious death and burial, his glorious resurrection, and triumphant ascension, and his most meritorious intercession; upon his sending another Comforter, to represent him, and leaving a pledge for his coming again in his own person at the last day, to subdue all things under his feet; upon the revelation of his Majesty and power in his miraculous triumphs over the spirits of darkness, and his constituting a spiritual kingdom on the earth, with proper officers and Ministers under him; upon the divinity of the HOLY SPIRIT, and unity both with the FATHER and the Soar; upon his manifold operations, gifts, and graces, and his government both of particular souls, and of the Church in general; upon the nature, causes, effects and signs of true repentance and conversion; upon the moral and eternal law, and the commandments given to ADAM, NOAH, ABRAHAM and MOSES; upon the Christian graces of faith, hope, and charity; upon the sacraments and other holy institutions of the New Testament; upon the ministration, under CHRIST, of angels and blessed spirits, and their attendance about our altars, and joining with our prayers and praises offered unto GOD; upon the immortality and intermediate state of all' souls, and the many mansions for the better sort of God's house, according to their degrees of sanctification here; upon the constitution of the Church on the foundation of the Apostles, CHRIST himself being the head cornerstone, and the HOLY GHOST the life thereof; upon the communion of saints, and the blessed fellowship of all the faithful of every degree both in heaven and earth, by a participation of the same life and spirit; upon the resurrection and judgment, and wonderful scenes that then shall be opened to all the world; and, Lastly, Upon the final destruction of all the wicked, and the glories and triumphs of the saints, when at the second coming of our LORD they shall receive their perfect consummation in bliss never to have end,

- John Wesley

-

The Office for Sunday.

Morning Prayer.

PREVENT, we beseech thee, O LORD, all our doings with thy most gracious inspirations, and further them with thy continual help, that every prayer and work of ours may begin always from thee, and by thee be happily ended, and more especially the service we are now entering upon, through JESUS CHRIST our LORD. Amen.

OUR FATHER, which art in heaven, hallowed be thy name. Thy kingdom come. Thy will be done in earth, as it is in heaven. Give us this day our daily bread. And forgive us our trespasses, as we forgive them that trespass against us. And lead us not into temptation: But deliver us from evil. For thine is the kingdom, the power, and the glory, for ever and ever. Amen.

PSALM 1.

BEHOLD the angels assembled in their choirs, and the blessed saints ready with their hymns; behold the church prepares her solemn offices, and summons all her children to bring in their praises.

Come, let us adore our gloried JESUS.

The King of heaven himself invites us, and graciously calls us into his own presence; he bids us suspend our mean employments in the world, to receive the honor of treating with him.

Come, let us adore our glorified JESUS.

To him we owe all the days of our lives; at least let us pay this one to his service; a service so sweet and easy in itself, and so infinitely rich in its eternal rewards.

Come, let us adore our glorified JESUS.

Let us cheerfully ascend to the house of our LORD, the place he has chosen for our sakes to dwell in: Let us reverently bow before his holy altar, where himself comes to meet us and our prayers.

Come, let us adore our glorified JESUS.

GLORY BE to the Father, and to the Son, and to the Holy Ghost. As it was in the beginning, is now, and ever shall be: world without end.

Amen.

HYMN 1

Behold we come, dear LORD, to thee,
And bow before thy throne: We come to offer on our knee,
Our vows to thee alone.
Whatever we have, whatever we are,
Thy bounty freely gave:
You dost us here in mercy spare,
And wilt hereafter save.
But, O! can all our store afford
No better gifts for thee
Thus we confess thy riches, LORD,
And thus our poverty.
'Tis not our tongue or knee can pay
The mighty debt we owe;
Far more we should than we can say,
Far lower should we bow.
Come then, my soul, bring all thy powers,
And grieve you have no more; Bring every day thy choicest hours,
And thy great GOD adore.

But, above all, prepare thy heart
On this his own blest day,
In its sweet task to bear thy part,
And sing, and love, and pray.
Glory to the eternal LORD,
Thrice blessed Three in One!
Thy name at all times be ador'd,
Till time itself be done! Amen!
"This is the day which the LORD has made; let us be
glad and rejoice therein." Hallelujah.

PSALM 2

WELCOME, blessed day, wherein the Sun of Righteousness arose, and chased away the clouds of fear.

Welcome, you birthday of our hopes, a day of joy, and public refreshment.

A day of holiness and solemn devotion; a day of rest and universal jubilee.

Welcome to us, and our dark world; and may thy radiant name shine bright for ever.

May all the earth be enlightened with thy beams, and every frozen heart dissolve and sing!

This is the day which our LORD has made; let us be glad and rejoice therein.

This is the day he has sanctified to himself, and called by his own most holy name:

That in it we may meet to "adore his greatness, and admire the wonders of his infinite power:

That we may remember his innumerable mercies, and deeply imprint them in our hearts:

That we may visit his holy temple, and humbly present our homage at his altar:

That sacred altar, where the sacrifice of the LAMB of GOD is shown forth, and the memory of our Savior's love continually renewed.

Worthy, O LORD, art you of all our time, worthy the praises of all thy creatures.

Every moment of our life is bound to bless thee, since every moment subsists by thy goodness.

Shall others labor so much for vanity, and shall we not rest for the service of our GOD

Shall we employ the whole week on ourselves, and not offer in gratitude one day unto thee

To thee, who bestowest on us all we have, and wilt give us hereafter more than we can hope.

O gracious LORD, whose mercy accepts such slender payment, as our poverty affords,

Whose bounty grants so liberally to us, and retains so small a part for thyself:

O make us faithfully observe our duty, and render so exactly the tribute we owe to thee,

That passing still thy days to thy honor, we may end our own in thy favor.

GLORY BE to the Father, and to the Son, and to the Holy Ghost. As it was in the beginning, is now, and ever shall be: world without end.

Amen.

Antiphon

"You have created all things, O LORD, for the use of man, and man for the enjoyment of thyself."

PSALM 3.

WHEN the harvest sun provides a cloud, and seems to rest his wearied beams;

He seeks not to save the journey of his light, but only spares the reaper's head.

Much leas seekest You, O LORD, who madest the sun the shadow of thy glory, and inspiredst all creatures to represent thy bounty;

Much less seekest You, by the reserve of a day, to procure thine own repose.

You, who createdst all things by a word of thy mouth, and sustainest them in thy hand;

Who governest the whole world without perplexing thy thoughts, and always remainest the same unchangeable fullness:

It is not to increase thine own eternity, that thus you takest a portion of our time.

Thy goodness friendly bears the name, but intends for us all the profit of the day:

That the wearied hands may be relieved with rest, and enabled to lift up themselves to thee:

That the guilty consciences may accuse their crimes on earth, to be pardoned in heaven:

That the love prepared souls may approach thy table,

and feast their hopes with that delicious banquet.

That all may speak to thee by prayer, and hear thy voice

by the mouth of their pastors:

O blessed LORD, what excellent arts has thy wisdom invented to bring us to thyself!

You takest our eyes by the beauty of thy house, and of thy solemn offices.

You quickenest our affections by our mutual devotions, and meltest our hearts with the sweetness of thy music.

You strengthenest our faith by thy public assemblies, and improvest our love both to thee, and one another.

Whilst we all meet for the same blessed end, and by mutual reflections increase out fervors:

Happy, thrice happy they, O merciful GOD, whom thy providence has favored with all these blessings.

But where you art pleased to deny these mercies, refuse not, O LORD, to extend a measure of thy grace:

And to all that live in such spiritual destitutions, grant extraordinary supplies from thy self;

That at least they may build a little chapel in their hearts, and consecrate themselves entirely unto thee.

Grant that the more they want of other helps, they may find the greater assistances from thee:

Make them sensible of the blessed opportunities they have had, and now want, to wait upon thee.

Forgive them the neglect, and ill improvement they have made of them, and wherever they meet in thy name, be you in the midst of them.

No farther motives shall they need to draw them, nor other temple to address their prayers.

Since every place, where you art not graciously present, is unholy; but where you art, is joy and peace.

GLORY BE to the Father, and to the Son, and to the Holy Ghost. As it was in the beginning, is now, and ever shall be: world without end.

Amen.

Antiphon

"You have created all things, O LORD, for the use of man, and man for the enjoyment of thyself."

PSALM 4.

COME, let us lay aside the cares of this world, and take into our minds the joys of heaven.

Let us empty our heads of all other thoughts, and prepare that room to entertain our GOD.

Retiring from the many distractions of this life, and closely recollecting all the forces of our souls,

So to pursue in earnest that one necessary work, the securing to ourselves the kingdom of heaven.

Why should we thus neglect that sacred science, and be busy in every thing but our own salvation

Why should we forsake the real substance, to embrace an empty fancy

Miserable are they, O LORD, who study all things else, and never seek to taste thy sweetness.

Miserable, though their skill can number the stars, and trace out the ways of the planets.

To know thee, O LORD, is to be truly wise, and to contemplate thee, the highest learning.

But, O you glorious GOD of truth, in whom the treasures of knowledge are all laid up!

Unless you draw the curtain from before our eyes, and drive away the clouds that intercept our sight,

Never shall we see those heavenly mysteries, nor ever discern the beauty of thy providence.

Send forth thy light, O you Morning Star! and lead us to thy holy hill.

Send forth thy truth, O untreated Wisdom! and bring us to thy blessed tabernacle.

Show us thyself, O glorious JESUS! and in thee we shall behold all that we can wish.

Only so much we beg to conceive of thy majesty, as may move our hearts to seek thee.

Only so much of thy unapproachable Deity, as may guide our souls to find thee.

So let us know and love thee here, O you sovereign bliss of our souls!

That hereafter we may know thee better, and love and enjoy thee for ever.

GLORY BE to the Father, and to the Son, and to the Holy Ghost. As it was in the beginning, is now, and ever shall be: world without end.

Amen.

Hallelujah.

O glorious JESUS, in whom we live, and without whom we die, mortify in us all sensual desires, and quicken our hearts with thy holy love; that we may no longer esteem the vanities of the world, but place our affections entirely on thee; who didst die for our sins, and rise again for our justification. O you our only hope and portion in the land of the living, may our thoughts and discourses still be of thee, our works and sufferings all for thee; who didst die for our sins, and rise again for our justification.

At Noon.

Antiphon

O how adorable are thy counsels, O Lone! How strangely endearing the ways of thy love!

PSALM 5.

SING unto our LORD a psalm of joy; sing praises to the GOD of our salvation.

Sing with a loud and cheerful voice; sing with a glad and thankful heart.

Say to the weak of spirit, Be strong; and unto the sorrowful, Be of good comfort.

Tell all the world this soul reviving truth, and may their hearts within them leap to hear it:

Tell them, the LORD of life is risen again, and has clothed himself with immortal glory.

He made the angels messengers of his victory, and vouchsafed himself to bring us the joyful news.

How many ways did thy mercy invent, O you wise Contriver of all our happiness!

To convince thy followers into this blessed belief, and settle in their hearts a firm ground of hope.

You appearedst to holy women in their return from the sepulchre, and openedst their eyes to know and adore thee:

You overtookedst in the way the two that discoursed of thee, and made their hearts burn within them to hear thee.

You showedst thyself on the shore to thy weary disciples laboring at sea.

Laboring all night, alas! in vain, without the blessing of their beloved JESUS;

You showedst thyself, and toldest them who you wert, in the kind known token of a beneficial miracle.

Through the doors, though shut, you swiftly passedst, to carry peace to thy comfortless friends;

To encourage their fears with thy powerful presence, and secure their faith by thy arguments.

How didst you condescend to eat before them, and invite them to touch thy sacred body!

How didst you sweetly provoke that incredulous servant to thrust his hand into thy wounded side!

How often, O my gracious LORD, in those blessed forty days, did thy love cast about to meet with thy disciples! That you might teach them still some excellent

truth, and imprint still deeper thy love in their hearts. Discoursing perpetually of the kingdom of heaven, and establishing means to bring us thither.

At last, when all thy glorious task was done, and thy parting hour from this earth approached,

You tenderly gatheredst thy children about thee, and, in their full sight, wentest up to heaven;

Leaving thy dearest blessing on their heads, and promising them a Comforter to supply thy absence.

O how adorable are thy counsels, O LORD! How strangely endearing are the ways of thy love!

Say now, my soul, is not this evidence clear enough to answer all our darkest doubts

Is not this hope abundantly sufficient to sweeten all our bitterest sorrows

What, though we mourn and be afflicted here, and sigh under the miseries of this world for a time

We are sure our tears shall one day be turned into joy, and that joy none shall take from us.

What, though our bodies are crumbled into dust, and that dust blown about over the face of the earth

Yet we know that our REDEEMER lives, and shall appear in brightness at the last great day.

He shall appear in the midst of innumerable angels, and with these very eyes we shall see him:

We shall possess him whom our souls have loved; and be united to him for ever, who is the only end of our being.

GLORY BE to the Father, and to the Son, and to the Holy Ghost. As it was in the beginning, is now, and ever shall be: world without end.

Amen.

Hallelujah.

PSALM 6.

RAISE thy head, O my soul, and look up, and behold the glory of thy crucified SAVIOR.

He that was dead and laid in the grave, low enough to prove himself man,

Is risen again and ascended into heaven, high enough to prove himself GOD.

He is risen, and made the light his garment, and commanded the clouds to be the chariot of his triumph.

The gates of heaven obeyed their LORD, and the everlasting doors opened to the King of Glory.

Enter, bright King, attended with thy beauteous angels, and the glad train of saints, who arose, and came out of their graves after thy resurrection.

Enter and repossess thy ancient throne, and reign eternally at the right hand of thy FATHER.

May every knee bow low at thy exalted name, and every tongue confess thy glory!

May all created nature adore thy power, and the church of thy redeemed exult in thy goodness!

Whom have we in heaven, O LORD, but thee, who wentest thither to make way for thy followers

What have we on earth but our hope, by following thee, to arrive at last where you art gone before us

O glorious JESUS, our strength, our joy, and the immortal life of our souls,

Be you the subject of all our studies, and the daily entertainment of our thoughts.

Draw us, O LORD, from the world and ourselves, that we be not entangled with any earthly desires.

Draw us after thee, and the odors of thy sweetness; that we may run with delight the ways of thy commands.

Draw us up to thee on thy throne of bliss; that we may see thy face, and rejoice with thee for ever in thy kingdom.

GLORY BE to the Father, and to the Son, and to the Holy Ghost. As it was in the beginning, is now, and ever shall be: world without end.

Amen.

Hallelujah.

PSALM 7.

WHY should our hearts still dwell upon earth, since the treasure of our hearts is returned to heaven

Since our glorified JESUS is ascended above; to prepare us a place in his own kingdom

A place of rest and secure peace, where we shall see, and praise, and adore him for ever:

A place of joy and everlasting felicity, where we shall love, and possess, and delight in him for ever.

How will our spirits be ravished within themselves, to reflect on the fullness of their own beatitude!

Flow shall we all rejoice in one another's felicity; but infinitely more in the infinitely greater felicity of our GOD!

O heaven! towards thee we lift up our languishing heads, and with longing hearts and outstretched hands, reach at thy glories.

When, O you finisher of all our hopes; when shall we once behold that incomparable light

That light, which illuminates the eyes of angels, and renews the youth of saints:

That light, which is thy very self, O LORD our GOD! whom we shall there see face to face.

O Light! shine you perpetually in our eyes; that thy brightness may darken the little lustre of this world.

O Light! shed you thy flames in our hearts; that thy light may consume all other desires;

That we may burn continually with the chaste love of thee; till thine own bright day appear;

Till we be called from this veil of darkness, into the glorious presence of the living Gov:

To see him that made the heavens and the earth: and disposes all things into such beauteous order:

To see Lim who first gave us our being, then governed us in our way, and brought us at length to so blessed an end.

Meanwhile, O gracious LORD, the crown of all thy saints, and only expectation of thy faithful servants! Make us entertain our life with the comfort of this hope,

and our hope with the assurance of thy promises.

Make us still every day more perfectly understand our great duty, and thy infinite love.

Make us continually meditate the advancement of thy glory, and invite all the world to sing thy praises.

Praise our LORD, O ye holy angels! Praise him, O ye happy saints!

Praise him, O ye faithful, departed in his grace! Praise him, O ye living, who subsist by his mercy!

Praise him in the vast immensity of his power! Praise him in the admirable wisdom of his providence!

Praise him in the blessed effects of his goodness! Praise him in the infiniteness of all his attributes!

Be you for ever thine own first praise, O glorious Gov! and to all the felicities you essentially possessest, may every creature say, Amen.

GLORY BE to the Father, and to the Son, and to the Holy Ghost. As it was in the beginning, is now, and ever shall be: world without end.

Amen.

Hallelujah.

 **GOD**, *who have glorified our victorious SAVIOR with a visible triumphant resurrection from the dead, and ascension into heaven, where he sits at thy right hand, the world's supreme Governor and final Judge; grant, we beseech thee, that his triumphs and glories may ever shine in our eyes, to make us more clearly see through his sufferings, and more courageously wade through our own; being assured by his example, that if we endeavor to live and die like him, for the advancement of thy love in ourselves and others, you wilt raise again our dead bodies too, and conforming them to his glorious body, call us above the clouds, and give us possession of thy everlasting kingdom; through the same LORD JESUS CHRIST, thy SON, who, with thee and the HOLY GHOST, liveth and reigneth one GOD, world without end.* Amen.

In the Afternoon.

In the name of' the FATHER, and of the ✠ SON, and of the HOLY GHOST. Amen.

Blessed be the holy and undivided TRINITY, now and fir evermore. Amen.

Antiphon

Glorious things are said of thee, you city of the King of heaven. **Hallelujah**.

PSALM 8.

LET them, O LORD, seek other delights, who expect no felicity from thee.

Let them fill up their time with other employments, who think thy rewards not worth their labor.

As for thy servants, our chief content shall be to meditate the glories prepared for us above.

All the few years we live, shall spend themselves to prepare for that one eternal day:

That day whose brightness knows no night; nor ever fears the least eclipse:

Whose cheerful brow no clouds overcast; nor storm molest the passage of its rays:

Which still shines on serene and clear; and fills with splendor that spacious palace.

It needs not the fading lustre of our sun, nor the borrowed silver of the moon.

The sun that rises there, is the LAMS; and the light that shines, is the glory of GOD.

O how beauteous truths are sung of thee, you city of the King of heaven!

Thy walls are raised with precious stone, and every gate is of one rich pearl.

Thy mansions are built with choicest jewels; and the pavement of thy streets is transparent gold.

Down in the midst runs a crystal river, perpetually flowing from the throne of GOD.

There all along those pleasant banks, deliciously grows the tree of life;

Healing all wounds with its balmy leaves, and making immortal all that taste its fruit.

Thus is the holy city built; thus is the New Jerusalem adorned.

O fortunate and glorious city! How free and happy are thy glad inhabitants!

Every head wears a royal crown; and every hand a palm of victory.

Every eye overflows with joy; and every tongue with psalms of praise.

Behold, O my soul, the inheritance we seek; and where can we find more riches to invite us

Behold the felicities to which we are called; and where can we meet such pleasures to entertain us

Away then, all vain and worldly desires; be banished for ever from molesting my peace.

Descend, you blessed heaven, into my heart, or rather take up my heart unto thee.

Thy joys are too great to enter into me; O make me fit to enter into them.

Make me still think on my country above; and there establish my eternal home,

Where I shall dwell perpetually in the view of my GOD; and be filled for ever with the sweetness of his presence.

GLORY BE to the Father, and to the Son, and to the Holy Ghost. As it was in the beginning, is now, and ever shall be: world without end.

Amen.

Antiphon

If these imperfect shadows so sweetly please, how will the real substance transport our hearts! **Hallelujah**.

PSALM 9.

BLESSED be thy gracious wisdom, O LORD, that so mercifully stoops to our low conceptions.

You hidest, or rather, so revealest thy sublime rewards,.. to take us with things we most admire.

Sceptres and crowns you knows are apt to win the hearts of us thy children:

Children, alas, in useful knowledge; O that we were so in love and duty!

What is a drop of water to the boundless ocean; or a grain of dust to this vast globe

Such, O my GOD, and infinitely less, are the richest kingdoms here below;

Should we compare their most pompous state, to the meanest degree in the court of heaven.

When you have fed us a while with milk, you invitest our appetite to stronger meat.

You tellest us of a sweet delicious life, in the blessed society of saints and angels:

With whom we shall dwell in perpetual friendship, and be loved and esteemed. of them all for ever.

You tellest us of a pure soulravishing joy, to behold the amiable face of JESUS;

Whose gracious smiles shine round about, and fill the heavens with holy gladness.

You tellest us still of incomparably higher delights; hearken, O my soul, and humbly adore thy GOD;

Whose bounty has provided thee large rewards; since they are no less than his very self.

Himself he will clearly unveil before us; and openly show us that great secret.

O happy secret, if once attained; if once we but see the face of our GOD!

What is it, LORD, to see thy glorious face, but to know thee as you art in thine own blessed being

To know the immensity of thy selfsubsisting essence and the infinite excellence of all thy attributes:

To know the power of the eternal FATHER, and the wisdom of the untreated Son:

To know the goodness of the HOLY GHOST, and the incomprehensible. glories of the undivided TRINITY.

This, O my soul, is the top of happiness; this is the supreme perfection of our nature.

This, this is alone the aim of our being; the hope and end of all our labors.

When we are come to this, we shall presently rest; and our satisfied desires reach no farther.

We shall be filled with overflowing bliss; and our utmost capacities hold no more:

But in one act of joy will be eternally fixed; and that one act spring fresh for ever.

GLORY BE to the Father, and to the Son, and to the Holy Ghost. As it was in the beginning, is now, and ever shall be: world without end.

Amen.

Antiphon

Never can we say too much of this glorious subject; never can we think enough of the felicities of heaven. **Hallelujah**.

PSALM 10.

ARISE, my soul, to thee these joys belong; arise, and advance thyself on high.

Leave here below all earthly thoughts, and fly away with the wings of the spirit..

Fly to that glorious land of promise, and gladly salute those heavenly regions.

Hail, happy Paradise of pure delights; you beauteous garden of never fading flowers!

Hail; blessed society of beatified spirits, who perpetually contemplate the eternal Deity!

Hail, and for ever may your glories grow, till they rise so high, they can grow no more.

Hail you, who, in your cheerful hymns, remember us who dwell below in this vale of tears.

We hope one,day to come up to you; and be placed, to sing in your holy choirs.

We hope to know all things produced; we hope to know that all producing Cause.

O what a fire of love will it kindle in our hearts, when we shall see those shining mysteries!

When our great GOD, like a burning mirror, shall strike his brightness on the eyes of our souls!

Under these veils you hidest those glorious mysteries, too high and spiritual for flesh and blood.

O what excessive joy will that love produce; a love so violently desiring, and so fully satisfied!

When our capacities shall be stretched to the utmost, and the rich abounding objects fill and overflow them!

O what profound repose will that joy beget; a joy so infinitely high, and so eternally secure!

When we shall sweetly dissolve into the blissful union with our first beginning!

When, without losing what we are, we shall become in a great measure even what he is!

We shall take part in all his joys, and share in the glories of all his heaven.

O what divine and ravishing words are these! How gently they enter and delight my ear!

How they diffuse themselves through all my heart, and strongly penetrate my very soul!

Methinks they turn to substance as they go; and I feel them work and stir through all my powers.

There, O my soul, we shall rest from all our labors, which are but the way to all that happiness.

There we shall rest for ever in the protection of our GOD, in the arms and bosom of our dearest LORD.

O heaven! the eternal source of all these joys, and infinitely more, and infinitely greater,

As the hart pants after the water brooks, so let my soul thirst after thee.

After thee let me daily sigh and mourn; and with a fixed and longing eye look up, and say,

When, O my GOD, shall I sit at that fountain head; and drink my fill of those living streams

When shall I be satisfied with that torrent of pleasures, which springs for ever from thy glorious throne

O that the days of my banishment were finished! How is the time of my pilgrimage prolonged!

Why any I still detained in this valley of tears Still wandering up and down in this wilderness of dangers Come, JESUS, my only hope, and sure deliverer out of all my sorrows.

Come You, and here begin to dwell in my heart; and fit me for the life I shall lead hereafter.

Come, O my LORD, and prepare my soul for thee; and then, when thou pleasest, take it to thyself.

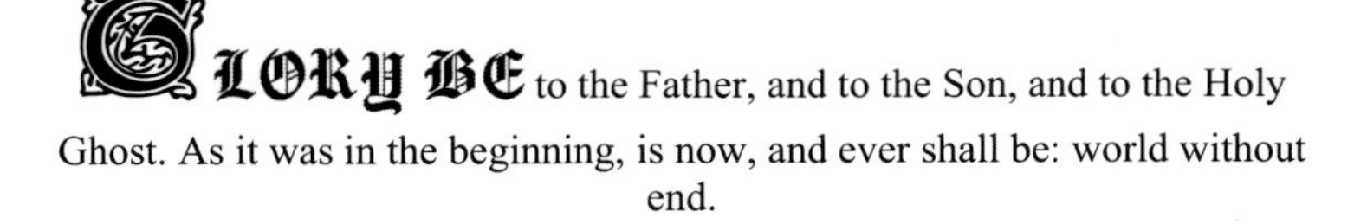

GLORY BE to the Father, and to the Son, and to the Holy Ghost. As it was in the beginning, is now, and ever shall be: world without end.

Amen.

In the Evening.

Antiphon

All is unquiet here till we come to thee, and repose at last in the kingdom of peace.

PSALM 11.

WHO will give me the wings of a dove, that I may fly away, Viand beat rest

That I may fly away from the troubles of this life, and be at rest, O LORD, with thee!

Here, alas! we are forced to sigh, and bear with grief the burden of our miseries.

Often we encounter dangers that divert our progress in the way to bliss.

Often we are assaulted with temptations, that set us back in the accounts of eternity.

How many times, O my soul, have we concluded that this earth affords no real joy!

How many times have we fully agreed, that heaven alone is the place of happiness.

Yet do these false allurements again deceive us, and steal away our hearts to dote on folly:

Yet do we forget our resolves, and wretchedly neglect our true felicity.

O you victorious Conqueror of sin and death! assist us in this dangerous warfare.

O you benign Refresher of distressed spirits! relieve us in this tedious pilgrimage.

Make us still thirst and sigh after thee, the living fountain of life giving streams.

Make us despise all other delights, and set our affections entirely on thy joys.

Since nothing, LORD, can satisfy our souls but thee, O let our souls seek nothing but thee.

GLORY BE to the Father, and to the Son, and to the Holy Ghost. As it was in the beginning, is now, and ever shall be: world without end.

Amen.

PSALM 12.

GIVE me, O LORD, the innocency of doves; and fill my soul with thy mild Spirit:

Then I shall need none of their wings; since heaven itself will dwell in my heart.

It is on the proud you lookest afar off; but inclinest thine ear to the humble and meek:

Who delight in the peace of a contented mind; and limit their thoughts to their own little sphere:

Never intermeddling with the actions of others; unless where charity and reason engage them:

But their beloved employment is to sit in silence; and think on the happiness they expect hereafter.

To meditate the joys of saints and angels; and the blissful vision of the face of JESUS.

O how secure and sweetly do they sleep, who go to bed with a quiet conscience!

Who after a day of faithful industry, in a course of just and pious living,

Lay down their wearied heads in peace, and safely rest in the bosom of Providence:

If they awake, their conscience comforts them in the dark; and bids them not fear the shadow of death

No, nor even death itself; but confidently look up, and long for the dawn of that eternal day.

This too, my soul, should be our care, to note, and censure, and correct ourselves:

To strive for mastery over the passions that molest us; and dismiss from our thoughts what no way concerns us.

Let then the worldly pursue their liberties; and say and do as they think fit.

What is that to thee, my soul! who shall not answer for others, unless you some way make their faults thine own.

Thy pity may grieve, and thy charity endeavor; but if they will not hear, follow you thy God.

Follow the way that leads to truth; follow the truth that leads to life.

Follow the steps of thy beloved JESUS, who alone is the way, the truth, and the life.

Follow his holiness in what he did; follow his patience in what he suffered.

Follow him that calls thee in a thousand promises; follow him that crowns thee with infinite rewards.

Follow thy faithful LORD, O my soul, to the end; and you art sure in the end to possess him for ever.

GLORY BE to the Father, and to the Son, and to the Holy Ghost. As it was in the beginning, is now, and ever shall be: world without end.

Amen.

PSALM 13.

MEEKNESS indeed is the heaven of this life; but the heaven of heavens, O LORD, is above with thee.

Meekness may qualify our miseries here, and make our time pass gentler away.

But to be fully happy, we must stay till hereafter; till thy mercy bring us all to our last end.

That glorious end for which our souls were made; and all things else, to serve them in their way.

It is not to sport our time in pleasures, that You, O LORD, have placed us here.

It is not to gain a fair estate, that thy kindness still prolongs our days.

But to do good to ourselves and others, and glorify thee in improving thy creatures.

To increase every day our longing desires of beholding thee in thine own bright self.

O glorious LORD, whose infinite sweetness provokes and satisfies all our appetites!

May my entire affections delight in thee, above all the vain enjoyments of this world:

Above all praise and empty honor; above all beauty and fading pleasure:

Above all health and deceitful riches; above all power and subtle knowledge:

Above all even thine own bounty can give, and whatever is not thy very self.

O! may my wearied soul repose in thee, the centre of eternal rest.

May I forget myself to think of thee; and fill my memory with the wonders of thy love.

That infinite love, which when my thoughts consider, not as they ought, alas! but as I am able,

The goods or ills of this world lose their name, and yield not either relish or distaste.

O my adored JESUS, let me love thee always; because from eternity you have loved me!

O let me love thee only, gracious GOD! because you alone deserve all my heart.

Always, and only, let me love thee, O LORD! since always my hope is only in thee.

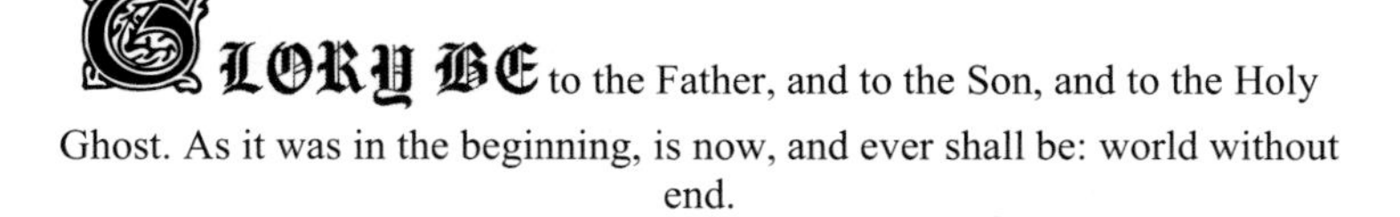

GLORY BE to the Father, and to the Son, and to the Holy Ghost. As it was in the beginning, is now, and ever shall be: world without end.

Amen.

Hallelujah.

Antiphon

All is unquiet here, till we come to thee, and repose at last in the kingdom of peace.

HYMN 2.

DEAR JESUS, when, when will it be That I no more shall break with thee!
When will this war of passions cease, And my free soul enjoy thy peace!
Here I repent, and sin again; Now I revive, and now am slain;
Slain with the same unhappy dart, Which, O! too often wounds my heart.
When, dearest LORD, when shall I be A garden sealed to all but thee
No more expos'd, no more undone; But live and grow to thee alone
'Tis not, alas! on this low earth, That such pure flowers can find a birth:
Only they spring above the skies, Where none can live, till here he dies.
Then let me die, that I may go, And dwell where those bright lilies grow;
Where those blest plants of glory rise, And make a safer Paradise.
No dang'rous fruit, no tempting EVE, No crafty serpent to deceive;
But we like GODs indeed shall be; O let me die that life to see.
Great everliving GOD, to thee, In essence One, in persons Three,
May all thy works their tribute bring, And every age thy glory sing. Amen.

Antiphon

Blessed be the holy name of the LORD our GOD who has spewed us the light of his countenance,and has caused us to see his goodness in the land of the living. **Hallelujah**.*For, behold, you art the light of the nations, O CHRIST, and the glory of thy church.* **Hallelujah**.

LORD, we beseech thee, forsake us not in the vanishing of our days but still continue thy gracious and fatherly protection unto us:

Be you our light and defense, our guide and guard, through the valley of misery and tears, and the shadow of death, to that holy hill where thine honor and our rest dwelleth: And give us the peace, and comfort, and communion of thy HOLY SPIRIT, that our eyes may see thy salvation, and we thy servants may depart in thy peace, for the merits and satisfaction of thy dear Son, JESUS CHRIST our LORD. Amen.

O GOD; whose gracious providence has particularly ordained the spirit of meekness to waft us safely through the turbulent sea of the world, to our heaven of bliss; vouchsafe, we beseech thee, that the clear experience we every day make of our own weakness and vanity, may so dispose us for this precious virtue, that our minds may never be discomposed with passion, nor our tongues break forth into violent expressions, but our temper may be always preserved calm and regular, and, as becomes those all whose powers are possessed of the joys of heaven, apt to feel in every thing only the sweet impulses of hope and charity, through our LORD JESUS CHRIST thy SON; to whom, with thee and the HOLY GHOST, be all honor and glory, world without end. Amen.

Vouchsafe us, we beseech thee, O LORD, a quiet night, and a happy end.

Visit, we beseech thee, O LORD, this habitation, and drive far away all snares of the enemy: Let thy holy angels dwell therein to preserve us in peace, and thy blessing be upon us for ever: through our LORD JESUS CHRIST thy SON.

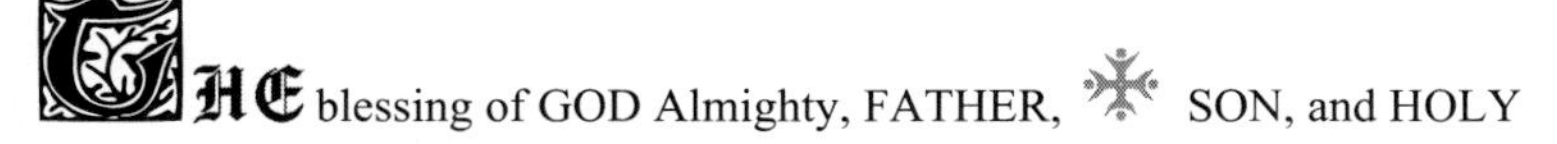

THE blessing of GOD Almighty, FATHER, ✠ SON, and HOLY GHOST, descend upon us, and dwell in our hearts for ever.

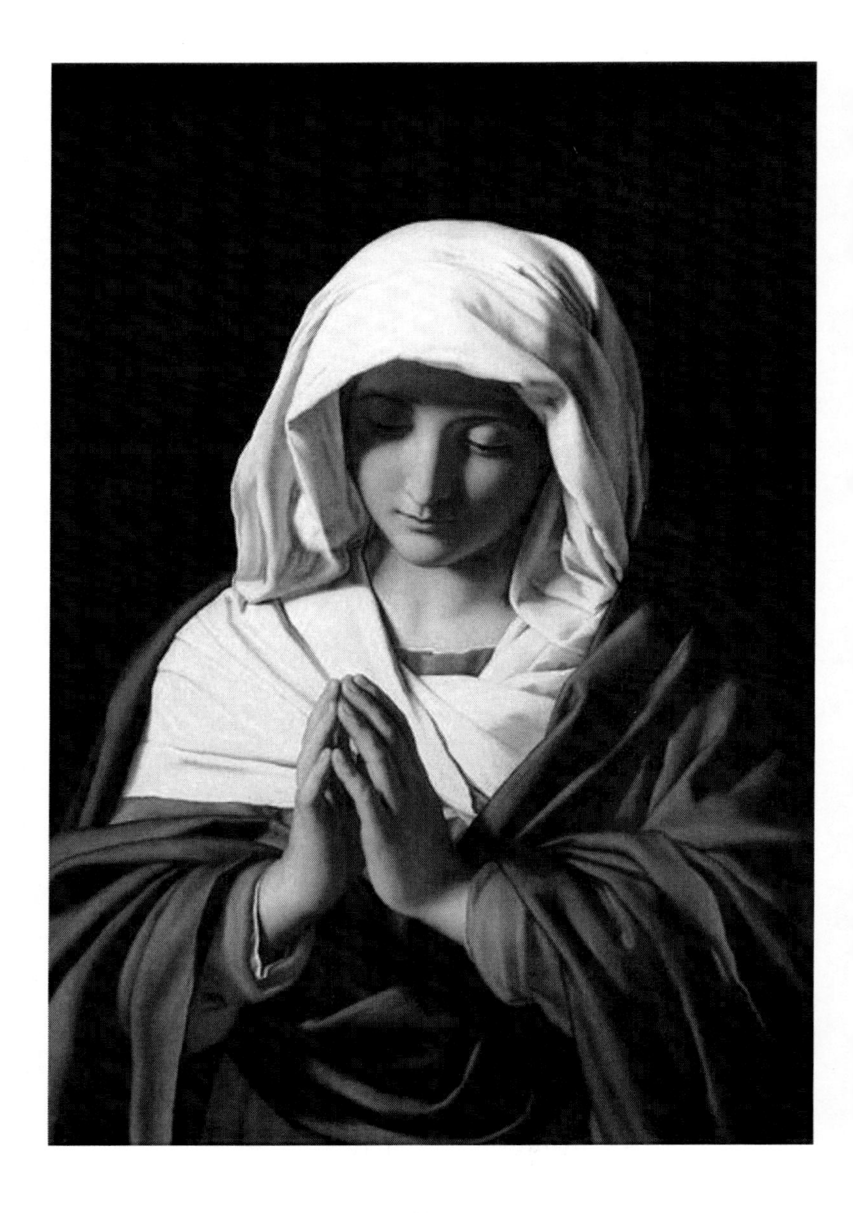

The Office for Monday.

Morning Prayer.

PSALM 1.

LET us with reverence appear before Him, and humble ourselves in the presence of his glory; Let us all bring forth our psalms of praise, and sing with joy to our great Creator.

Come, let us adore our GOD that made us.

He made us, not we ourselves, and freely bestowed on us all the rest of his creatures, to engage our hearts to love his goodness, and to admire the riches of his infinite bounty.

Come, let us adore our GOD that made us.

Our bodies he framed of the dust of the earth, and gave us a soul after his own likeness; a soul which all created nature cannot fill; nor any thing below his own immensity.

Come, let us adore our GOD that made us.

For himself he made us, and for his glorious kingdom, that we might dwell with him in perfect bliss, and sing his praises for ever.

GLORY BE to the Father, and to the Son, and to the Holy Ghost. As it was in the beginning, is now, and ever shall be: world without end.

Amen.

Antiphon

"All things he open to the eyes of GOD. All things are naked to Him with whom we speak."

PSALM 2.

Happy are they, O glorious LORD! who every where adore thy presence.

Happy, who live on earth, as in the sight of the King of heaven; and every moment say in their heart, Our GOD is here.

Here is the centre of our souls, to witness all our thoughts, and judge exactly our most secret intents.

Though his throne of state is established above; and the splendors of his glory shine only on the blessed:

Yet his unlimited eye looks clown to this world, and beholds all the ways of the children of ADAM.

If we go out, He marks our steps; and when we retire, our closet excludes not him.

While we are alone, he minds our contrivings; and the ends we aim at in all our studies.

When we converse with others, he observes our deportment, and the good or ill we do them, or ourselves.

In our devotions he notes our carriage; and regards with what attention we pray.

All the day long he considers how we spend our time; and our darkest night conceals not our works from him.

If we deceive our neighbor, he spies the fraud; and hears the least whisper of a slandering tongue:

If we in secret oppress the poor; or by private alms relieve their wants:

If in our hearts we murmur at the rich; or live contented with our little portion:

Whatever we do, he perfectly sees us; where ever we are, he is with us.

Why, O you Sovereign LORD of heaven! why dost you stoop thus low thy glorious eye?

What can you find that here deserves thy sight, among the trifles of our empty world?

What can you find, alas! that should not fear thy sight among the follies of our lives?

It is not thyself, O LORD, you seekest to satisfy; but all thy design is for our advantage.

You graciously stand by to see us work; that thine awful eye may quicken our diligence.

You art still at hand to relieve our wants; that so friendly a nearness may increase our confidence.

You appearest still ready to punish our sins; that the shake of thy rod may prevent our miseries.

Sure, O my GOD, thy favors must needs be sweet; since even thy threatenings have so much mercy.

Sure we must needs be worse than blind; if in the face of heaven we dare be wicked.

Henceforth, O gracious LORD! as children rejoice in the indulgent presence of their tender Father,

So make us still,with humble boldness, rejoice before thee our merciful Creator.

And as new pardoned subjects justly fear the angry brow of their offended Prince;

So let our forgiven souls continually tremble to provoke the wrath of thy dread Majesty.

O temper thus our love with reverence; and thus allay our fear with hope.

GLORY BE to the Father, and to the Son, and to the Holy Ghost. As it was in the beginning, is now, and ever shall be: world without end.

Amen.

Antiphon

Happy we, who have our GOD so near us; happy, if our pious lives keep us near him.

PSALM 3

MY GOD! since you art never absent from us; let us be always present with thee.

Let us go up to the throne above; and there contemplate and admire thy glory.

Let us attend on thy holy altars; and there adore and praise thy mercy.

Every where let us seek to meet thee; every where let us delight to find thee.

All our wants let us spread before thee; all our petitions let us offer unto thee.

You willingly inclinest thy gracious ear to the prayers that come from a fervent heart.

You loves to hear us treat of heaven; as if we made it our business indeed to go thither.

All other things we must ask with submission to thee; since we know not what is good for ourselves:

But thy eternal joys we may beg without restraint; and urge and press for thy assistance to gain them.

Heaven we may wish, without the check of resignation; heaven we may pray for, without fear of importunity.

O wise and gracious LORD, whatever you doest, thy love intends it all for the good of thy servants.

If you deferrest sometimes to grant our requests, it is only in love to make us repeat them.

That we may feel more sensibly our own poverty, and be more strongly convinced of our dependence on thee.

That we may practice our hope while we expect; and increase our gratitude when we receive.

Sure, no easier work than to ask what we want; no cheaper purchase than to have for asking.

Sure, no sweeter pleasure than to converse with GOD; nor greater profit than to gain his favor.

O you blessed End of all our labors, and only Centre of all our wishes!

Do you reclaim our wandering fancies; and guide and fix them on thy service.

Night and day let us call on thee, and never cease knocking at the doors of thy palace.

Let no delay discourage our hope; nor even refusal destroy our confidence,

But let this foundation still sustain us; and on this let our peace be established for ever.

What is necessary thy goodness will not deny; the rest our obedience submits to thy pleasure.

GLORY BE to the Father, and to the Son, and to the Holy Ghost. As it was in the beginning, is now, and ever shall be: world without end.

Amen.

PSALM 4

DELIVER us, O LORD, from asking of thee, what we cannot receive without danger to ourselves.

Deliver us from receiving what we cannot use, without offending others, or ruining our own souls.

Deliver us from so presuming on thy bounty, as to omit our own duty.

Still to our devotions let us join our best endeavors; and make our earth comply with thy heaven.

If we desire of thee to relieve our necessities, let us faithfully labor with our hands;

And not expect a blessing from the clouds on the idle follies of an undisciplined life.

If we beg grace for victory over our passions, let us constantly resist their assaults.

Let us wisely foresee our particular dangers, and use the proper weapon against every sin.

In vain we approach thy holy altar, if our lives prepare not the way for our offerings.

You shuttest thy ears to our loudest prayers, if we open not ours to the voice of the poor.

You deniest to pardon our trespasses against thee, unless we forgive our enemies.

O the extreme benignity of our glorious GOD; who treats with his creatures upon equal terms!

Who deals no otherwise with us, miserable wretches, than we ourselves with one another.

He promises to give the same measure we give our neighbors, and performs incomparably more than he promises;

Pressed down and shaken together, and running over into the bosoms of them that love him.

Such, O my GOD, is the bounty of thy goodness, and no less the patience of thy generous hand.

You holdest thy blessings hovering over our heads, still watching the time when we are fit to receive them.

Then you immediately sendest them down to enter our hearts, and dwell with us for ever.

Even that very temper which thus disposes us, entirely depends on the favor of thy providence:

Every condition you requirest on our part, being nothing else but thine own free gift.

Thy mercy alone is the fountain of all our blessings; and _in what channel soever they flow to us, they spring from thee.

You art the GOD of nature and reason; you art the GOD of grace and religion.

Give, gracious GOD, what you art pleased to command, and then command what you pleasest.

GLORY BE to the Father, and to the Son, and to the Holy Ghost. As it was in the beginning, is now, and ever shall be: world without end.

Amen.

MY *soul, what cause you wish for more? Behold, thv gracious LORD offers thee to choose what you wilt, and promises to give thee what you choosest. O infinite Goodness! it is thyself alone I choose, for you art my only happiness for ever. I see my portion hereafter depends on my choice here; but my choice, O LORD, depends on thee. Guide me with thy holy grace, that I withdraw my affections from all vain and perishable creatures, and fix them entirely on thee, my LORD and my GOD, and my eternal felicity.*

SEND *down, O GOD of our fathers, and LORD of mercy! send down thy wisdom from thy holy heaven, and from the seat of thy greatness, to be in us, and labor with us, and teach us what is acceptable unto thee; that we may know our end, and wisely choose our way, and order our actions to our true felicity. Our thoughts are fearful and our prudence uncertain: We se. conjecture the things that are on earth, and find with pains the things that are in sight. Give us, O LORD, the wisdom that sits at thy throne, and reject us not from among thy children.*

DELIVER *us, O LORD, from relapsing into the sins we have repented of: Deliver us free all malice and enmity with our neighbors, and from oppressing the poor who have none to defend them. Then may we confidently expect thy protection, while we serve thee and love one another. You art our strength; O LORD, whom shall we fear? You art our salvation, of what shall we be afraid? Nothing can hurt us, but our own vicious desires; nothing can endanger us, but disobedience to our GOD.*

O GOD*, who art ever present to all that you have made, still watching to improve us, as we grow fit for greater bounty; keep, we beseech thee, cur eyes continually fixed on thine over us, at once awfully checking our inclination to folly., and tenderly encouraging our pursuit of true good: Make us always feel ourselves under thy sure protection in our dangers, and within the reach of thy glorious ear, for whatever good we faithfully ask, and* *use our just endeavors, according to thy discipline, to attain, through our LORD JESUS CHRIST, thy Son.* Amen.

At Noon.

Antiphon

Bless the LORD, O my soul, and all that is within me, praise his holy name.

PSALM 5

COME, let us sing the praises of GOD, and joyfully recite his divine perfections.

His being is of himself alone, and no dependence his eternal essence knows.

His knowledge fathoms the extent of all things, and his power commands them as he pleases.

His goodness is supremely infinite, and all his glorious attributes transcendently adorable.

Come, let us sing the praises of our GOD, and joyfully recite his divine perfection.

He is the source of all felicity; eternally full of his own unchangeable bliss.

Before time began, he was; and when the sun must lose his light, his day will remain the same for ever.

The heaven of heavens is the palace of his glory, and all created nature the subject of his dominion.

In his presence the brightest seraphims cover their faces, and all the blessed spirits bow down their heads to his footstool.

Come, let us sing aloud the prerogatives of our GOD, and stretch our utmost thoughts to exalt his greatness.

But, O most glorious and dreadful Deity! how dare we wretches undertake thy praises?

How dare our sin polluted lips pronounce thy name? Or where shall we seek expressions fit for thee?

All that we can say is nothing to thy unspeakable excellencies; all we can think, but a faint shadow of thy inconceivable beauty.

Even the voice of angels is too low to reach thy worth, and their highest strains fall infinitely short of thee.

Only in this shall thy servants rejoice, and all the powers of our soul be glad;

That thyself alone art thy own full praise; be to thyself thine own glory.

Live, our great GOD, eternally encompassed with the beams of thine own inaccessible light.

Live, our adored Creator, and reign for ever on the throne of thine own immortal kingdom.

GLORY BE to the Father, and to the Son, and to the Holy Ghost. As it was in the beginning, is now, and ever shall be: world without end.

Amen.

PSALM 6

TOO glorious art You, O LORD, in thyself; and thy direct rays shine too bright for our eyes.

Yet may we venture to praise thee in thy works; and contemplate thee at least reflected from the creatures.

In them we may safely behold our mighty Maker; and freely admire the magnificence of our GOD.

Heaven and earth are full of his greatness; heaven and earth were created by his power.

From him all the host of angels receive their being; from him they have the honor to assist in his presence.

He kindleth warmth and brightness in the sun; and beauteously garnisheth the firmament with the stars.

He spread the air, and stored it with flocks of birds; he gathered the waters, and replenished them with shoals of fishes.

He established the earth on a firm foundation, and richly adorned it with innumerable varieties.

Every element is filled with his blessings; and all the world with his liberal miracles.

He spoke the word, and they were made; he commands, and they are still preserved.

He governs their motions in perfect order; and distributes to each his proper office.

Contriving the whole into one vast machine, a spacious theatre of his own unlimited greatness.

O glorious architect of universal nature; who disposest all things in number, weight, and measure!

How does thy wisdom engage us to admire thee! How does thy goodness oblige us to love thee!

Not for themselves alone, O gracious GOD, did thy hand produce those happy spirits.

But to receive in charge thy little flock; and safely conduct them to the folds of bliss.

Not for themselves, O bounteous LORD, were the rest of this huge creation framed.

But to sustain our lives in the way; and carry us on to our eternal home.

O may our souls first praise thee for themselves, and employ their whole powers to improve in thy service.

May we praise thee, O LORD, for all thy gifts; but infinitely above all still value the Giver.

May every blessing be a motive of gratitude, and every creature a step of approach towards thee.

So shall we faithfully observe their end, and happily arrive at ours.

Using them only to entertain us here, till our souls be prepared for the life of heaven,

Till they become full ripe for thee, and then fly away to thy holy presence.

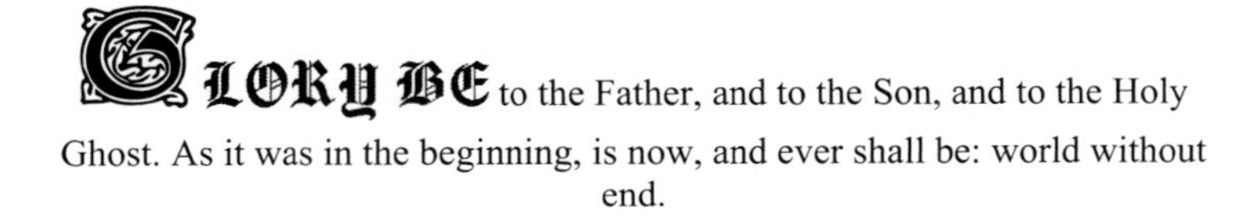

GLORY BE to the Father, and to the Son, and to the Holy Ghost. As it was in the beginning, is now, and ever shall be: world without end.

Amen.

PSALM 7

HOW admirable is thy name, O LORD, over all the earth! How wise and gracious the counsels of thy providence!

After you hadst thus prepared the world as a house ready furnished for man to inhabit;

Thy mighty hand framed our bodies of the dust, and built them of a shape of use and beauty,:

You didst breathe into us the spirit of life, and fit us with faculties proportionable to our end.

You gayest us a soul to govern our bodies, and reason to command in this our soul.

You revealedst unto us a law for the improvement of our reason;
and enabledst us by thy grace to observe that law. You compelledst whole

nature to serve us without reward, and invitedst us to love thee for our own happiness. You designedst us an age of pure delights in that sweet and fruitful garden; And, after having led there a long and pleasant life, thou resolvedst to transplant us thence to thine own Paradise. All this you didst, O glorious GOD, the full possessor of universal bliss!

Not for any need you hadst of us, or the least advantage you couldest derive from our being.

All this you didst, O infinite Goodness, the liberal Bestower of whatever we possess!

Not for any merit, alas! of ours, or the least motive we could offer to induce thee.

But for thine own excessive love, and the mere inclination of thine own rich nature.

That, empty, we might receive of thy fullness; and be partakers of thy overflowing bounty.

So sheds the generous sun his beams, and freely scatters them on every side;

Gilding all the world with his beauteous light; and kindly cherishing it with his fruitful heat.

And so dost You, and infinitely more, O you GOD of infinitely more perfections!

So we confess you doest to us; but we, what return have we made to thee?

Have we well considered the end of our being; and faithfully complied with thy purpose to save us?

Ah, wretched we! we forget our GOD that made us; and fill our heads with thoughts that undo us.

Pardon, O gracious LORD, our past ingratitude, and mercifully direct our time to come;

Teach every passage of our yet remaining life, how to express an acknowledgment fit for thy mercies.

O make our senses subject to our reason, and our reason entirely obedient unto thee.

O make the whole creation conspire to thy honor, and all that depend on thee join together in thy praise.

This is the only praise you expectest from us; and the whole honor you requirest of thy creatures.

That by observing the orders you appointest them here, in this lower region, we may all grow up to be hereafter in the state of permanency and eternal rest.

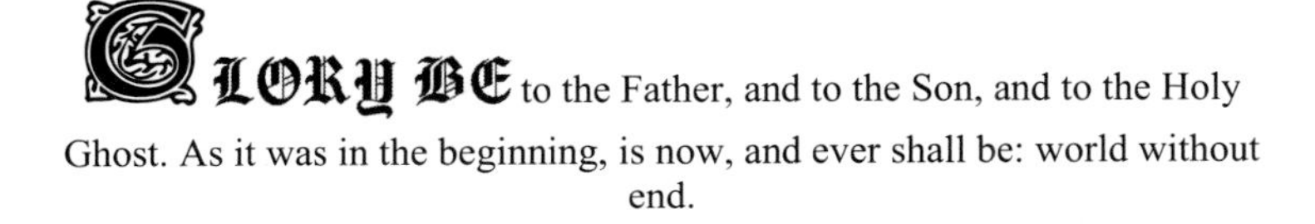

GLORY BE to the Father, and to the Son, and to the Holy Ghost. As it was in the beginning, is now, and ever shall be: world without end.

Amen.

Antiphon

You art worthy, O LORD, to receive glory, and honor and power; for you have created all things, and for thy pleasure they are and were created.

HYMN 1

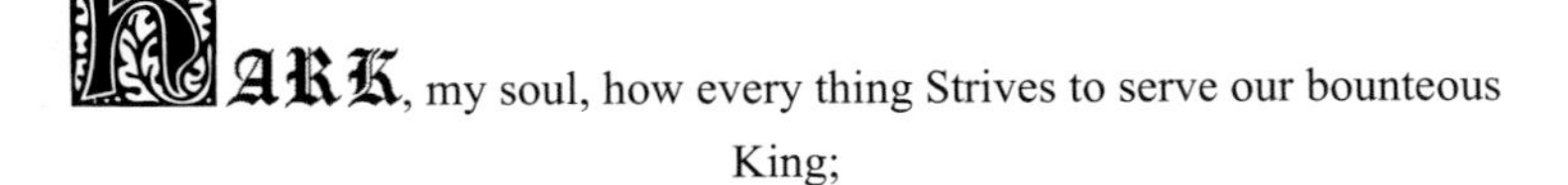

HARK, my soul, how every thing Strives to serve our bounteous King;

Each a double tribute pays, Sings its part and then obeys.

Nature's sweetest, loveliest choir, Him with cheerful notes admire;

Chanting every day their lauds; While the grove their song applauds.

Though their voices lower be, Streams too have their melody;

Night and day they warbling run, Never pause, but still sing on.

All the flowers that gild the Spring, Hither their still music bring; If heaven bless them,

thankful, they Smell more sweet, and look more gay.

Wake for shame my sluggish heart, Wake, and gladly sing thy part:

Learn of birds, and springs, and flowers, How to use thy nobler powers.

Call whole nature to thy aid, Since twas He whole nature made;

Join in one eternal song, Who to one GOD all belong.

Live for ever, glorious LORD! Live by all thy works adored;

One in Three, and Three in One, All thins bow to thee alone. Amen.

THE *boundless ocean of being could not contain his streams, but overflowed upon pure nothing; and behold a bounteous world appeared: Heaven and earth, and all therein, from the highest angel to the least grain of dust.*

O *Almighty LORD, the only wise and good Creator of the universe, who madest all corporeal nature for the use of man, and man for his own felicity! Enlarge our souls, we beseech thee, humbly to adore thy infinitefulness of being in thyself, and thy immense liberality to us; and mercifully carry on the whole creation to its end, vouchsafing so to order thy creatures by thy grace, that they may attain their perfection in duly serving us, and we ours in eternally enjoying thee, through our LORD JESUS CHRIST:* Amen.

In the Afternoon

Antiphon

To know thee, O LORD, is the highest learning; and to see thy face, the only happiness.

PSALM 8

LET us now consider, O LORD our GOD, let us thankfully remember what you art to us.

You art the great Beginning of our nature; and glorious End of all our actions.

You art the overflowing Source from whence we spring; and the immense Ocean to which we tend.

You art the free Bestower of all we possess; and faithful Promiser of all we hope.

You art the strong Sustainer of our lives; and ready Deliverer from all our enemies.

You art the merciful Scourger of our sins, and bounteous Rewarder of our obedience.

You art the safe Conductor of our pilgrimage, and the eternal Rest of wearied souls.

Such, alas' our narrowness is constrained to use; when we' endeavor to speak thy bounties.

Wider a little can our thoughts extend; yet infinitely less than the least of thy mercies.

Tell us thyself, O you mild Instructor of the ignorant! what you art to us.

One word of thine expresses more than all the eloquence of men and angels. _

Say to our souls, you art our Salvation; but say it so, that we may hear thee, and feel it so.

Gladly will we run after the sound of that voice; and by following it, find out thee.

When we have found thee once, O you joy of our hearts! never let us lose thy sight again.

Never let us turn our eyes from thee; but steadily fix them upon thy glorious face.

Suffer us not to go, till you have given us thy blessing; and then may thy blessing bind us faster unto thee.

GLORY BE to the Father, and to the Son, and to the Holy Ghost. As it was in the beginning, is now, and ever shall be: world without end.

Amen.

Antiphon

To know ourselves is the truest wisdom; to see our own poverty, the safest riches.

PSALM 9

LET us now consider, O LORD our Gov! let us humbly remember what we are to thee.

We, who, alas! are nothing in ourselves; what can we be to thy immensity?

You, who art all things in thine own rich self; what can you receive from our poverty?

This only we are to thee, O great Creator! the unthankful objects of all thy bounties.

This only we are to thee, O dear Redeemer! the unworthy cause of all thy sufferings.

Guilty we committed the crime, and You,
with thine innocency, undertookest the punishment.

We went astray from the path of life; and thy mercy came down from heaven to seek us:

To seek us in the wilderness where we had lost ourselves; and bring us home to the discipline of thy love.

LORD, what are we, that you should thus regard such poor, and vile, and inconsiderable wretches?

What can our goodwill avail thy bliss; that with so many charms
you wooest us to love thee?

What can our malice prejudice thy content; that you threatenest so violently, if we love thee not?

Is there not, O my FATHER, felicity enough in the sweetness alone of loving thee?

Is there not misery enough in living deprived of thy blissful love?

Yes, LORD, and that you knows, and that is the only cause which moved thy goodness to court our affections.

You knewest, we else should cast away ourselves, by doting on the follies of this deceitful world.

You knewest the danger of our wilful nature, and therefore strivest by the greatest fears and the greatest hopes,

And all the wisest arts of love and bounty, to draw us to thyself, and endow us with thy kingdom.

Unhappy we, whose frowardness required so strange proceedings, to force upon us our own salvation!

Happy we, whose wants have met so kind a hand, that needed but our emptiness to engage him to fill us!

Happy yet more, that our LORD, that thus favors us now, will at last give us himself.

GLORY BE to the Father, and to the Son, and to the Holy Ghost. As it was in the beginning, is now, and ever shall be: world without end.

Amen.

Antiphon

Vanity of vanities, all is vanity, but to love GOD, and to serve and enjoy him.

PSALM 10.

LORD, without thee what is all this world, but a flying dream of busy vanities?

It promises, indeed, a paradise of bliss; but all it performs is an empty cloud.

Thine are the joys that shine fixed as the stars, and make the only solid heaven.

LORD, without thee what are we to ourselves, but the wretched causes of our own ruin?

We, till you gayest us being, were pure nothing; more removed from happiness, than the miscrablest of thy creatures.

And now you halt made us, we wholly depend on thee, and perish immediately if you forsake us.

You, without us, art the same allglorious essence, full of thy own eternal felicity.

Without us, thy royal throne stands firm for ever; and all the powers of heaven obey thy pleasure.

Pity, O gracious LORD, our imperfect nature; whose every circumstance is so contrary to thine.

You dwellest above in the mansions of glory, and we below in houses of clay.

You art immortal, and thy day outlives all time; we every moment go downwards to our grave.

You art immense, and thy presence fills the heavens; but the greatest of us, alas, how little are we!

When, O my Go)), shall these distances meet together? When will these extremities embrace each other?

We know they were once miraculously joined in the sacred person of thy eternal SON,

When the King of heaven stooped down to earth, and grafted in his own person the nature of man.

We hope they once again shall be happily united, in the blissful vision of thy glorious self;

When the children of the earth shall be exalted to heaven; and made partakers of the Divine nature.

But are there no means for us here below; O you infinitely high and glorious GOD?

Is there no way to approach to thee; and diminish at least this uncomfortable distance?

None but the way of holy love; which none can attain but by thy free gift.

Yet, O LORD, unless you first love us, and sweetly draw us by thy gentle hand:

Never shall we be so happy as to love thee; nor ever be happy unless we do love thee.

O bounteous GOD! to all thy favors add this one, of making us esteem thee above them all.

Be you to us our GOD and all things; and make us nothing in our own eyes.

Be you our whole and everlasting delight; and let nothing else be any thing unto us.

GLORY BE to the Father, and to the Son, and to the Holy Ghost. As it was in the beginning, is now, and ever shall be: world without end.

Amen.

HYMN 2

GLORY to thee, O bounteous LORD!
Who givest to all things breath; Glory to thee, eternal WORD!
Who says us by thy death.
Glory, O blessed SPIRIT, to thee!
Who fill'st our hearts with love;
Glory to all the mystic Three!
Who reign one GOD above.

HE *that framed The heart of man, designed it for himself, and bequeathed it unquietness till possessed of its Maker.*

O GOD, who alone art all in all things to us, and to whom we are nothing but wretched objects of thy bounty, which the more it flows upon us, the more we feel our own emptiness, and want of it; increase, we humbly beseech thee, this happy sense in thy servants, by the experience we every day have how unsatisfactory this world is; and grant,that finding it ordained by thee to increase and widen, not fill our capacity, we may make this only use of all thy creatures here, to raise and heighten our desires of thy infinite self in eternity, through our LORD JESUS CHRIST, who, with thee and the HOLY GHOST, liveth and reigneth one God, world without end. Amen.

In the Evening.

Antiphon

All thy ways, O LORD, are mercy and wisdom; and all thy counsels tend to our happiness.

PSALM 11.

MY GOD, in every thing I see thy hand; in every passage thy gracious providence.

You wisely governest the house you have built, and preventest with thy mercies all our wants.

You tallest us up in the early morning, and givest us light by the beams of thy sun,

To labor every one in their proper office, and fill the place appointed them in the world.

You providest a rest for our weary evening; and favorest our sleep with a shady darkness.

To refresh our bodies in the peace of night, and repair the waste of our decaying spirits.

Again you awakest our drowsy eyes, and biddest us return to our daily task.

Thus has thy wisdom mixed our life, and beauteously interwoven it of rest and work,

Whose mutual changes sweeten each. other, and each prepare us for our greatest duty,

Of finishing here the work of our salvation, to rest hereafter in thy holy peace.

GLORY BE to the Father, and to the Son, and to the Holy Ghost. As it was in the beginning, is now, and ever shall be: world without end.

Amen.

PSALM 12.

LORD, how thy bounty gives us all things else, with a large and open hand!

Our fields at once are covered with corn; and our trees bow under the weight of their fruit.

At once you fillest our magazines with plenty, and sendest whole showers of other blessings.

Only our time you distillest by drops, and never givest us two moments at once:

But takest away one when you lendest another, to teach us the price of so rich a jewel:

That we may learn to value every hour, and not childishly spend them on empty trifles:

Much less, maliciously murder whole days, in pursuing a course of sin and shame.

LORD, as you have taught our ignorance; so let thy grace enable our weakness,

Wisely to manage the time you givest us, and still press on to new degrees of improvement;

That with our few, but wellspent years, we may prepare ourselves for our blessed eternity.

GLORY BE to the Father, and to the Son, and to the Holy Ghost. As it was in the beginning, is now, and ever shall be: world without end.

Amen.

PSALM 13

IT was thy mercy too, O gracious LORD, to dispense by parcels our portion of time;

That the succeeding day may learn to grow wise, and correct its faults by experience of the past.

Else were our being unchangeable, and free from time's vicissitude, as it shall be in eternal life,

Our sins could not be repented of; and then, alas! how desperate were we!

We, who are borne in the way to misery, and unless we change, can never be happy.

We, who so often wilfully go astray, and unless we return, must perish for ever.

O You, in whose indulgent hands are both our time, and our eternity;

Whose providence gives every minute of our life; and governs the fatal period of our death!

O make us every evening still provide to pass with comÂfort that important hour!

Make us still balance our account for heaven, and strive to increase our treasures with thee:

That if we rise no more to our acquaintance here, we may joyfully awake among thy blessed angels,

There to unite our hymns with theirs; and join altogether in one full choir.

GLORY BE to the Father, and to the Son, and to the Holy Ghost. As it was in the beginning, is now, and ever shall be: world without end.

Amen.

The Office for Tuesday.

Morning Prayer.

PSALM 1.

FROM Thee, O LORD, we derive our being, and from the same goodness our continuance to be: If you with drawest thy hand, but a moment, we instantly return to our first nothing.

Come, let us adore our GOD that preserves us.

From all our enemies his providence defends us, and covers our heads in the day of danger; he sends his grace to relieve our weakness, and disappoints the temptations that threaten to undo us.

Come, let us adore our GOD that preserves us.

Here his almighty power sustains our life, and mercifully allows us space to repent, that by well employing the time he lends, we may wisely provide for our own eternity.

Come, let us adore our GOD that preserves us.

He still repeats blessings to us, and shall we neglect our duty to him? He freely bestows on us all our day, and shall we not spend half an hour in his service?

Come, let us adore our GOD that preserves us.

If we receive all we have of GOD, why do we boast, as' if we had it of ourselves?

PSALM 2.

NOT unto us, O LORD, not unto us, but to thine own blessed name give all the glory.

When we have applied our utmost cares, and used all the diligence that lies in our power;

What can we do but look up to thee, and second our endeavors with prayers for thy blessing?

When we have obtained thy gracious mercy, and, to obtain it, have presented before thee the meritorious offering of thy Son;

What can we do, but submit our hopes, and expect the event from thy own free goodness?

We know, and you thyself has taught us, unless you defendest the city, the guard watches in vain.

We know, and our own experience tells us, unless you reach forth thy hand, we are presently in danger of sinking.

Every moment of our day subsists by thee, and every step we take moves by thy strength.

Even the life we now repeat must beg its breath of thee, and stop if you deniest it.

If you deniest it, who can compel thy will, or call in question thy decrees?

Are we not all thy creatures, O gracious God! and as helpless children hanging on the breast of thy providence?

Are we not all as clay in thy hands, to frame us into vessels of what use you pleasest?

Behold, we confess, O LORD, in thee we live and have our being.

All our sufficiency proceeds from thee, and all our success depends on thy favor.

Others may tell us the way we should go; but you alone can enable us to walk.

Others may tell us the way; but even they must first be taught by thee.

They must be moved by thee to act that charity; and so at last. all is resolved into thee.

Should we, O LORD, presume to divide thy grace, and proudly challenge any share to ourselves:

Thy mighty truth stands up against us, and our own infirmities plainly confute us.

Should you severely examine our hearts, and ask who works all their actions in them?

Sure we must needs bow down our heads, and from our low dust humbly say:

Nothing are we, O LORD, but what you have made us; nothing have we but what you have given us.

Only our sins are entirely our own, which O may thy grace extinguish for ever!

O may all presumption die in us, and our whole confidence live only in thee!

May even our frailties make us more strong, and our being nothing teach us to be humble.

So shall thy power, O LORD, be magnified in our weakness; and thy mercy triumph in relief of our misery.

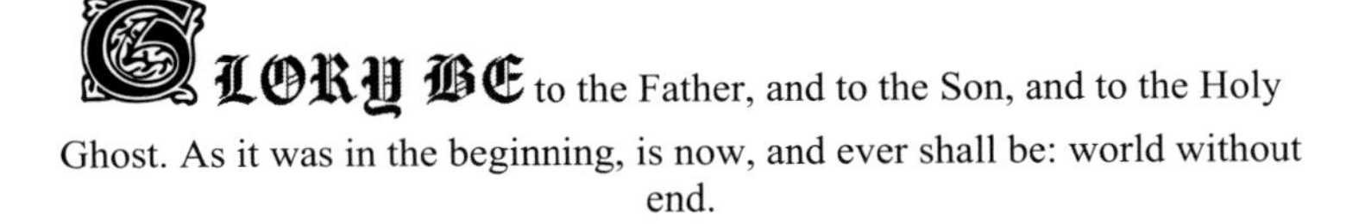

GLORY BE to the Father, and to the Son, and to the Holy Ghost. As it was in the beginning, is now, and ever shall be: world without end.

Amen.

Antiphon

GOD is my Savior, whom should I fear? GOD is my Protector, of what should I be afraid?

PSALM 3

THUS we depend, and happy we are in this dependence, did we but know our own true interest.

We and our whole concerns are deposited with GOD; and where can we find a better hand to ensure them?

Is he not wise enough to choose safely for us, who disposes all nature in so admirable an order?

Has he not power enough to go through with his purpose, who commands the wills of men and angels?

Wants he an inclination to favor us, who desires our felicity more than our own hearts can do?

He feeds the fowls of the air, and curiously clothes the lilies of the field.

And without his providence not a sparrow falls to the ground; and shall we mistrust his care for his children?

Under his government we have lived all this while; and can we now suspect he will forsake us?

He has shown his bounty in extraordinary graces, and will he deny us his lesser blessings?

He has freely bestowed on us his dearest SON; how shall he not give us all things else?

All that are truly useful to carry us on our way, and bring us at length to his eternal rest.

Ask but the former ages, and they will tell you the wonders he wrought in favor of his servants.

He multiplied the oil in the poor widow's cruse, and fed his Prophet by the service of a raven.

He dried the sea into a path for his people, and melted the rocks to refresh their thirst.

He made his angels stewards of their provision, and nourished them in the wilderness with the bread of heaven.

Still, O my GOD, thy eternal love retains the same affection for those that rely on thee.

Still thy all seeing wisdom governs the world with the same immense unalterable goodness.

Nay, surely now the streams of thy mercy run more strong, and have wrought to themselves a larger channel;

Since you broughtest down the waters from above the heavens, and openedst in thine own body a spring of life;

A spring of joy and bliss, to revive our hearts, and overflow them with a torrent of everlasting pleasures.

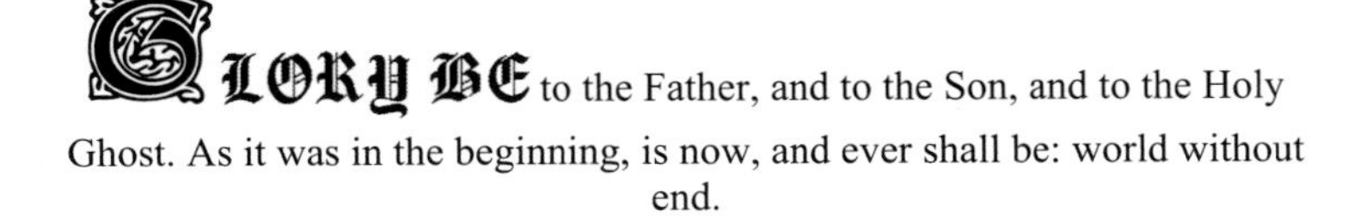

GLORY BE to the Father, and to the Son, and to the Holy Ghost. As it was in the beginning, is now, and ever shall be: world without end.

Amen.

PSALM 4.

LET us then sit down in peace, O my soul, and rest secure in the bosom of Providence.

Let us not disturb the order of those mercies, which our GOD has designed us in his eternal counsel.

If our affairs succeed, let us praise our great Benefactor, and think what he will give us hereafter, who so favors us here.

If they miscarry, let us yield to the will of Heaven, and learn by our crosses in this world to betake us to the other.

Whatever happens, let this be our constant rule, to provide for the future life, and be content with the present.

Shall we not patiently accept a little evil from him, that has given us so much good?

Shall the being without some one thing we need not, more sensibly affect us, than the having of all we need?

Ingrateful we! the common benefits we all enjoy, deserve the thanksgiving of a whole life.

The air we breathe, the sun that shines upon us, the water and the earth that so faithfully serve us:

The exercise of our senses, and the use of our reason, if not in excellence, at least to some degree:

All these, O LORD, you givest to the good and to the bad; and for the least of these none can praise thee enough.

What shall we say to those high supernatural blessings; the SOLI of GOD to redeem us, and heaven to reward us?

What shall we say? Can we yet complain, because some few are more prosperous than we?

Should we not rather look down on the many below us, and be thankful to see ourselves more favored than they?

Should we not reckon over the miseries of mankind, and bless our GOD that has so far preserved us.

Had we some desperate canker breeding on our face, or noisome leprosy spreading over our skin,

What would we give to be as now we are? How gladly change for a moderate affliction?

It is but interpreting our worst condition well, to find motives enough for our gratitude.

It is but interpreting our best condition frowardly, and we find defects enough to think ourselves miserable.

Did we adore as we ought the wisdom of our GOD, we should easily trust him to rule his own world.

Could we understand the secret character of his decrees, we should read in each syllable a perfect harmony.

Teach us, O you blessed Enlightener of our minds, teach us to expound thy actions in a fairer sense.

Suffer us not to follow our private spirit, lest we create to ourselves a voluntary misery.

Still let us construe the afflictions you sendest us, as meant to correct, not to destroy us:

To prevent some sin, or beget some virtue in us, and when we need our crosses no longer, you wilt take them away.

Meanwhile, O gracious LORD, make us wait thy time, and not impatiently prescribe limits to thee.

Make us rejoice that our lots are in thy hands; but O let thy mercy choose favorably for us.

Dispose as you please our condition here; only our portion hereafter let that be with thy blessed.

GLORY BE to the Father, and to the Son, and to the Holy Ghost. As it was in the beginning, is now, and ever shall be: world without end.

Amen.

WHAT can infinite Power and Goodness do, but that which is best? LORD, I submit and adore thy providence, which scatters these temporal things with a seeming negligence, as trifles of so little importance, that they signify neither love nor hatred. Nothing, indeed, but heaven is considerable; nothing but eternity deserves our esteem. Fix you our steps, O LORD, that we stagger not at the uneven motions of the world, but steadily go on to our glorious home; neither censuring our journey by the weather we meet with, nor turning out of the way for any thing that befalls us.

GLORY BE to the Father, and to the Son, and to the Holy Ghost. As it was in the beginning, is now, and ever shall be: world without end.

Amen.

O GOD, *the eternal source and necessity of being, on whose free overflowing that of the whole creation every moment depends! Strike, we beseech thee, our hearts with a continual dread and reverence of thy absolute dominion, which should it but never so little suspend thy bounty, we should instantly vanish into nothing; and grant that we may by thy grace so husband our time here, as in the next life to possess thy eternity, through our LORD Jesus CHRIST.*

At Noon.

PSALM 5.

BE YOU eternally adored, O GOD of our salvation, and may thy praises be sung by thy servants for ever.

When our first parents had disobeyed thy precepts, to the ruin of themselves and their whole posterity;

Thy mercy immediately provided a remedy, and graciously promised a powerful Redeemer, who should suffer as man, and satisfy as GOD.

A meritorious Redeemer that should conquer sin and death; and crush in pieces the serpent's head.

A Redeemer that should fully repair the breaches of mankind, and die as a piacular oblation, to procure atonement for our sins:

Enlightening our eyes with a clearer view of those excellent truths that concern our peace, and his all sufficient merits, for purification and satisfaction:

And supporting our nature with a stronger grace, to bear us safely on through all encounters;

Till we arrive at the land of rest; and be received for ever into that glorious kingdom.

O blessed JESUS! our strength and our guide; who knows and pitiest our weak capacities;

Who in thy tender care have contrived such means, that nothing can undo us but our own perverseness;

How easy have you made the way to heaven! How light the burden you layest upon thy followers!

It is but to love thee, our greatest Benefactor, and we perfectly fulfil every branch of thy law.

It is but desiring to see thee, our supreme Beatitude, and we are sure to possess an eternity of joy.

Blessed, O my GOD, be the wisdom of thy providence, which alone knows the way to draw good out of evil;

Which not only restores us to our first degree, but makes even our fall rebound us to a greater height.

LORD, as thy goodness turns all things to the advantage of thy elect; O may thy elect praise thy goodness in all things.

PSALM 6.

ADMIRABLE, O LORD, wert you in thy merciful promise; but infinitely more in thy wonderful performance. You didst not depute an angel to supply thy place;

nor entrust so tender a work to the management of a seraph.

But thyself didst bow the heavens, and come down, and

with thy own blessed hands work our redemption.

Thyself didst take upon thee our frail nature; and

vouchsafe to be born of an humble VIRGIN.

Condescending to the weaknesses of a child; a child whose parents were poor, and unesteemed in the world.

Not declining the mean entertainment of a stable; O how unfit for the birth of the King of heaven!

But contenting thyself with the cradle of a manger, and the uneasy lodging of a bed of straw.

Refusing the soft accommodations of the rich, to undergo the inconveniences of a poor stranger.

Only the faithful JOSEPH stood waiting on thee, and provided, as he was able, for his helpless family.

Only thy pious Mother dearly embraced thee, and wrapped thy tender limbs in swaddling clothes.

Wonder, O heavens! and be amazed, O earth! and every creature humbly bow your heads.

Bow, and adore this incomprehensible mystery, " the Word was made flesh, and dwelt among us."

But most of all, we, who are most concerned, the banished children of unfortunate ADAM:

Let us bow down our faces to the dust; and, prostrate, adore so unspeakable a mercy.

Behold, thus low my SAVIOR stooped for me, to check the pride of my corrupted nature.

Behold, thus low he stooped to take me from the ground; and raise me to the felicities of his own kingdom.

Lift up thy voice with joy, O my soul; and sing Hosanna to the newborn JESUS.

Call all the blessed angels to celebrate his birth, and repeat afresh that heavenly anthem;

"Glory be to GOD on high, on earth peace, goodwill towards men."

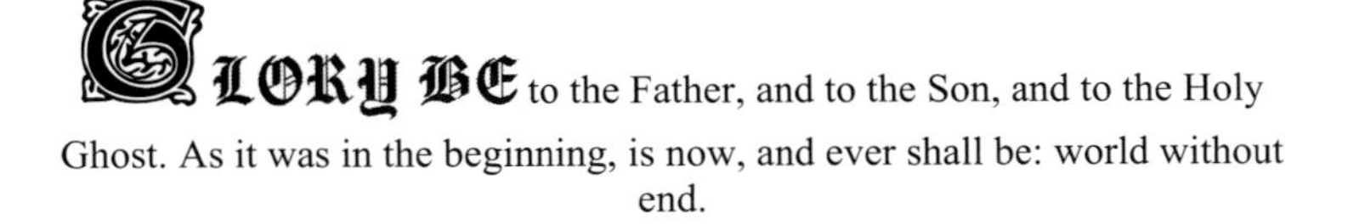

GLORY BE to the Father, and to the Son, and to the Holy Ghost. As it was in the beginning, is now, and ever shall be: world without end.

Amen.

PSALM 7.

REJOICE all you faithful nations of the earth, when you hear the sweet name of your dear REDEEMER.

Rejoice, and, with your bended knees and hearts, adore the blessed JESUS.

He is the SON of the everliving GOD; equally participating the glories of his FATHER.

He is the great MESSIAH whom the Prophets foretold, and all the ancient saints so long expected.

At length in fullness of time he came to visit in person our miserable world.

He came with his hands full of miracles; and every miracle full of mercies.

He made the crooked become straight; and the lame to walk and leap for joy.

He opened the ears of the deaf to hear, and gave sight to them that were born blind.

He loosened the tongues of the dumb to speak: O may he govern ours to sing his praise!

He cleansed the lepers with a word of his mouth, and healed their diseases who but touched his garment.

To the poor he revealed the treasures of his Gospel; and taught the simple the mysteries of his kingdom.

He cast out Devils by the command of his will, and forced them to confess and adore his person.

He raised the dead from the grave to life; the dead that was four days buried and corrupted.

Nay, even himself being slain for us upon the cross; and his tomb made fast and secured with a guard;

He raised again by his own victorious power, and carried up our nature into the highest heavens.

All these stupendous signs, O glorious JESUS! were done by the hand of thy almighty mercy:

To witness thy truth with the seal of heaven, and endear thy precepts with gracious miracles.

That thus engaged we might believe in thee; and obeying the Law, he eternally saved.

O let not all this love be lost, by so many tokens so kindly expressed!

One miracle more we humbly beg; but one as strange, and hard as any of the rest:

Soften our stony hearts into a tender sense of thy great goodness, and their own true duty.

Raise our dead spirits from this heavy earth, to dwell with thee in the land of the living.

That as we here admire thy bounteous power, and daily sing the wonders of thy grace:

We may hereafter adore thy blessed self, and sing eternally the wonders of thy glory.

GLORY BE to the Father, and to the Son, and to the Holy Ghost. As it was in the beginning, is now, and ever shall be: world without end.

Amen.

O GOD, *who, to preserve in reach of happiness those whom you preserve in being, didst send down in the fullness of time (as thy mercy, as ancient as our misery, promised) the true MESSIAS to save the world from the ruin into which it was plunged by ADAM'S fall; fill our souls, we beseech thee, through deep admiration of this thy excessive bounty, with an overflowing love of thyself, infinitely fuller of thy goodness than can be expressed; and grant that this love to us may so powerfully endear to us our heavenly Master's gracious precepts and example, that our perfect observing, them, through our LORD JESUS CHRIST.* Amen.

In the Afternoon.

Antiphon

Who is like thee, O LORD, among the gods? Who is like thee, terrible in judgments?

PSALM 8.

SPEAK no more proudly, vain dust, nor provoke any longer the living Got.

Seal up thy lips in humble silence; and tremblingly remember his dreadful judgments.

Remember how the earth opened itself, and swallowed up alive so many thousands.

Remember how the clouds rained fire and brimstone, and buried whole cities in their own ashes.

Remember how the general deluge overspread the world,

and swept away almost all mankind.

Remember, and ask the cause of all this ruin, and tell it aloud to the bold offender.

Tell him, it was sin, and such as his, that drew upon these so swift destruction.

Sin threw the angels down from heaven, and chained them up in eternal darkness.

Sin banished ADAM out of Paradise, and turned that delicious garden into a field' of weeds.

O GOD, how terrible is thy mighty arm, when you stretchest it forth to be avenged on thine enemies!

O sin, how fatal is thy desperate malice, that pulls on our heads all the thunder of heaven!

O my soul, how dull and senseless are we, to sleep secure as if all were safe!

Can we repeat those amazing truths, and not tremble at the wrath of the divine justice?

Even while we sing thy praises, O glorious GOD! for our very duty we should fear before thee.

What should corrupted nature then do, when it sees itself ready to offend thee?

What should a guilty conscience do, when it sees itself ruined by offending thee?

Strike you our hearts, O you infinite Majesty! With an awful reverence of thy great name.

Correct our many levities into a pious sadness, and break our proud spirits to bow to thee.

Still may our consciences cry aloud within us, Dare you commit this evil, and sin against Go])?

Dare you commit this evil, and undo yourselves, and plunge your souls into everlasting torments?

Forbid so rash a madness, gracious LORD, and make thy judgments on others mercies to us.

GLORY BE to the Father, and to the Son, and to the Holy Ghost. As it was in the beginning, is now, and ever shall be: world without end.

Amen.

Antiphon

Who is like thee, O LORD, among the gods? Who is like thee, amiable in mercies?

PSALM 9.

WIPE away the tears from thine eyes, O my soul; and clear thy heart from all clouds of despair.

He that is thus infinite in power to punish, is full as infinite in goodness to save us.

How often have we broken his divine commands! yet still his earth sustains, and serves us.

Himself, with his own Almighty Word, confined the waters, and reproved their officiousness to destroy.

Hitherto shall you come, and no farther; and here will I stay your proud waves.

Only the ambitious angels find no forgiveness, because their obstinacy and immutable pride refuses to seek it of GOD.

But O! the inestimable love vouchsafed to AD AM, and to us dust and ashes his posterity.

For whom the Sovereign King of heaven humbled himself to descend upon earth:

Leading a poor laborious life, and suffering a painful ignominious death.

To make expiation for our sins, and teach us how to live, and how to die.

Thy mercies, O LORD, are above all thy works, and this above all thy mercies.

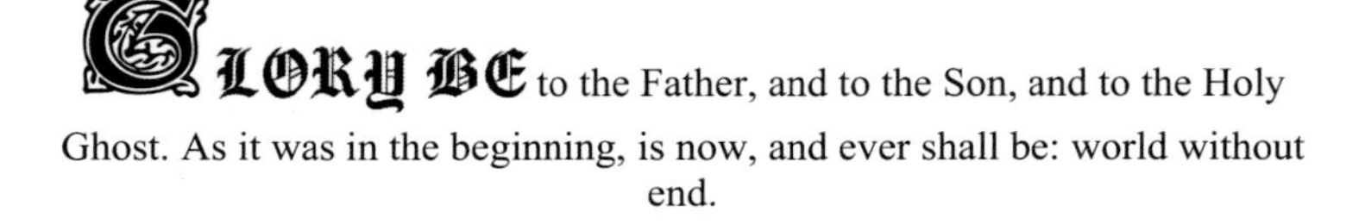

GLORY BE to the Father, and to the Son, and to the Holy Ghost. As it was in the beginning, is now, and ever shall be: world without end.

Amen.

Antiphon

Dreadful art You, LORD, in the terror of' thy judgments; but infinitely more amiable in the sweetness of thy mercies.

PSALM 10.

STILL let us sing the mercies of our GOD, and hold a little longer this sweet key.

When we, alas! lay buried in the abyss of nothing, his free goodness called us into being.

He fashioned our limbs in our mother's womb, and filled our nurse's breast with milk.

He enlarged our little steps when we began to go, and carefully preserved our helpless infancy.

Commanding even his angels to bear us in their hands, lest we should dash our feet against a stone.

How many dangers have we happily escaped; and not

one of them but was governed by his providence!

How many blessings do we daily receive; and not one of

them but proceeds from his bounty!

He provided tutors to instruct our youth, and to plant in our tender minds the seeds of virtue.

He appointed pastors to feed our souls, and safely to guide them in the ways of bliss.

He founded his church on an immovable rock, to render our faith firm and secure.

He sealed his love with sacraments of grace, to breed and nourish up in us the life of love.

All this you have done, O merciful LORD! the wise Disposer of heaven and earth.

All this you have done, and still goest on, by infinite ways, to gain us to thy love.

You commandest us to ask, and promisest to grant; you invitest us to seek, and assurest us to find.

You vouchsafest even thyself to stand at the door and knock; and if we open, you enterest and fillest our hearts with joy.

If we forget thee, you renewest our memory; if we fly from thee, you still findest means to recal us.

If we defer our amendment, you patiently stayest for us; and when we return, you openest thy arms to embrace us.

We know thy ways are in the deep abyss, and none can sound the bottom of thy counsels.

Yet may we safely look on the flowing streams, and gather this comfort from their gentle course.

When we were not, you freely lovedst us; you wilt not forsake us now we strive to love thee.

When we had lost our way, you soughtest after us; you wilt not refuse us now we seek after thee.

LORD, all we have is derived from thee; all that we can expect can come from none but thyself.

Accomplish thine own blessed purpose in us; and finish these happy beginnings towards us.

GLORY BE to the Father, and to the Son, and to the Holy Ghost. As it was in the beginning, is now, and ever shall be: world without end.

Amen.

WHAT *heart can resist the great King of kings, terrible and amiable, and mightily shown both in glorious miracles of vengeance and love?*

In the Evening.

Antiphon

You art, O LORD! All goodness and patience, and we, alas! All sin and disobedience.

PSALM 11.

GOOD GOD! How extremely ingrateful are we; how strangely insensible of our manifest duty!

Every creature hears thy voice but we; every thing lives by rule but we.

The sun observes his constant rising, and sets exactly at his appointed time.

The sun stands still if you commandest, and even goes back to obey thy will.

And we who expect those glorious promises, and aim no lower than the heaven of heavens:

Shall we forget the law of GOD, that only instructs us to perfect ourselves?

We, who are bought by the blood of JESUS, and freely redeemed by his sacred cross!

Shall we neglect so gracious a SAVIOR, whose only design is to draw us to his love?

Shall we neglect so generous a love, whose only effect is to make us happy?

O may thy holy will, be all our rule, and thy gracious hand our only guide.

O may thy infinite goodness engage us to love thee; arid. thy blessed love prepare us to enjoy thee.

GLORY BE to the Father, and to the Son, and to the Holy Ghost. As it was in the beginning, is now, and ever shall be: world without end.

Amen.

PSALM 12.

WHAT did I say, O LORD My GOD! we guide not our lives by thy straight rules?

It was too mild and gentle a reproof for us, who quite contradict thy laws.

What you forbiddest we, left to ourselves, eagerly pursue; and what you commandest, our frowardness still resists.

We boldly converse with temptation and sin, which thy love adviseth` us to fly like death.

We fear a loss or a frown, where you biddest us proceed with undaunted courage.

We govern our actions by our own wild fancies, and expect thy providence should comply with our humors.

We would have thee relieve us when we list; and rain, and shine, as we think fit;

Pardon, O gracious LORD, this rude perverseness, and fashion our spirits to submit to thee.

Make us exactly observe what you prescribest, how bitter soever it taste to our sense.

We are assured thy wisdom knows our infirmities; we are sure thy goodness delights in our relief.

GLORY BE to the Father, and to the Son, and to the Holy Ghost. As it was in the beginning, is now, and ever shall be: world without end.

Amen.

PSALM 13.

IT was not alone to make the day, that You, O LORD, didst make the sun;

But to teach us these pious lessons, and write them plain as its own beams.

So should our light shine forth to others; and so our love warm their coldness.

So when they say we are under a cloud; we should, like the sun, be really above it,

And though we appear sometimes eclipsed, or even extinguished in a night of sorrow,

Still we should shine to ourselves, and thee; and still go on in the ways of light.

Only in this we gladly disagree; and blessed be our GOD who made the difference:

Not like the sun, that every night goes down, and must at last be quite put out:;

When we have finished here our course, and seem to set to this dark earth:

We hope to rise, and set no more; but shine perpetually in a brighter heaven.

GLORY BE to the Father, and to the Son, and to the Holy Ghost. As it was in the beginning, is now, and ever shall be: world without end.

Amen.

O *gracious GOD, whose laws are but necessary rules of saving love, and whose commands are but efficacious advices of what our nature needs to make it happy; quicken, we beseech thee, the slackness of our obedience, by often reflecting on this thy generous goodness; and grant that the ready observance paid by all other creatures to thy holy will in serving us, may so reproach our perverse resisting the guidance of thy sweet SPIRIT towards our own only good, which you kindly callest thy service, that we may feel ourselves confounded with shame at our notorious follies, and be henceforth apter to learn, by all the world about us, our duty to thee, through our LORD JESUS CHRIST.* Amen.

The Office for Wednesday.

Morning Prayer.

HE is our great and sovereign LORD, the absolute King of heaven and earth; he sees at once the whole frame of all things, and throughly comprehends their various natures.

Come, let us adore our GOD that governs us.

To every creature he appoints a fit office, and guides all their motions in perfect order; till he has wrought his glorious design to finish the world in a beauteous close.

Come, let us adore our GOD, &c.

All these he governs by his infinite wisdom, and all for the good of them that love him; his counsels are deep, and beyond our reach, but all his ways are just and merciful.

Come, let us adore our GOD, &c.

He governs his enemies with a rod of iron, and punishes their willfulness with eternal miseries; but his servants he blesses with the privilege of children, and provides for their duty a rich inheritance.

Come, let us adore our GOD that governs us.

PSALM 1.

WHY do you laugh, unhappy wretches! who tire yourselves in the ways of sin

Ways that indeed seem smooth at first; but lead to danger, and end in ruin.

Why do you boast your pleasant life, who he asleep in the arms of death

Awake, and chase the dream away, that deludes your sick heads with empty fancies.

Awake, and fill your eyes with tears, and sadly look on your real miseries.

Whither, alas! will your souls be hurried, when you sigh away your last faint breath

They shall fly away amazed from the sight of heaven, and hide their guilty selves in eternal darkness.

There shall they dwell with intolerable pains, weeping, and wailing, and lamenting for ever.

Their understanding shall sit as in a deep dungeon, and think on nothing but its own calamities.

Their will shall be heightened to a madness of desire, and perpetually racked with despair of obtaining.

Their memory shall serve but to renew their sorrows; and their whole souls be drowned in the sea of bitterness. They shall wish the mountains to fall on them; and cry to the hills to cover them.

But nothing shall fall on them but the wrath of GOD; nor cover them, but their own confusion.

There every vice shall have its proper torment, prodigiously bred out of its own corruption.

The lascivious shall burn with unquenchable fire, perpetually flaming from their own passions.

The glutton and drunkard shall vainly sigh for a drop of water to cool their tongues.

The choleric shall rage like mad dogs; and the envious gnaw their own bowels.

But O, what horrid pangs shall seize them all; and wound, and pierce the very centre of their souls!

When they shall see themselves eternally deprived of the bright and blissful vision of GOD.

When they shall see themselves eternally banished from the sweet and gracious presence of JESUS.

That GOD, who made them to enjoy his glory; that JESUS, who redeemed them to be heirs of his felicity! Then shall they curse the day of their birth, and the

unfortunate companions that inveigled them to sin.

They shall curse this vain deceitful world; and cry out with desperate fury, Are these the effects of those fond desires, whose enjoyments we made our chief felicity

Alas! what avail now our wanton liberties, and the fugitive pleasures we so eagerly pursued

What comfort receive we from those empty honors, and faithless riches we so highly esteemed

They all are vanished away like a shadow, and as a cloud of smoke scattered with the wind.

But the remorse and punishment endure for ever, and torture our spirit with perpetual anguish.

Thus shall they cry, and none regard; thus shall they mourn, and none shall be found to pity them.

O sad expectance of a dissolute life! O dreadful consequence of an impenitent death!

Eternally to long for what they never can enjoy; eternally to suffer what they can never avoid.

Blessed be thy gracious providence, O GOD, that with such tender care forewarns us of our dangers.

O save us too from all those dangers; save us for thy mercy's sake.

Save us, and make us fearful to do what, when we have done, will make us miserable to suffer.

Quicken our apprehensions of the ruinous effects of sill; and with thy terrible threatenings check our unbridled passions.

That if thy glorious promises move not our hearts, the fear at least of hell may fright us into heaven.

GLORY BE to the Father, and to the Son, and to the Holy Ghost. As it was in the beginning, is now, and ever shall be: world without end.

Amen.

Antiphon

The day will come, it will infallibly come, when GOD will crown all that love his glory.

PSALM 2.

WHY do you mourn, you children of the light, to whom belong the promises of bliss

Who feed on the pleasant fruits of piety, and the continual feast of a good conscience.

Who taste already the sweetness of hope; and hereafter shall be satisfied with the fullness of fruition.

What can molest your happy state, whom the GOD of, glory has chosen for himself

Whom he has adopted into his own family, and designed for heirs of the kingdom of heaven

That blessed kingdom where all delights abound, and sorrow and tears are banished away.

Where none are sick, or grow old, or die; but flourish in health, and youth, and immortal life.

Where none are perplexed with cares or fears, but dwell secure and free for ever.

Where we no more shall be subject to pain; no more exposed to the danger of temptation.

Where we no more shall be crossed by others, no more disquieted by our own passions.

But a serene tranquility shall be perpetually within us, and innumerable joys all round about us.

Joy in the excellences of our glorified bodies; joy in the perfections of our enlarged souls.

Joy in the sweet society of saints; joy in the glorious company of angels.

Joy in the ravishing sight of our beloved JESUS; joy is the blissful union with the adored Deity.

All shall be joy, and love, and peace; and all endure for eternal ages.

Let then the impenitent sinner be in fear; and the obdurate heart break with grief;

But for the innocent, let them always be glad; and the servants of JESUS rejoice and sing.

Sweet is the yoke of thy love, O LORD! light is the burden of thy commands.

But O! how far more rich are thy faithful promises! How infinitely greater thy glorious rewards!

When every virtue shall wear its proper crown, and shine with a diadem fit for its own head.

The humble there shall be highly exalted; and the poor in spirit preferred to be Kings.

The meek shall possess the Holy Land, and the mourners be comforted with eternal refreshments.

The pure in heart shall see the GOD of purity; and the lovers of peace have the privilege of his children.

They who hunger and thirst after heaven shall be filled! and the merciful entertained with embraces of mercy.

They who suffered persecution shall be abundantly rewarded; and the enlighteners of others shine bright as the stars.

They who relinquished any thing for GOD shall receive a hundred fold; and all the just shall be in glory for ever. Then shall they bless the true friend that reproved them, and the charitable hand that assisted them to their happiness.

They shall bless the provident mercies of their GOD, and sing aloud the victories of his grace.

Is this the effect of those little pains we took Are these the repairs for those petty losses we suffered.

Happy we, who denied ourselves toys, and now are advanced to these high felicities!

Millions of years shall pass away, and our glory shall seem then but to begin.

Millions of millions shall pass away, and our glory shall be no nearer its end.

Thus shall they rejoice, and none disturb them; thus shall they sing, and all the heavens join with them.

O sweet expectance of a pious life! O happs consequence of a holy death!

Eternally to be free from whatsoever can afflict; eternally to enjoy whatever can delight.

Blessed be thy gracious providence, O GOD, that with so large a bounty wooes us to our happiness:

Wooes us in a way we are so apt to be taken, the love of ourselves, and our own great interest.

As you have prepared such felicities for us, O may thy grace prepare us for them.

O may this best of works take up all our time, at least take up the best of our time.

At least every morning let us renew our hopes, and close the evening with the same sweet thoughts.

Let us not. faint, and we surely shall see a prosperous issue of all our sorrows.

Still let us labor, still let us suffer; our troubles are short and our joys eternal.

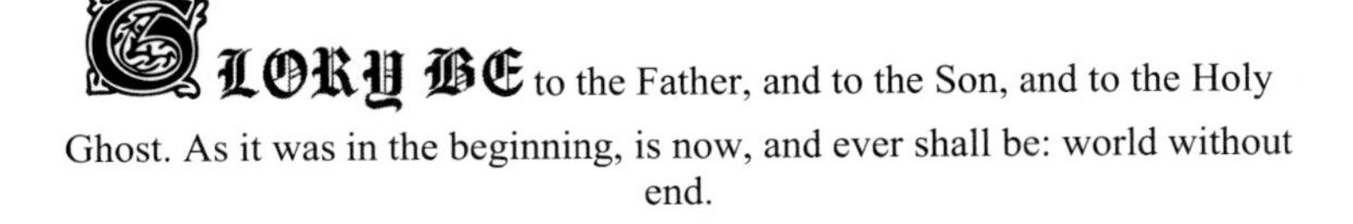

GLORY BE to the Father, and to the Son, and to the Holy Ghost. As it was in the beginning, is now, and ever shall be: world without end.

Amen.

Antiphon

What will it Profit a man to gain the whole world, and lose his own soul Or what shall we give in exchange, or our souls

PSALM 3.

COME now, my soul, and choose; for life and death are set before thee.

Choose whilst thy gracious LORD allows thee day; lest the night of darkness overtake thy neglect.

Choose, but remember eternity is concerned; and examine well ere you make thy resolve.

Call all the pleasures of the world before thee, and ask if any of them be worth such pains.

Ask, if to satisfy some irregular passion, can recompence the forfeiture of such felicities

Ask, if the vain forbidden things you loves, deserve thy affection better than thy Maker

Are they more worthy in themselves, or beneficial unto thee, that you can prefer them before thy Redeemer

Dost you expect to be quiet by enjoying them; or everlastingly happy in their procurement

Will they protect thee at the hour of death; or plead thy cause at the day of judgment

O no! they but deceive me with a smiling look; which I too oft have proved by dear experience.

It is heaven alone that yields a true content; it is heaven alone that fills us with delight.

Take then away your flatteries, false world, and leave me free for better thoughts.

Turn you thy face to me, O JESUS; and keep mine eyes still turned towards thee:

That I may look continually on thy glorious beauty, and be ravishes for ever with the charms of thy sweetness.

It is thee, chaste Spouse of souls, it is thee alone I choose, and dedicate myself entirely to thy service.

You art my sole and absolute LORD; be you my part and inheritance for ever.

But, O my LORD, do you choose me, and guide my uninstructed soul to choose thee.

O make me choose to love thee, till I come to see thee; and then I am sure I cannot choose but love thee, and be ravished with thee for ever.

Here, alas! we move slowly in the dark, led on by the evidence of things not seen.

Did we but clearly see what we say we believe, we should certainly change the course of our lives.

Did we but see the damned in their flames, or hear them cry in the midst of their torments;

How should we fear to follow them in their sin, which we know has plunged them into all those miseries!

How should we strive against the next temptation, and cast about to avoid the danger!

Did we but see the glories of the saints, or hear the sweet hymns they continually sing;

How should we study to imitate their lives, which, we know, have raised them to all their happiness!

How should we seek all occasions of improvement, and make it our business to work out our salvation!

Nay, did our faith but firmly believe the truths we every day recite in our creeds,

What would we do to attain those joys; what would we do to escape those sorrows!

Would half an hour be too long to pray, or once a week too often to last

Would the pardon of an injury be too hard a law, or the making restitution too dear a price

Durst we return to our sins again, or spend our time in idleness and folly

Yet is all this as sure as if we saw it; and would move us as much if we seriously considered it.

Which of us doubts but ere it be long we shall all be dust; yet which of us lives as if we thought to die

Pity, O gracious LORD, the frailties of thy servants, and suffer not our blindness to lead us to ruin.

Supply our want of sight by a lively faith; and strengthen our faith by thy powerful grace.

Make us choose wisely, and pursue our choice; and as well use the means as pursue the end.

O set you right the bias of our hearts, that in all our motions we may draw off from the world:

That they may still incline towards the, and rest at last in thy holy presence.

You art our LORD, and we will serve thee in fear; you art our GOD, and we will love thee in hope, and humble confidence too of enjoying thee for ever.

GLORY BE to the Father, and to the Son, and to the Holy Ghost. As it was in the beginning, is now, and ever shall be: world without end.

Amen.

At Noon.

PSALM 5.

LET them neglect thy praises, O LORD, who never consider thy mercies.

Let them be silent to thee, O gracious GOD, whose mouths are full of themselves.

But as for us, who subsist by thy gifts, and thankfully acknowledge the riches of thy goodness,

Our hearts shall continually meditate on thee, and our lips delight to sing thy glory.

Blessed for ever be thy name, O JESU; and blessed be the sweetness of thy wisdom:

Whose infinite love has vouchsafed our earth such excellent rules to guide us to heaven.

You taughtest us that happy skill of finding our lives, by losing them to follow thee.

You taughtest us to trample this world under our feet; and use it as a step to climb up to the next.

From thee we learn those glorious mysteries, that exalt our faith so high above reason.

From thee alone, and from thy school of discipline and grace, all know we, all learn we, and all we receive.

How long, alas! might we have wandered here, in the midst of darkness and error,

Had not thy love and pity, O merciful LORD, brought down thyself to become our light!

Never else should we have learned to deny ourselves, and take up our cross, and follow thee.

Never should we have known that great secret, to forgive our enemies, and do good to those that despitefully use us. On the unsatisfying things of this low earth should we blindly have set our whole affections:

Hadst you not told us of the kingdom of heaven, and bid us lay up our treasures there;

Hadst you not terrified us to fear thy wrath, by declaring the miseries that attend our sins:

Hadst you not invited us to obey thy commands, by proposing the felicities of a pious life.

What host you promised, gracious LORD, to the meek and poor in spirit!

What have you promised, LORD, to the weepers here; to those that hunger and thirst after holiness!

How many joys has thy bounty prepared, for the lovers of mercy, and makers of peace!

How many blessings for the pure of heart, and those who with patience bear their crosses!

O you all seeing Wisdom of the Eternal Father, and sovereign King of men and angels!

Who from thy glorious throne descendedst on our earth, familiarly to teach us the oracles of heaven:

Write these sacred words in the tables of our hearts, and suffer not at any time our passions to break them.

Make us still study thee, our heavenly Master, and continually admire the beauty of thy law

A law, that so clearly shows us our end, and so plenteously furnishes us with means to attain it.

A law, that so safely cures our infirmities, and so fitly supplies all our defects.

A law, so exactly conformable to true reason, and so highly perfective of human nature.

A blessed law, that makes even here our life more sweet, and leads us hereafter to everlasting felicity.

GLORY BE to the Father, and to the Son, and to the Holy Ghost. As it was in the beginning, is now, and ever shall be: world without end.

Amen.

PSALM 5.

NEVER will we cease to exalt thy goodness, O JESU, since you never ceasest to oblige us with new blessings.

Thy generous love could not thus be satisfied, to have only spoken to us the words of life.

It was not enough for thy excessive love, that thy heavenly sermons told us our duty;

But thou must urge and provoke our obedience, by the sweet enforcement of thine own example.

You forbiddest thy followers to affect superfluities, and thine own provision was a few barley loaves.

You biddest us not fear them that kill the body, and yieldest up thine own to the death on the cross.

You enjoinest us to love our fiercest enemies, and thy dying breath prayed for thy crucifiers.

Thy perfect soul needed not, as our weak natures, the outward forms and discipline of religion:

Yet you vouchsafest to observe the common feasts, and assist at the public offices of the temple,

To watch, and pray, and fast with so fervent a zeal, that thy practice outdid thine own precepts.

This life, and death itself, our merciful Lord undertook, to mark out for us the way to heaven, and purchase everlasting happiness for us.

Shall we not then, O my soul, rejoicingly follow that path which we see our SAVIOR has trod before us

Which we see, though spread all over with thorns, yet carried him directly to the glories of Paradise.

Shall we not confidently rely on so gracious a Leader, who promises, if we faint, to look back and relieve us!

O LORD, bow down thy gracious eye, and pity the frailties of our imperfect nature.

Reach forth thy hand, and strengthen us with thy grace, that, nothing may divert our advance towards thee.

But in this dangerous labyrinth of the world, and the whole course of our pilgrimage here, Thy heavenly dictates be our map, and thy holy life be our guide.

GLORY BE to the Father, and to the Son, and to the Holy Ghost. As it was in the beginning, is now, and ever shall be: world without end.

Amen.

PSALM 6.

MAY every age sing praises to our GOD, and all generations adore his providence.

From the beginning, his mercy has still laid means to raise us to those blessed objects above our nature.

At first he created ADAM with all necessary knowledge, and then ordained the Patriarchs to inform their families.

Afterwards he charged the angels to bring us his commands, and often inspired the Prophets to declare his will.

When he had done all this, and found it not enough to guide untoward man to his true end,

What did he do then to save the perishing world O strange excess of the divine goodness!

He sent his own beloved Son to dwell amongst us, and teach us the art of working out our salvation:

That sacred art of training up our souls for heaven, and fitting them for the blissful union with himself.

But, O you King of glorious sweetness, whose flowing tongue drops milk and honey!

We were not so happy as to behold thy person, nor our ears to hear thy voice.

Yet ere we were born, you hadst us in thy thoughts, and didst provide a method to supply that defect:

Selecting a number, of choice disciples, and throughly instructing them in thy heavenly doctrine;

That they might keep alive the memory of thee, and witness to all nations thy stupendous works.

You didst verify their mission with the power of miracles, and enflamedst their hearts with the fire of thy SPIRIT.

Deep in the breasts of the faithful did they write thy Gospel, and sealed it before their eyes with their own blood.

Their successors deposited the same precious treasure in the common magazine of the universal church:

Enjoining their children to guard it with their lives, and convey it unchanged to future ages.

Blessed be thy goodness, O gracious GOD, who have thus made known thy will to us.

Blessed be thy power, O LORD, who by thy Apostles have wrought such miracles to confirm thy faith, and inclined our hearts to believe it.

How many souls are unhappily seduced, and lose themselves in the wilderness of error and heresy!

While we, by thy providence, are directly led in the strait way to bliss.

How many nations are miserably involved in the darkness of barbarism and unbelief!

While we enjoy a clear noonday, and safely walk in the light of truth.

O infinite Goodness! who freely choosest to pour forth thy blessings on us, though unworthy of them,

As it is alone from thee we receive these favors, to thee alone let us return our praises.

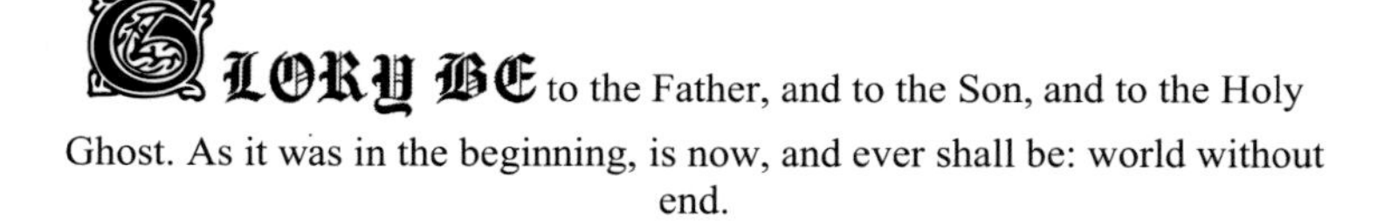

GLORY BE to the Father, and to the Son, and to the Holy Ghost. As it was in the beginning, is now, and ever shall be: world without end.

Amen.

In the Afternoon.

Antiphon

A good conscience is a continual feast, and a Peaceful mind the antepast of heaven.

PSALM 7.

LORD, how secure and quiet they live, whom thy grace preserves in innocence!

The day goes smoothly over their heads, and silent as the shadow of a dial.

Their spirits run calm and even, and ebb and flow in obedience to reason.

All their delight is to think of heaven, and reckon the joys they shall one day possess:

Till some unruly passion presses to come in, and by its fawning outside gains admittance.

It promises at first all joy, all happiness; but soon discovers its pernicious effects.

Soon it grows bold to undermine their repose, and open a door to all their enemies.

So at a little breach of the city wall, an whole army pours in:

Enslaving all that submit to their violence, and destroying all that resist it.

And such, alas! is their confusion, when once they have, yielded to the first assault;

Immediately a throng of tumultuous thoughts crowd in, and utterly consume their peace.

Vain at the best, and short are the enjoyments of this

world; and, after a little flattery, betray us into ruin.

Save us, O blessed JESUS, or else we perish; awake,

and with thy speedy mercy rescue thy servants.

Send down thy powerful grace to sustain us, and thoroughly reduce these unquiet disorders;

That we again may return to our former rest, and constantly enjoy an universal peace.

Peace with the had, by bearing their injuries; peace with the good, by conforming to their virtues.

Peace with ourselves, by subduing sense to reason; and peace with thee, by improving reason with religion.

GLORY BE to the Father, and to the Son, and to the Holy Ghost. As it was in the beginning, is now, and ever shall be: world without end.

Amen.

Antiphon

You art, O LORD, the only anchor of our hope; save us, O JESUS, or we perish.

PSALM 8.

THUS are they miserably tossed up and down, who float on the waves of their own passions.

Their wearied souls soon faint within them, when they see their LORD has withdrawn his presence.

They seek him, but cannot find him; they call upon him, but he gives them no answer.

O still seek on, still call upon your GOD; for his mercy will surely awake at last.

Though he seem sometimes to slumber for a while, to try your duty, or punish your disobedience;

Though he suffer a while the fury of the tempest, to show you your hopeless state, if left unto yourselves:

Yet be assured he will hear your prayers at last; he will not permit you to perish for ever:

For he is a Gm) hearing prayer, and the hope of the poor destitute; and when they cry unto him, he delivereth them out of their distress.

When they are even at their wit's end, they cry aloud, " LORD," save us, or we perish;" and their soul even melts away because of the trouble.

And now, when all their fears are grown to the height, and no means appear to sustain their patience:

When the proud waves beat violently against them, and cover their little vessel with despair and ruin:

Behold his blessed voice commands a calm, and immediately the sea and winds obey him:

Immediately his sun arises in their hearts, and with its gentle beams revives their hopes.

Then is their darkness turned into light, and the clouds dispersed into a bright day.

Then they recollect their scattered thoughts, and range them again in their ancient order.

Often they look back on the dangers they have escaped, and as often bless the mercy that delivers them.

Often they look forwards on the course they are going, and as often sing with joy for their happy change.

Welcome again that easy yoke of CHRIST, and the light burden of loving our SAVIOR.

Welcome the holy offices of sweet devotion, and that soul enflaming fervent prayer.

Now, now we discern this beauteous truth; and O may we print it deeply in our minds:

That the pleasures of virtue are pure and constant, and

infinite blessings attend to reward it.

But the pursuit of vice is troublesome and intricate, and finishes its course in an abyss of misery.

Pity, O LORD, you Raiser of them that fall, and sole

Sustainer of them that stand!

Pity thy children's weakness, who look up to thee, and know we are nothing in ourselves.

Let us not lose this experience; but teach us wisdom from our own miscarriage.

Teach us to observe where our error was, and fortify ourselves against that defect.

To suppress our temptations in their first approach; when their power is weak, and our grace is in full strength.

To remember how formerly their flatteries have abused us; and when they counterfeit again, be no more deceived:

Never to look on the face of pleasures, as they come dressed up and smiling towards us:

But always reflect how sadly they go off, and leave nothing behind, but their venomous sting.

So shall we gain the best of victories, whilst we master our own corrupt inclinations.

So shall we be honored with the noblest of triumphs, whilst our conquered passions draw us up to heaven.

GLORY BE to the Father, and to the Son, and to the Holy Ghost. As it was in the beginning, is now, and ever shall be: world without end.

Amen.

Antiphon

All our lots are in the hands of GOD, and all our safety in the assistance of his grace.

PSALM 9.

LORD, as thy all wise providence seems to sleep sometimes and permits the storm to grow high and loud;

Yet never fails to relieve thy servants, who faithfully call on thee in their day of trouble:

So let thy favorable hand still bear us up, when you seest us charged with any strong assault.

Leave us not then to our own infirmities, lest the enemy of our souls prevail against us.

Forsake not our misery when we are fallen, lest we he for ever grovelling on the earth.

Suffer not our frailties to become a custom, lest we die impenitent, and perish without recovery.

Deliver us, O LORD, from the occasions of sin, and the importunities of such as delight in folly.

Deliver us from the snare of enticing company, and the dangerous infection of ill example:

Infection, that spreads in every place its poisonous air; and wherever it enters, corrupts and kills.

Once more, my soul, let us repeat this prayer; and humbly implore again so necessary a blessing.

Deliver us, O LORD, from the occasions of sin, and " the importunities of such as delight in folly.

Deliver us from the snare of enticing company, and the dangerous infection of ill example."

Set a strict watch continually over our eyes, and diligently keep the door of our lips.

Govern all our senses, that they seduce not our mind; and order every motion of our heart.

Perfect the work you have begun, and make our passions servants of thy grace.

Change our anger into a severity against ourselves, and a prudent zeal for others.

Convert our fear into a timorousness to offend, and art awful reverence of thy sacred name.

Let our affections be turned into love, that our hearts may desire nothing but thee:

Whom we may safely love with our whole strength; whose heaven we may covet, and fear no excess.

O You, whose blissful vision is the joy of angels, and sovereign happiness of all saints!

O that our souls could love thee without limits, as you art in thyself infinitely amiable:

That we could fix all our thoughts on thee; and never take them off from the memory of thy sweetness.

At least, O you fountain of eternal bliss and bounty, that flowest so freely with perpetual blessings!

Let every day we receive of thee, still set apart some portion of itself,

Seriously to meditate thy infinite mercies, and heartily rejoice in thy glorious rewards:

Mercies that give us all we have, and rewards that reserve for us all we can wish.

GLORY BE to the Father, and to the Son, and to the Holy Ghost. As it was in the beginning, is now, and ever shall be: world without end.

Amen.

HYMN 1.

WHEN, O my soul, did we ever follow our passions, bin they instantly wrought our disturbance, and threatened at last our ruin
When did we ever turn our thoughts to piety, but it presently brought us peace, and refreshed our minds with new hopes of felicity
The winds are often rough, and our own weight presses us downwards.
Reach forth, O LORD, thy hand, thy saving hand, and speedily deliver us.

O GOD, *whose grace it is that mightily rescues our reason from the desperate rebellion of our passions! Grant, we beseech thee, that the experience of the miserable effects of yielding to their allurements, may make us warier in observing, and severer in repressing their first motions; and let thy grace so strongly fortify us against all their assaults, that reason may more and more recover its due force, and calmly join with faith to secure and exalt in our hearts the blissful throne of thy love, through our LORD*

JESUS CHRIST, thy Son, who liveth and reigneth with thee and the HOLY GHOST, one GOD, blessed for ever. Amen.

In the Evening.

Antiphon

Repent now, my soul, for the evils you heist done, and bless thy GOD for the goods you have received.

PSALM 10.

WELL! we are so much nearer our grave, and all the world is older by a day.

The portion of the wicked is so much less, and the time of their punishment so much approached.

The sufferings of the patient so much diminished, and their hopes of deliverance so much increased.

They who have spent this day in sin and folly, see all their thoughts now vanish like a dream.

They see all is past, but the fear of justice, and the best that can follow is a bitter repentance.

LET others court what joys they please, And gain whatever they court:; For me, I find but little ease

In all their gayest sport.

Be you alone but with my heart, My GOD, my only bliss, I shall not murmur at my part, Nor envy their success.

They talk of pleasure, talk of gain, None must their humor cross; But well I know their pleasure's pain, Their greatest profit's loss.

Let them talk on; for have not we Our gains, our pleasures too

Pleasures that spring more sweet, more free.

Gains that more fully flow. Nay, well endured, our very pains.

To us a pleasure are; And all our losses turn to gains, If hopes may have their share.

And sure they may, such hopes that cheer the heavenespoused breast:

Hopes that so strangely charm us here,

What will they be, possessed

All glory to the sacred Three, All honor, power and praise;

As twas at first, still may it be Beyond the end of days. Amen.

But such as have wisely bestowed their time, and made another step towards heaven:

They see their joys come to meet them in the way, and

still grow bigger as they come:

Till by a holy death they join in one, and dwell together for eternal ages.

O you blessed Author of all our hopes, and perfect

Satisfier of all our wishes;

Do you instruct us in this great and wise truth, and let every evening renew it in our minds:

That the things of this world are of little import; since its joys and griefs last but for time.

But that the future state infinitely concerns us, where life and death endure for ever."

GLORY BE to the Father, and to the Son, and to the Holy Ghost. As it was in the beginning, is now, and ever shall be: world without end.

Amen.

.

PSALM 11.

WE ARE nearer indeed the end of our life; but are we nearer the end for which we live

What have we done, my soul, today, that truly advanceth us to our last great home

Have we increased our esteem of heaven, and settled its love more strongly in our hearts

Have we avoided any known temptation, or faithfully resisted when we could not avoid

Have we interrupted our customary faults, and checked the vices we are most inclined to

Have we embraced the opportunities of good, which the mercy of providence has offered to us

Have we industriously contrived occasions to improve, as we are able, ourselves and others

Alas, LORD! what do we see, when seriously we look into our guilty selves

When we reflect upon our former years; nay, even the follies of this one day

O meek Redeemer, what our passions have done; and favorably supply what our weakness has omitted.

Make us hereafter more carefully watch, that our time slide not unprofitably away.

Make us select every day some fit retreat, to study the knowledge of ourselves and thee:

Of ourselves, to correct our many infirmities; and of thee, to adore thy infinite perfections.

GLORY BE to the Father, and to the Son, and to the Holy Ghost. As it was in the beginning, is now, and ever shall be: world without end.

Amen.

PSALM 12.

LITTLE, you knows, O LORD, is the good we do; and every grain of it is derived from thee.

Great, we confess, are the evils we commit; and all be charged entirely upon ourselves.

Tell me, my soul, when first you have well examined the innumerable circumstances that concern thy state;

Tell me, and let not pride deny the truth; nor any thing divert thy free confession:

Could we have saved ourselves from any dangerous temptation, unless our GOD had powerfully sustained us

Could we have carried on any pious purpose, unless his hand had blessed our endeavors

No! To thyself, O LORD, we give all the praise, if thv creatures have performed the least good work.

Take to thyself all the glory, O LORD, if they have not committed the worst of sins.

Thy hand alone directs us to do well; and the same blessed hand restrains us from ill.

It is not in us to esteem those unseen joys, and despise the flatteries of this deceitful world.

It is not the work of nature to mortify our senses, and patiently bear the crosses we meet.

Of ourselves we are inclined to none of these; but the grace of GOD enables us to do all.

Grace gives us strength to overcome our passions; and the world and the flesh shall be subject unto us.

Grace gives us faith to fortify our reason; and heaven it itself shall be conquered by us.

GLORY BE to the Father, and to the Son, and to the Holy Ghost. As it was in the beginning, is now, and ever shall be: world without end.

Amen.

The Office for Thursday.

Morning Prayer.

Antiphon

Come, let us adore our GOD that feeds us.

PSALM 1.

HE freely opens his bounteous hand, and fills with his blessings every living creature; he gives even Kings their daily bread, and all the world is maintained with his provisions.

Come, let us adore our GOD that feeds us.

He feeds our understanding with the knowledge of truth, and strengthens our wills with his holy grace; he refreshes our memories with a thousand benefits, and feasts our whole souls with everlasting hopes.

Come, let us adore our GOD that feeds us.

With himself, and his sacred body, and blood, he feeds us, and nourishes us up to immortal life; beginning even here that blessed union, which shall be fully perfected his own kingdom.

Come, let us adore our GOD that feeds us.

Come, all ye servants of so gracious a LORD; whom he daily entertains with innumerable mercies: Come, all ye children of so loving a Father; for whom he has provided an eternal feast.

Come, let us adore our GOD that feeds us.

GLORY BE to the Father, and to the Son, and to the Holy Ghost. As it was in the beginning, is now, and ever shall be: world without end.

Amen.

PSALM 2.

HE who made the sun to enlighten our steps in the pilgrimage of this short life.

Has he ordained no guide to conduct our souls, in the difficulty to their eternal home

He who feeds the ravens that call upon him; has he not provided bread for his children

He has, and still his mercy furnishes us with means to perform whatever he commands.

At first he espoused to himself by the preaching of his Apostles, a glorious, faithful, spotless church;

Which he built upon the foundation of the Apostles, and Prophets, himself being the chief cornerstone.

He promised to be with it, and preserve it, and the faith delivered to it, unto the end of the world:

Establishing his truth on a firm pillar; a solid foundation to sustain our faith.

That we waver no longer as children; nor be carried about with every wind of doctrine:

Nor consume all our days with studying to believe, without ever proceeding to life and action.

This spouse, O you glorious King of heaven, and admirable Lover of poor ruined man!

This humble spouse, you camest down to woo, and dearly purchase with thine own blood.

You have endowed her with eminent prerogatives and powers, above the rest of the daughters of the earth.

Preserving her in the midst of Pagans and Jews, and against more subtile and dangerous enemies than they; worldly politicians, and the authors and maintainers of heresy and schism:

Preserving thy truth in her, and the Holy Scriptures committed to her, bright and conspicuous as the sun; that every open willing eye may see her light.

You have adorned her with the beauty of order, when thy church is in splendor; and with peace and patience, under an eclipse.

You didst introduce her with the power of miracles, and cement her with the blood of martyrs.

You have given her the keys of thy treasures, and opened unto her the mysteries of heaven.

Mysteries that free our souls from the dominion of sense, and place them above the reach of reason.

These thy whole church unanimously confesses and attests, as derived from thee, their original source.

Whence running along through every age, they have always maintained their constant channel.

O may they still bear on their course, and still spread wider their wholesome streams.

May all the world be watered with this dew of heaven, and bring forth fruit to everlasting life.

May the faith, which was once delivered to the saints, continue in an happy progress to the end of all things.

GLORY BE to the Father, and to the Son, and to the Holy Ghost. As it was in the beginning, is now, and ever shall be: world without end.

Amen.

PSALM 3.

SAFE in the hands of the Apostolic Catholic church, as our provident lot, deposited the richest treasures of his kingdom.

Commanding his Bishops and Priests to conserve them with reverence, and in unity; and dispense them to others with a prudent charity.

Soon as we are born into this world of danger, his pastors are ready to dispense his baptism to save us:

To wipe out the guilt of our birth, our original sin, and write our new name in the book of life.

What all eternity could not have worn off, a little washing of water cleanses away.

Healed by the bitter waters of penitence, we are invited to all the sweetness of Paradise:

To taste the delicious bread of angels, offered in the holy Eucharist;

And spiritually, in full effect and virtue, to eat the flesh and drink the blood of the SON of GOD.

Thereby to become entirely one with him; while we feed on his body, and are governed by his SPIRIT.

That the world may continue in a blessed succession, he in the beginning instituted marriage;

And adorned that holy estate with his presence, and first miracle, which he wrought in Cana of Galilee.

lie also made it a symbol of that mystical union, that is between himself and his church.

Exalting that state to the honor of a mystery, that we might the more regard the holiness of its duties.

To prevent the failing of governors in the church, the church for which the world continues;

Themselves are empowered to kindle fresh successive lights, who still may shine on when the old ones are spent.

Thus by thy wise indulgent care, O you sweet Conductor of our souls!

Every station of our pilgrimage has a fit entertainment, and every defect a proper remedy.

GLORY BE to the Father, and to the Son, and to the Holy Ghost. As it was in the beginning, is now, and ever shall be: world without end.

Amen.

PSALM 4.

BEHOLD He comes to us in the symbols of bread and wine; who is, indeed, both GOD and man;

He, whom the Seraphim prostrate adore, and fly with all their wings to perform his commands;

He, who came down to die for us sinners, and ascended again above the highest heavens;

Himself is there, and graciously stays our coming, to receive our prayers, and send us home with a blessing.

All the faithful, that approach him with prepared hearts, feel the virtue of his divine love;

Going out of him to heal their infirmities, and warm their souls, and inflame their affections:

And thus a lively faith passes through the veil, and confidently enters into the holy of holies.

A faith that works by love may enter, and fill itself with celestial manna.

Behold, O LORD, we believe; perfect by thy vigorous grace our faint endeavors.

Bring us where our dark faith shall cease into vision, and our hope expire into full enjoyment;

Where all our affections shall be contracted into love, and love shall be extended to all eternity.

GLORY BE to the Father, and to the Son, and to the Holy Ghost. As it was in the beginning, is now, and ever shall be: world without end.

Amen.

Antiphon

We confess, we are bound to do many things against our will; why not believe some few above our understanding

OUR FATHER, which art in heaven, hallowed be thy name. Thy kingdom come. Thy will be done in earth, as it is in heaven. Give us this day our daily bread. And forgive us our trespasses, as we forgive them that trespass against us. And lead us not into temptation: But deliver us from evil. For thine is the kingdom, the power, and the glory, for ever and ever. Amen.

At Noon.

Antiphon

How great is the multitude of thy loving kindnesses, which you host laid upon them that fear thee!

PSALM 5.

WHERE, O you boundless Ocean of Love, where will thy overflowing streams stay their course

We and our ingratitude strive to oppose thee; but nothing can resist thine almighty goodness.

When the impiety of men was at the height, and their treacherous heads plotting to betray thee,

Then did thy wisdom mercifully consult to overcome our malice with thy bounty.

Immediately you contrivedst an admirable way, to invite all the world to a feast of miracles:

A feast where thy sacred body should be our food, and thy precious blood our drink:

A feast in which are continually wrought new miracles of love for us.

And, as if it had not been love enough to have given thyself on the cross for us,

You have found out a way to give thyself to us in the holy Sacrament;

To unite us to thyself with the most intimate union that it is possible to conceive, and which we can better feel that express.

For what greater mercy and bounty can be extended to us, poor mortals, than for our Redeemer to become the very food of our souls'

To become the life, the strength, the support, and comfort of our beings:

Nay, to become even one with me, and be unto me the very soul of my soul

O LORD My GOD, this is so inconceivable a blessing, this is so divine a union,

That the very angels, who so much desire to look into the great mystery of our redemption,

Do crowd about our altars, and with awful admiration contemplate thy wonderful condescension in it.

What thanks then, gracious LORD, can I return thee for those wonders of love you have showed to me a wretched sinner; which those blessed angels above, who never sinned, so much admire!

A feast, where thy whole all glorious self is freely given to the meanest guest:

A feast of peace, and love, and incomparable sweetness, to which thine own blessed mouth thus calls us,

Come to me all ye that labor for holiness, and are oppressed under the weight of your sins:

Come to me ye that hunger after heaven, and thirst to drink at the fountain of bliss:

Come to me, and I will refresh you with the wine of gladness and the bread of life:

Come you that are weak, that you may grow strong; and you that are strong, lest you become weak:

Come you that have leisure, and here entertain your time: Come you that are busy, and here learn to sanctify your employment:

Come all, and gather freely of this celestial manna, and fill your souls with the food of angels.

GLORY BE to the Father, and to the Son, and to the Holy Ghost. As it was in the beginning, is now, and ever shall be: world without end.

Amen.

PSALM 6.

THUS does our gracious LORD invite; and shall we go Shall sinners dare to sit down at his table

Thus he invites, and shall we not go Shall wretches presume to refuse his call

Rise then, my soul, and take thy swiftest wings, and fly to the presence of this great mystery.

Soon as you comest, bow low thy head, and humbly adore thy blessed Redeemer;

Our GOD that comes so far to meet us, and brings along with him a whole heaven to entertain us.

Arise, and leave the world behind thee; and run with gladness to salute thy LORD.

Enter the palace of his glorious residence, the place where his honor dwells.

There shall we see the Eternal One, who descended from heaven to become man for us;

There we shall see the Prince of Peace sacrifice himself to reconcile us with his FATHER;

There shall we see, O stupendous mercy! the Sow of GOD with food entertaining the sons' of men.

Can we believe the wonders of this mystery, and not be ravished with admiration of thy goodness

Can we acknowledge thy supreme veracity, and not believe this wonder of thy love

What, though our eyes see nothing but bread and wine! our faith, yea experience too, assure us, that you art there also.

For, O the joy and overflowing comforts the just find herein!

Producing nothing but praises and thanksgivings; but love, and joy, and fear;

And care of offending that blessed Loin, who meets them at this holy and mysterious feast.

What earnest supplications do they make, that their LORD will take possession of their hearts, and never depart from them more!

Let us not then refuse to believe our GOD, because his mercies transcend our capacities.

No, no, it is thy very self, O blessed JESUS; and it is thine own light by which we see thee.

And it is thine HOLY SPIRIT, the Comforter, by which we feel and find thee.'

None but infinite wisdom could ever have invented so strange and high a mystery.

None but an inconceivable goodness would ever have imparted so dear, and tender, and rich a blessing.

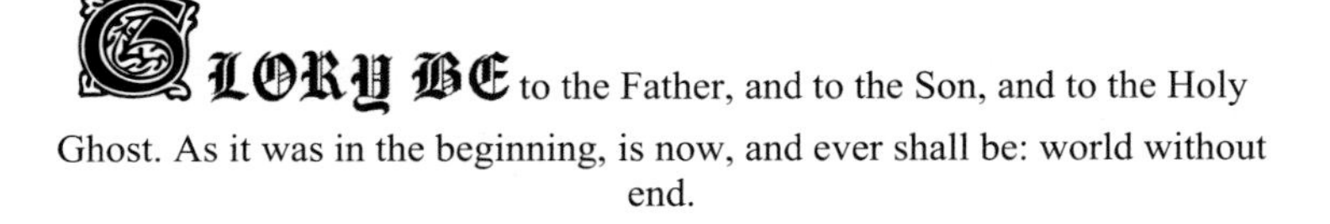

GLORY BE to the Father, and to the Son, and to the Holy Ghost. As it was in the beginning, is now, and ever shall be: world without end.

Amen.

PSALM 7.

LORD, who are we, unworthy sinners, that thus you regardest our wretched dust

What is all the world compared to thee, that thus you seemest to disregard thyself

It was for our sakes, and to draw us up to thy love, that you have commanded us to commemorate, and represent thy passion;

And present the merits of it before thy FATHER on earth, as you dost present them to him in heaven.

It was for our sakes, and to help the infirmities of our nature, that you didst appoint a commemorative sacrifice,

Of that one oblation of thyself once offered upon the cross; and bread and wine so offered, and blessed, as symbols of thy body and ✠ blood.

Blessed are the eyes, O JESUS, that see thee in these holy signs; and blessed is the mouth that reverently receives thee.

Blessed yet more is the heart that desires thy coming, and longs to see thee in thy beauteous self.

O you eternal LORD of grace and glory, our joy and portion in the land of the living!

What have you there prepared for thy servants, who bestowest such pledges of thy bounty here!

What dost you there reserve in thine own kingdom, who givest us thyself in this place of banishment!

How will thy open vision transport our souls; when our dark faith yields us such delights!

Nothing on earth so sweet as to kneel whole hours before thee, and one by one consider thy innumerable mercies.

What must it be in heaven to shine continually before thee; and all in one contemplate thy unspeakable goodness and glories!

O my adored Redeemer! when will that happy day appear, when mine eyes may behold thee without a veil

When will the clouds and the shadows pass away; that thy beams may shine on me in their full brightness

Object not against me, gracious LORD, that none can see thy face, and live.

Those fears thy love has changed, and all my hope is now to live by seeing thee.

Say not, O you mild and gracious Majesty, if I approach thy presence I must die.

Rather instruct me so to die, that I may live for ever in thy presence.

In the Afternoon.

Antiphon

Whither, O my GOD, should we wander, if left to ourselves Where should we fix our hearts, if not directed by thee

PSALM 8.

UNHAPPY man! at first created just; as every work comes fair from the hands of GOD.

At first endowed with dominion over the earth, and which was more, with dominion over thyself.

At first not only made sole LORD of Paradise; but heir apparent of the heaven of heavens.

All this was lost by one rash act of thine; disobeying the law of thy wise Creator.

All this, alas! we lost by thy transgression, which brought in sin, and death, and universal misery.

Our bodies were depraved by thy distemper; and our souls by such depraved bodies.

Our senses quickly rebelled against reason; and both together conspired against grace.

Dullness and ignorance overspread the world; error and vice possessed mankind.

The law they observed was their own unruly appetite; and the deity they worshipped, the work of their own hands.

Even the selected people of the true GOD; the favorite nation of, the Almighty Providence:

They who were brought out of Egypt with so many wonders, and seated in a country flowing with milk and honey:

They who had seen the sea divide before them; and stand on each side as a wall to defend them:

They who had tasted the quails and the manna from heaven; and drunk of the streams that came gushing out from the rock.

Even they forgot their great Deliverer; and set up for their GOD a golden calf.

Thus lay the miserable world, all covered with darkness; and with the thickest mists of gross idolatry.

Thus had poor man lost his way; and all he could do was to wander up and down awhile:

Till, when his few vain years were spent, he suddenly descended into everlasting sorrows.

This moved thy pity, gracious LORD! who often art found by those that seek thee not.

Who never withdrawest thy hand in time of need; but constantly suppliest us in all our distresses.

This moved thy pity to undertake our relief; to come down thyself to dwell amongst us.

To rescue the deluded world from idolatry, and call men from darkness to thy marvelous light.

GLORY BE to the Father, and to the Son, and to the Holy Ghost. As it was in the beginning, is now, and ever shall be: world without end.

Amen.

O bounteous LORD, the continual Supplier of thy creatures with all convenient sustenance to advance our growth and strength, till we are fit to take heaven by violence, and rise at length to be eternal enjoyers of thyself: Fix, we beseech thee, our eyes and adoration on that open hand, which thus graciously gives us our daily bread. And grant that the wonderful feast of thy Son's body and ✠ blood may duly sanctify our tastes to all other thy bounties, that they may only relish, and feed upon thy dear love to us, through the same our LORD JESUS CHRIST. Amen.

YOU *camest first to thine own, and didst dwell among them, that they might see thy glory:The glory as of the only begotten Son of GOD, that God man, GOD manifested in flesh, whom they might safely worship.But you must again ascend into thy FATHER'S bosom, to prepare a place for thy faithful followers.Yet even then, O you wise and infinite Goodness! Thou didst not wholly forsake our earth; you didst not leave us comfortless.But didst send forth thy HOLY SPIRIT to guide and comfort us; and give thyself in the Holy Eucharist to feed and nourish" our hungry souls with' that sacramental food.Still you art really present to us in that holy mystery of love; hence we offer up our devotions in it, with our utmost reverence, wonder, and love.We know it is impossible to adore and love our GOD too much; O that it were possible to love, and admire him, and adore him enough.*

GLORY BE to the Father, and to the Son, and to the Holy Ghost. As it was in the beginning, is now, and ever shall be: world without end.

Amen.

In the Evening

Antiphon

Blessed be thy providence, O GOD, that so tenderly nurses up the Church, that it may still grow on to new degrees of perfection.

PSALM 9.

LORD, what a happy change has thy coming wrought! what glorious effects has thy doctrine produced!

Once in a populous city not ten that were just! and on the whole earth but eight that were saved!

But O what a happy change did thy coming work in the world! O what glorious effects in a little while did thy doctrine produce!

When, by thy abundant grace, thousands, with a strong and vigorous love, ran swiftly after thee in the ways of thy commands.

Now we see Kings and mighty nations submit to thee; and hope ere long that all the world will adore thee.

Whence could this strange improvement come Whence could all those blessings spring

But from thy holy life, O blessed JESUS, and the infinite merits of thy painful death!

Both which are united, and the fruits thereof abridged, in this holy Sacrament of thy blessed body and ✠ blood. These sacred things, thy word and sacraments, breed in us not only profound veneration and adoration to thee: But also a great and due respect to thy Pastors and Priests, the dispensers thereof.

These saving mysteries keep alive our clear Redeemer's death and apply to our souls all the merits of his passion.

These fill our hearts with heroic courage; to do and suffer for the name of JESUS.

These are the food of faith, and hope, and love, which fit us for eternal happiness.

O blessed memorial of my Savior's love, and faithful seal of all his promises!

If I forget to sing of thee, let my tongue cleave to the roof of my mouth.

If I forget to meditate on thee, let my head forfeit its power to think.

All the short time that I remain in thy presence I will wholly employ to adore thy Majesty.

Thee will I bless for all thy mercies; to thee will I open all my necessities.

Begging thy pardon for my past offences, and thy gracious assistance for the time to come.

Imploring the preservation of thy Church, and thy blessing upon all the world.

O spotless Lamb, once slain for us on the cross; and duly commemorated on, and communicated to us at thy holy altar!

Be you our powerful Advocate with thy heavenly FATHER; and solicit, by thy merits, his mercy for us.

Offer thyself before his throne, and turn away the wrath we deserve for our sins.

So slaves are rescued from their chains, from the doom of death.

Whilst they appease their offended King, with the pleasing remembrance of his beloved SON.

And so we hope, and infinitely more, from the infinitely greater mediation of JESUS

If You, O LORD, shall thus restore our liberty, and clothe thy servants with the robes of thy righteousness,

Then shall we delight to be still in thy presence; and follow thee, O Lamb of GOD, whithersoever you goest.

Wherever you art, we will never forsake thee; and wherever we are, our hearts shall always be with thee.

Neither death, nor life, nor angels, nor principalities, nor any of the powers either of this or the invisible world, nor indeed any other creatures whatever,

Shall be ever able,' we firmly hope, to separate us from thee, or diminish that love which draws us after thee, O GOD of our life.

GLORY BE to the Father, and to the Son, and to the Holy Ghost. As it was in the beginning, is now, and ever shall be: world without end.

Amen.

PSALM 10.

AND does our glorious GOD not only visit, but dwell perpetually with us then upon earth

He whom the heaven of heavens cannot contain; does he make his residence in our little tabernacles,

Where are you, ye holy angels, that you fly not swiftly down, and in your whitest robes attend your LORD

Where are you, ye careless men, that you run not quickly hither; and with your lowest homage bow to your King

Who though he shines out clear to the blessed above; and the beams of his glory strike bright upon their faces:

Yet have his mercies to us far more of miracle, far more of care, and tender providence:

Whilst he not only is pleased to be among us, but condescends to become even one with us:

While he is not only our GOD to go before us; but our very food to enter into us.

O souls redeemed by the blood of JESUS; and nourished with the flesh and blood of his sacred body:

Why melt you not away into tears of joy, for being so regarded by the King of heaven

'Why not at least dissolve ye into tears of sorrow, for so little regarding him

Who will not tremble with loving reverence, that stands in the sight of so great a Majesty

Who can forbear to be transported with joy, that thinks in himself, I am a guest at the table of my GOD

Who can contain the overflowings of his heart, whilst his breast can say, I have the honor to be entertained by my God

My great and glorious GOD, who, merely out of love, thus gives me himself in a mystery of grace, and leaves me the pledges of my salvation.

O infinite Sweetness! How good it is for us to be here, and, as it were, behold our LORD transfigured before us!

Here let us make a thousand tabernacles; one, O my JESUS, for thee, and one for each of us.

That in our little tents we may dwell about thee; and sing, and bow, and rejoice before thee.

What should the captive wish but liberty, and the weary pilgrim but to be at rest

What should the sick desire but health; and what can I, but to be with my GOD

But have I considered how chaste those eyes should be, which go to behold the GOD of purity

Have I considered how clean that mouth should be, which presumes to eat the bread of heaven

But most, how celestial that soul should be, which aspires to an union with the body of our Lou])

Look, look, my heart, look well into thyself; and strictly search every corner of thy breast.

Alas! How poor, and dull, and empty are we! How infinitely unworthy of so divine a mystery

Yet are we called by him that can command; by him that sees and pities our miseries.

He bids us come, he will surely receive us; and with his bounteous fullness supply our defects.

Go then, my soul, go to that sacred table, and take thy part of that delicious banquet.

Go all enflamed with love, and joy, and hope; and quench thy holy thirst at that spring of bliss.

When you have tasted the sweetness of thy GOD, and feelest his heavenly streams flow gently on thee,

Open thy happy breast, and suck those waters in; and let them freely run over all thy powers.

Let them soak deep to the root of thy heart, and turn the barren heath into a fruitful land.

Fruitful in holy thoughts, and pious words; fruitful in good, and just, and charitable deeds:

Fruitful in thyself in thine own improvement; fruitful to others in thy good example.

No more ingratitude to so gracious a GOD; no more neglect of so glorious a Majesty.

Away false pleasures, sin and vanity; for the GOD of holiness has touched my heart.

He has himself gone in and taken full possession, and sealed it up for his own service.

GLORY BE to the Father, and to the Son, and to the Holy Ghost. As it was in the beginning, is now, and ever shall be: world without end.

Amen.

PSALM 11.

Who will give me this happy favor, that I may find my GOD alone

That I may find him in the silence of retirement, where the noise of' this world can no way interrupt us; And that my GOD may speak to me, and I to him, as

dearest friends converse together: That I may unfold before him all my wants, and freely ask his counsel.

What shall I do, O my gracious LORD, to be happy here What shall I do to be happy hereafter

Nature already has thus far taught me, that in all I undertake I should seek my own good.

Only I have cause to fear I may mistake that good, and set up an idol instead of thee:

Unless my GOD vouchsafe to instruct me, and show my soul its true felicity.

Hark! how the Eternal Wisdom gives thee advice! And let every word sink deep into thy soul:

"Seek with thy first endeavor the kingdom of heaven, " and all things else shall be added to thy wish.

"Love with thy whole affections the enjoyment of thy ` GOD; and all things else shall conspire to thy happiness."

These, my lips confess, are excellent truths; but when, O my GOD, shall my life confess them

When shall I perfectly overcome my passions, and guide them so that they may draw me to thy light

While they are mine, alas! I cannot govern them behold, LORD, I offer them all to thee.

Check you their lawless motions by thy grace, lest they' carry me away from my duty.

Wean you my heart from the follies of this world, and quicken its appetite to thy solid joys:

That I may hunger and thirst perpetually after thee, and those glorious promises you have made to thy servants

That my whole soul may seek thee alone; since you alone art all my heaven.

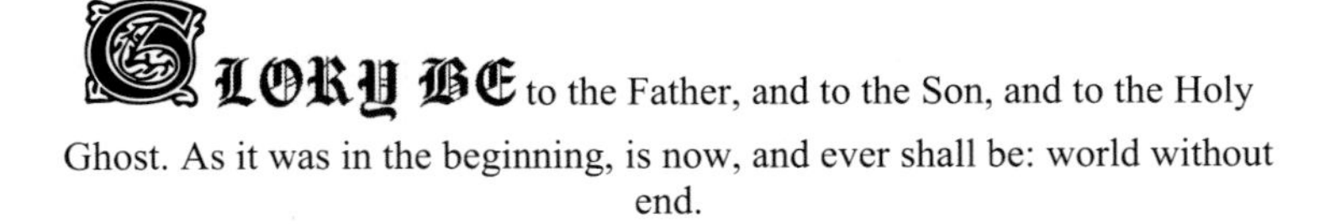

GLORY BE to the Father, and to the Son, and to the Holy Ghost. As it was in the beginning, is now, and ever shall be: world without end.

Amen.

PSALM 12.

WHEN, O my soul, shall thy GOD find thee alone; free from those busy thoughts that fill thy head

O with what ready love would he then instruct thee, and let thee into his blessed secrets!

Himself would become thy familiar guest, and dwell with thee in thy perpetual joy.

LORD, you must enter first, and chase those fancies away, and consecrate my soul a temple to thyself.

Take you entire possession, and hold it fast for ever and suffer not the enemies of my peace to return.

Sit you as sovereign King, and absolutely command; for thy government is mild, and thy rewards are infinite.

What have you promised, gracious LORD, to him that receives thee with an humble love

All that is contained in those sweet and mystic words; " He dwells in me, and I in him."

O blessed words, if once my soul can say, " He dwells " in me, and I in him!

"He is my refuge in all temptations! He is my comfort " in all distresses!

"He is my security against all my enemies! He dwells " in me, and I in him.!"

What can an infinite bounty give greater than itself And what can an empty creature receive greater than his GOD

O glorious GOD, my life, my joy, and the only center of all my hopes!

Were my unsteady soul once united to thee; or once had relished the sweetness of thy presence:

How would all other company seem dull and tedious, and the whole world be bitter to my taste!

How would my thoughts cleave fast to thee, and gladly seal thine everlasting covenant!

If You, O LORD, wilt dwell with me, my heart shall continually attend on thee.

Night and day will I sing thy praises, and all my life long adore thy mercies.

GLORY BE to the Father, and to the Son, and to the Holy Ghost. As it was in the beginning, is now, and ever shall be: world without end.

Amen.

PSALM 13

THOU art my only hope, O blessed JESUS; and thy favor alone is all things to me.

In thee I find the providence of a father, and the tender kindness of an indulgent mother.

In thee I enjoy the protection of a King, and the rare fidelity of a constant friend.

In thee I possess whatsoever I want; and thy fullness exceeds even my utmost desires.

You art, O JESUS, My GOD, and all things; what can I think, or wish for more

Already enough is said for them that love, and know the value of those precious words.

Sweet words, My GOD, and all things! Sweet in excess to those that taste them.

Not to the corrupted palates of the world, who relish nothing but the food of sense.

Words that revive the fainting mind, and fill its darkest thoughts with light and joy.

O may these blessed words dwell on my tongue, and live for ever in my faithful memory!

Wherever I am in this inconstant world, and whatever business entertains my hands,

Still let my inward eye look up to thee, and fix its sight on thy glorious face;

Still may I wish and long for that happy day, which opens to my soul so blessed a view;

Where I shall see, and no longer darkly believe, " that You, O LORD, art my GOD, and all things."

GLORY BE to the Father, and to the Son, and to the Holy Ghost. As it was in the beginning, is now, and ever shall be: world without end.

Amen.

The Office for Friday

Morning Prayer.

Antiphon

Come, let us adore our GOD that redeemed us.

PSALM 1.

WHEN we had sold ourselves to sin, and were all become' the slaves of Satan, our blessed JESUS descended from heaven, and brought a vast price to buy out our freedom.

Come, let us adore our GOD that redeemed us.

The price was no less than his own dearest blood, which he plenteously shed on the holy cross, depositing so his inestimable life, to rescue us sinners from eternal death.

Come, let us adore our GOD that redeemed us.

Let us consecrate this day to his sacred memory, and tenderly compassionate his unparalleled sufferings; repenting from our hearts of our many sins, and thankfully admiring his infinite mercies

Come, let us adore our GOD that redeemed us.

Let us wean our minds from unbecoming delights, and mortify our senses with a prudent restraint; that, carried on the wings of fasting and alms, our prayers may mount up more swiftly to heaven.

Come, let us adore our GOD that redeemed us.

GLORY BE to the Father, and to the Son, and to the Holy Ghost. As it was in the beginning, is now, and ever shall be: world without end.

Amen.

PSALM 2.

MY GOD, who can complain of doing too much, if they consider the labors of JESUS

Those painful labors he so freely undertook, and mildly stooped to his humble task.

When he might have flown on the wings of Cherubim, he chose to walk with us worms in the dust.

When he might have commanded manna from heaven, in the sweat of his brows he would eat his bread.

When he might have made the angels his footstool, he rather became the servant of his parents:

Living with them in their little cottage, and readily obeying even their least command.

There in that humble privacy he increased in wisdom, and grew in favor both with GOD and man.

O that the same sweet Smut' of grace might draw our minds, O LORD, to thee

O that we could, in every passage of our lives, still actually reflect on the example of thine.

Thy retirements were filled with holy speculations, and in the midst of business thy life was free for heaven.

Thy converse with others misspent no time, but bestowed every moment in excellent charity:

To instruct the ignorant, to reduce the deceived, to comfort the afflicted, and heal the diseased;

To convince the froward, and absolve the penitent, and persuade all the world to be truly happy.

It was thy meat and drink to do thy FATHER'S Will; O make it ours to perform thine!

Make us in every action still think on thee, what thou wouldest counsel us to do:

What you thyself wouldest do, O blessed JESUS, if you again wert here amongst us.

And when we thus have learned our duty, LORD, make us do what you have made us know.

GLORY BE to the Father, and to the Son, and to the Holy Ghost. As it was in the beginning, is now, and ever shall be: world without end.

Amen.

PSALM 3.

MY GOD, who can repine at suffering too much, if they remember the afflictions of JESUS

Those many afflictions he so patiently endured, and bore with silence all their weight.

Even from his humble cradle in the manger of Bethlehem, to his bitter cross on the Mount of Calvary.

Sometimes abandoned by his dearest friends, and left alone among all his discomforts:

Sometimes pursued by his fiercest enemies, and made the common mark of all their spite:

Sometimes they plot to snare him in his words, and enviously slander his miraculous deeds:

Sometimes tumultuously they gather about him, to gaze at, and abuse this Man of Sorrows:

Sometimes they furiously seize on his person, and hale and drag him along the streets:

At last they all conspire to take away his life, and condemn him to a sharp and cruel death.

Have you not seen a harmless lamb stand silent in the midst of ravening wolves

So stood the Prince of Peace and innocency, compassed with a rout of savage Jews.

When they provoked him with their utmost malice, he pleaded their excuse; and when they murdered him, he earnestly prayed for their pardon.

O strange ingratitude of human nature, thus barbarously to crucify the world's Redeemer!

O admirable love of the world's Redeemer, thus patiently to die for human nature!

'Say now, my soul, for whom thy dearest LORD endured all this, and infinitely more,

Can you complain of thy little troubles, when the King of glory was thus afflicted

Can you complain of a meanly furnished house, when the Son of GOD had not where to lay his head

We wear the badge of a crucified Savior, and shall we shrink back at every cross we meet

We believe in a LORD that was crowned with thorns; and shall we abide to tread on nothing but roses

Before our eyes, O JESUS, we see thee humble and meek; and shall thv servants be proud and insolent

We see thee travel up and down, poor and unregarded; and shall thy followers strive to be rich and esteemed

Thy labors were maliciously slandered; and shall not our faults be reproved

O how unlike are we to that blessed Original, who descended from heaven to become our Pattern!

How do we go away from the sacred path, which the holy JESUS traced with his own steps!

Pity, O Redeemer! the infirmities of thy children; strengthen with thy grace our fainting hearts:

Arm us, O glorious Conqueror of sin and death! against all the fears and terrors of the world.

Arm all our powers with those celestial virtues of faith, and hope, and invincible love:

That we may still go on, and resolutely meet whatever stands in our way to heaven.

Since we must suffer as Christians, and deserve to suffer as sinners, LORD, let us bear our sufferings as becomes thy servants.

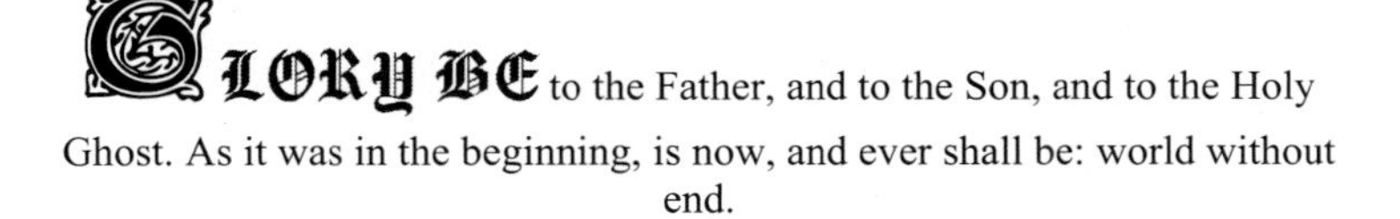

GLORY BE to the Father, and to the Son, and to the Holy Ghost. As it was in the beginning, is now, and ever shall be: world without end.

Amen.

Antiphon

Unworthy are we, O LORD, of the least of thy, favors; O let thy passion make us worthy of the greatest!

PSALM 5.

MY GOD, when I consider what you have suffered for us, and what we have done against thee,

I am amazed at the wonders of thy goodness, and confounded at the vileness of our misery.

Our sins were the cause of thy cruel death, yet still we permit them to live in us.

We entertain the worst of thy enemies, and treacherously lodge them in our own bosoms.

Preferring a petty interest before thy heaven, and transitory pleasure before eternal felicity.

Many, we confess, are the follies of our life, and our consciences tremble at them.

Many are the times you have graciously pardoned us, and still we relapse, and abuse thy clemency.

The memory of our transgressions is bitter unto us, and the thought of our ingratitude extremely afflicts us.

But is there, O holy JESUS, any stain so foul, which thy precious blood cannot wash away

Is there any number of sins so vast, to exceed the number of thy mercies

O no; you can forgive more than we can offend; but you wilt not forgive, unless we fear to offend;

Unless we seek to thee for peace and reconciliation, and. humble ourselves in thy holy presence.

Wherefore behold, O LORD, we fall down at thy crucified feet, and there ask pardon for our perverse affections.

Reverently we kiss thy pierced hands, and implore forgiveness for wicked actions.

All we can offer thy offended Majesty is an humble eye hased in tears, and a penitent heart broken with contrition_

Only a firm resolve to change our lives, and even all this we must beg of thee.

O You, our gracious and indulgent LORD! who freely pardonest all that truly repent,

Who givest repentance to all that ask, and invitest all to ask, by promising to give,

Make us look seriously in our own breasts, and heartily lament our many failings.

Make us search diligently for our bosom sins, and strive to cast them out with prayer and fasting.

Open You, O LORD, our lips to accuse our crimes; that we blush not to confess, what we feared not to do.

Correct our past sins with the works of repentance, that the stains they leave may be quite taken away.

Preserve us hereafter with thy powerful grace, that no temptation surprise or overcome us.

Extend thy mercy, O LORD, over all our works, since thyself have declared it is above all thine own.

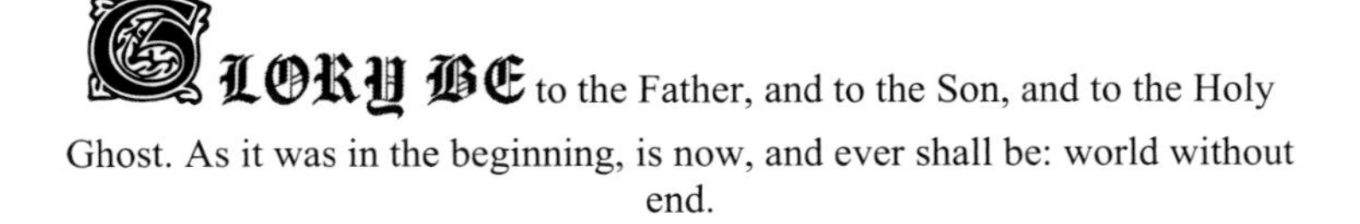

GLORY BE to the Father, and to the Son, and to the Holy Ghost. As it was in the beginning, is now, and ever shall be: world without end.

Amen.

MY *God! never let me rely upon any outward performances, so as to neglect the improvement of my mind; lest my fasting become an unprofitable trouble, and my prayer a vain liplabor. The soul and the body make a man, and the spirit and discipline make a Christian. Never let me so pretend to inward perfection, as to slight the outward observances of religion; lest my thoughts grow proud and fantastic, and all my arguments but a cover for licentiousness.*

O GOD*, who by our great Master's example, have taught us what labors and sufferings heaven deserves, and that we are to take it by force; confound in us, we humbly beseech thee, the nice tenderness of our nature, which is averse to that discipline and hardship we ought to endure, as disciples and soldiers of JESUS CHRIST; help us in our way thither, by selfdenial and mortification, for the sake of our LORD JESUS CHRIST, who liveth and reigneth with thee and thy HOLY SPIRIT, ever one GOD, world without end.* Amen.

At Noon.

Antiphon

Come, let us glory in the cross of our LORD JESUS CHRIST, in whom is our life, and health, and resurrection.

PSALM 5.

SHALL we rejoice, my soul, today Shall we not mourn at the funeral of our dear Redeemer

Such, O my LORD, was the excess of thy goodness, to derive joys for us from thine own sorrows.

You forbadest thy followers to weep for thee, and reservedst to thyself alone the shame and grief.

You invitedst all the world to glory in thy cross, and commandest us to delight in the memory of thy passion.

Sing then, all you dear bought nations of the earth; sing hymns of glory to the holy JESUS.

Sing, every one who pretends to felicity; sing immortal praises to the GOD of our salvation;

To him, who for us endured so much scorn, and patiently received so many injuries:

To him, who for us sweat drops of blood, and drank the dregs of his FATHER'S wrath:

To the eternal LORD of heaven and earth, who for us was slain by the hands of the wicked;

Who for us was led away as a sheep to the slaughter; and, as a meek lamb, opened not his mouth.

Whither, O my GOD, did thy compassions carry thee

How did thy love prevail with thee

Was it not enough to become man for us, but must thou expose thyself to all our miseries

Was it not enough to labor all thy life; but must thou suffer even the pains of death for us

You sufferedst them to expiate for our sins, and purchase eternal redemption for us.

You sawest our fondness of life needed thy parting with it, to reconcile us to death.

You sawest our fear of sufferings could no way be abated, but by freely undergoing them in thine own person.

O blessed JESUS, whose grace alone begins, and ends, and perfects all our hopes!

How are we bound to praise thy love! how infinitely obliged to adore thy goodness!

At any rate you wouldest still go on, to heal our weak and wounded nature.

Even at the price of thine own dear blood, you wouldest finish for us the purchase of heaven.

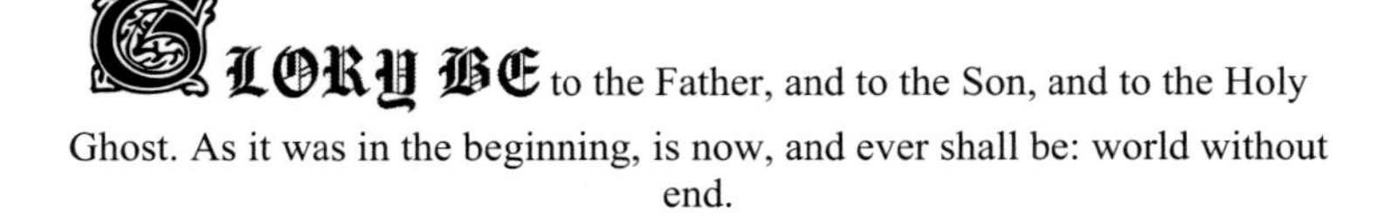

to the Father, and to the Son, and to the Holy Ghost. As it was in the beginning, is now, and ever shall be: world without end.

Amen.

PSALM 6.

AWAKE, my soul, and speedily prepare thy richest sacrifice of humble praise.

Awake, and summon all thy thoughts, to make haste and adore our great Redeemer.

For now it is time we should reverently go, and offer our hearts at the foot of his cross.

Thither let us fly from the troubles of the world; there let us dwell among the mercies of heaven.

Under the shade of that tree let us kneel, and often look up to our dearest LORD.

Let us remember every passage of his love, and be sure that none escape our thanks.

Let us compassionate every stroke of his death, and one by one salute his sacred wounds.

Blessed be the hands that wrought so many miracles, and were so barbarously bored with cruel nails.

Blessed be the feet that so often traveled for us, and were at last unmercifully fastened to the cross.

Blessed be the head that was crowned with thorns, the head that so industriously studied our happiness.

Blessed be the heart that was pierced with a spear, the heart that so passionately loved our peace.

Blessed be the entire person of our crucified LORD; and may all our powers join in his praise t

In thy eternal praise, O gracious JESUS! and the ravishing thoughts of thy incomparable sweetness.

O what excess of kindness was this! What strange extremity of love and pity.

The LORD is sold, that the slave may go free; the innocent condemned, that the guilty may be saved.

The physician is sick, that the patient may be cured; and GOD himself dies, that man may live.

Tell me, my soul, when first you have well considered, and looked about among all we know,

Tell me, who ever wished us so much good Who ever loved us with so much tenderness

What have our nearest friends done for us, or even our parents, in comparison of this love

No less than the SON of GOD came down to redeem us; no less than his own life was the price paid for us.

What can the favor of the whole world promise us, compared to his miraculous bounty

No less than the joys of angels are become our hope; no less than the kingdom of heaven is made our inheritance.

GLORY BE to the Father, and to the Son, and to the Holy Ghost. As it was in the beginning, is now, and ever shall be: world without end.

Amen.

PSALM 7.

TO thee, O GOD, we owe our whole selves, for making us after thine own image.

To thee, O LORD, we owe more than ourselves, for redeeming us with the death of thine only Son.

Nor were our ruins so soon repaired, as at first our being was produced.

Thy Power to create us said but one word, and immediately we became a living soul:

But thy Wisdom to redeem us, both spoke much, and wrought more, and suffered most of all.

To redeem us, he humbled himself to this low world, and the infirmities of this miserable nature.

He patiently endured hunger and thirst, and the malicious affronts of enraged enemies.

How many times did he hazard his life, to sustain with courage the truths of heaven!

How many tears did he tenderly weep, in compassion of his blind ungrateful country!

How many drops of blood did he shed in the doleful garden, and on the bitter cross!

The cross, where, after three long hours of grief, and shame, and intolerable pains,

He meekly bowed his fainting head, and, in an agony of pain, yielded up the ghost.

So sets the glorious sun in a sad cloud, and leaves our earth in darkness and disorder;

But goes to shine immediately in the other world, and soon returns again, and brings us light:

And so dost You, O LORD, and more; thy very darkness is our light.

It is by thy death we are made to live, and by thy wounds our sores are healed.

O my adored Redeemer, who tookest upon thee all our miseries, to impart to us thine own felicities!

Can we remember thy labors for us, and not be convinced to our duty to thee

Can our cold hearts recount, thy sufferings, and not be inflamed with the love that suffered

Can we believe our salvation cost thee so dear, and live as if to be saved were not worth our pains

Ungrateful we! How do we slight the kindness of our God! How carelessly comply with hi gracious design!

For all his gifts he requires no other return than to hope still more, and desire still greater blessings.

For all his favors he seeks no other praise, than our following his steps to arrive at glory.

O glorious JESUS! behold to thee we bow, and humbly kiss the dust in honor of thy death.

Behold, thus low we bow, to implore thy blessings, and the sure assistance of thy special grace;

That we may wean our affections from all vain desires, and clear our thoughts from all impertinent fancies.

Then shall our lives be entirely dedicated to thee, all the faculties of our souls to thy holy service.

Our minds shall continually study thy knowledge, and our wills grow every day stronger in thy love.

GLORY BE to the Father, and to the Son, and to the Holy Ghost. As it was in the beginning, is now, and ever shall be: world without end.

Amen.

O GOD, *who didst severely punish our first parents for eating the forbidden fruit, and has so often recommended us the necessary duties of abstinence and fasting! Grant, we beseech thee, that by observing diligently thy holy discipline, proposed to us in thy laws, we may correct our levities, and revenge our excesses, and subdue our irregular appetites, and frustrate the temptations of the enemy, and secure our perseverance, and daily proceed to new degrees of virtue and devotion, till in the end of our lives we receive the end of our labors, the salvation of our souls, through our LORD JESUS CHRIST.* Amen.

In the Afternoon.

PSALM 8.

LORD, how the world requites thy love! How ungrateful are we to thy blessed memory!

We negligently forget thy sacred passion; or rather, our sins renew thy sufferings.

While we deprive others of their right, what do we but divest thee of thy clothes!

While we delight in strife and schisms, what do we else but rend thy seamless coat!

If we despise the least of thy servants, are we not as so many HERODS that scorn thee

If we for fear proceed against our conscience, how are we better than PILATE that condemned thee

By forsaking thy will to follow our own, do we not choose a murderer before thee

By retaining sharp anger, or bitter malice, do we not give thee vinegar and gall to drink

By showing no mercy to the poor and afflicted, do we not pass by thy cross, as strangers unconcerned

Thus we again crucify the LORD of Glory, and put him afresh to an open shame.

Is this the duty we pay to the sacred memory of our dear Redeemer

Are these the thanks our gratitude returns for that strange excess of our Savior's love

When we sat in darkness he took us by the hand, and led us unto his own light.

We sought not him, but he came from far to find us; we looked not towards him, but his mercy called after us.

He called aloud in words of tenderness, Why will ye perish, O ye children of men

Why will ye run after empty trifles, as if there were no joys above with me

Return, O ye dear bought souls, and I will receive you; repent, and I will forgive you.

Behold, O blessed JESUS, to thee we come; and on thy holy cross fasten all our confidence.

Never will we unclasp our faithful hold, till thy grace has sealed the pardon of our sins.

Never will we part from that standard of hope, till our troubled consciences be dismissed in peace.

There will we stand, and sigh, and weep; and every one humbly say, To thy mercy;

JESUS, my GOD, I suffer violence; answer, I beseech thee, O answer you for me.

GLORY BE to the Father, and to the Son, and to the Holy Ghost. As it was in the beginning, is now, and ever shall be: world without end.

Amen.

PSALM 9.

BE silent, O' my soul, and thy LORD will answer for thee; be content, and he is thy security.

Be innocent, and he will defend thee; be humble, and he will exalt thee.

He will forgive thee all you repentest of, the will bestow on thee more than you askest.

Never let us fear the favor of our GOD; if we can but esteem and desire it.

He that so freely gave us himself, will he not with himself give us all things else

Is not his painful life and bitter death a sufficient pledge of his love to us

Is not his infinite love to us a sufficient motive of our duty to him

A duty to which we are so many ways obliged, and wherein our eternity is so highly concerned.

Surely they have little faith, and far less hope, who doubt the mercies of so gracious a Gov!

Mercies confirmed by a thousand miracles, and dearly sealed with his own blood:

That innocent blood, which was shed for us, to appease the wrath of his offended FATHER.

O blessed and all redeeming blood, which flowed so freely from the source of life,

Bathe our polluted souls in thy clear streams, and purge away all our foul impurities.

Cleanse us, O merciful LORD, from our secret faults, and from those darling sins that most abuse us.

Wash off the stains our malice has caused in others, and those which our weakness has received of them.

Let not them perish by our occasions, nor us be undone by theirs.

But let our charity assist one another, and thy clemency pardon us all.

Pardon, O gracious JESUS, what we have been; with thy holy discipline correct what we are!

Order by thy providence what we shall be; and, in the end, crown thine own gifts.

GLORY BE to the Father, and to the Son, and to the Holy Ghost. As it was in the beginning, is now, and ever shall be: world without end.

Amen.

PSALM 10.

SHOULD You, O LORD, have dealt with us in rigour, we had long since been sentenced to eternal death.

Long since our guilty souls had been snatched away, and hurried down to everlasting torments.

But thy gracious mercy has reprieved our lives, and given us space to work out our pardons.

Now is the time of acceptance with thee; now is the day of salvation for us.

Now let us mourn our former offences, and bring forth fruits meet for repentance.

If we, O Jesus, have hitherto persecuted thee, and with our sins nailed thee to the tree of death:

Now let our whole endeavors attend thy service, and loyally aspire to our LORD.

Let us ascend to the Mount of Calvary, and, as often as we go, kiss thy holy steps.

We kiss thy steps when we love thy way; and humble ourselves, and follow thee.

Let us there on our knees approach thy cross, and reverently cover thy naked body.

We cover thee when our charity clothes thy servants, and hides the infirmities of thy little ones.

Let us there, with the tenderest care, unfasten the nails, and gently draw them out of thy hands and feet.

We draw them out when we freely obey thy will, and loosen our affections from cleaving to the world.

LORD, when we have thus rescued thee, and placed thee again in thy throne of glory:

Instead of thyself, nail you us to thy cross, who deserve what you didst endure.

Crucify our flesh with the fear of thee, and give us our portion of sorrow here.

Crucify the world to us, and us to the world; that, dead to it, we may live to thee.

At least, live you in us, O holy Jesu, and fit our souls for so glorious a guest.

Enter into our hearts, and fill them with thyself, that no room be left for any thing but thee.

One only hope we have, thy care of us; one only fear, the neglect of, ourselves.

GLORY BE to the Father, and to the Son, and to the Holy Ghost. As it was in the beginning, is now, and ever shall be: world without end.

Amen.

 **GOD**, *who, at the price of thy only SON's last drop of blood upon the cross, have won our hearts from this life, and all the goods of it, to the sole pursuit and hopes of thyself in eternity: Possess, we beseech thee, and absolutely dispose of what you have so dearly paid for, mortifying us to this world, and confirming our courage, to fight manfully under the banner of our crucified Savior; that we may be able to stand the shock of all temptations, and nothing either in life or death may ever separate us from thy love in him our glorious Redeemer; who, with thee and the HOLY GHOST, liveth and reigned), one GOD, blessed for ever.* Amen.

 **LORD CHRIST**, *who, by thy holy doctrine, has taught us to fast, and watch, and pray; and, by thy blessed example, have powerfully engaged us to follow thy steps! Vouchsafe, we beseech thee, by thy grace, so to mortify our bodies, withdrawing the fuel from our unruly passions, and reducing our immoderate sleep to the measures of necessary refreshment, that our minds may be better disposed for prayer and meditation, devoutly to celebrate the fasts and festivals of thy church, and eternally to rejoice with thee hereafter, in the kingdom of thy glory, where, with the FATHER and the HOLY GHOST, you live and reignest, one GOD, world without end.* Amen.

In the Evening.

PSALM 11.

COME, let us now call off our thoughts from ranging abroad, where they do but lose themselves.

Let us diligently examine the accounts of our time, and sum up the profit we have made today:

What we have gained by all that we have heard or seen, since nothing is so barren but may yield some fruit,

Had we the art to cultivate it right, and fitly apply it to our own advantage.

If we have seen some good examples, which our gracious LORD presents to excite us, Did we immediately entertain the motion, and resolve in our hearts effectually to follow it

If we have fallen among vicious company, which too often engages us to folly; Did the danger increase our care, and the sin of others breed virtue in us

We have heard perhaps some melancholy news of sudden sickness or unexpected deaths: But do we fear to be surprised ourselves, and provide betimes for that day of trial

Order thy whole affairs with the utmost skill, and, which is seldom seen, let all succeed: Still you shall find something to trouble thee, and even thy pleasures shall be tedious unto thee.

Wherever you goest, still crosses will follow thee; since wherever you goest, you carriest thyself.

Who then, my GOD, is truly happy or rather, who comes nearest happiness

He that with patience resolves to suffer, whatever his endeavors are not able to avoid.

Happy yet more is he that delights to suffer, and glories to be like his crucified SAVIOR.

When you art come to this, my soul, that thy crosses seem sweet for the love of JESUS;

Think then thyself sublimely happy; for you have found a heaven upon earth.

GLORY BE to the Father, and to the Son, and to the Holy Ghost. As it was in the beginning, is now, and ever shall be: world without end.

Amen.

PSALM 12.

MY SOUL, when you art thus retired alone, and fitly disposed for quiet thoughts;

Never let the greatness of another molest thy peace, not. his prosperous condition make thee repine.

Say not in thy heart, Had I that fair estate, or were entrusted with so high a place:

I should know how to contrive things better, and never commit such gross mistakes.

Tell me, how dost you manage thy own employments; and fit the little room you boldest in the world

If you have leisure, art you not idle, and spendest thy precious time in unprofitable follies

If you art busy, art not you so too much; and leavest no time to provide for thy soul

Do thy riches make thee wise, and generously assist the poor

Does thy poverty make thee humble; and faithfully to labor for thy family

Dost you in every state give thanks to Heaven; and contentedly subscribe to its severest decrees

Can you rejoicingly say to God, O my adored Creator! I am glad my life is in thy hands

You art all wisdom, and seest my wants; you art all goodness and delightest to relieve me.

Under thy providence I know I am safe; whatever befalls me, you guidest to my advantage.

If you wilt have me obscure, and low; thy blessed will, not mine, be done.

If you wilt load my back with crosses, and embitter my days with grief and sickness;

Still may thy blessed will, O LORD, be done; still govern thy creatures in thine own best way.

Place where you pleasest thy favors; but secure to my soul a portion of thy love.

Take what you wilt of the things you host lent me; but leave in my heart the possession of thyself.

Let others be preferred, and me neglected; let their affairs succeed, and mine miscarry.:

Only one thing I humbly beg; and may my gracious GOD vouchsafe to grant it:

Cast me not away from thy presence for ever; nor wipe my name out of the book of life.

But my eternal hopes, let them remain, and still grow quicker as they approach to their end.

GLORY BE to the Father, and to the Son, and to the Holy Ghost. As it was in the beginning, is now, and ever shall be: world without end.

Amen.

PSALM 13.

WE WEARY ourselves with running after flies, which are hard to catch, and trifles when they are caught.

This we pursue, and follow that; but nothing we meet can fill our hearts:

Till we have found thee out, O gracious LORD! our only fulfill satisfying good:

Till we have found out thee, not by a dark belief, but clearly as you art in thine own bright self.

Remember, O my soul, this truth, which our own experience evidently proves:

The eye is not filled with seeing varieties, nor the ear with hearing all harmony.

Remember this truth of the world we hope, made sure our faith by the word of JESUS.

The eye has not seen such beauteous glories, nor has the ear heard such ravishing charms

Nor can the heart itself conceive such incredible joys, as our GOD has provided for them that love him:

As our blessed JESUS has purchased for his servants; and even for thee, my soul, to crown thy patience. Wherefore in peace lay down thy head, and rest secure in the protection of thy GOD.

GLORY BE to the Father, and to the Son, and to the Holy Ghost. As it was in the beginning, is now, and ever shall be: world without end.

Amen.

O GOD, *whose provident mercies make every day a new branch of the tree of knowledge to us, whence the evening may fresh gather variety of fruit, fit to nourish those souls whom thy grace has brought to feed on the tree of life, the cross of JESUS! Grant, we humbly beseech thee, that no experience of good or evil, which this day has afforded, may be lost on us; but whatever of moment has happened to ourselves or others, may render us more skilful in discerning the true value and use of this estate in all the scenes of life, and ready to resign (with our Savior) our whole concerns, and beings here to thy will, and the sole advancement of thy glory, which at length will crown thy servants with immortal bliss, through our LORD JESUS CHRIST.*

THE LORD *bless us, and keep us this night; the LORD make his face to shine upon us, and keep us under the shadow of his wings; the LORD lift up his countenance, and give us peace and rest in him, now and ever.* Amen.

The Office for Saturday

Morning Prayer.

Antiphon

Come, let us adore our victorious Redeemer.

PSALM 1.

COME, all ye powers of my delivered soul, and pay your homage to the Prince of peace, to the Prince of our salvation; cast your unworthy selves at his sacred feet, and renew your vows of following his steps.

Come, let us adore our victorious Redeemer.

He triumphed over death in his own body, and enables us to conquer it in ours; imparting to us his heavenly skill, and provoking our courage with infinite rewards.

Come, let us adore our victorious Redeemer.

He changed the corrupted government of the world, and established a new and holy law, that as we were vassals to sin before, we might now become the free subjects of grace.

Come, let us adore our victorious Redeemer.

Let us live and die in his blessed obedience, and may no temptation separate us from him; who, if we resist, will make us overcome; and when we have overcome, will crown us with peace.

Come, let us adore our victorious Redeemer.

GLORY BE to the Father, and to the Son, and to the Holy Ghost. As it was in the beginning, is now, and ever shall be: world without end.

Amen.

Antiphon

This is, alas, the land of the dying; but we hope to see the glory of GOD in the land of the living.

PSALM 2.

PROSTRATE before thy tomb, O LORD! behold we freely confess our misery; And in the lowest posture of afflicted pilgrims, humbly implore thy mercy.

Peacefully in the grave thy holy body was reposed, and thy soul went triumphing to redeem thy captives. But we, alas, thy helpless orphans; how are we left in the midst of our enemies!

To how many dangers are our lives exposed! With how many temptations are we besieged!

Temptations in meat, temptations in drink, temptations in conversing, temptations in solitude.

Temptations in business, temptations in leisure, temptations in riches, temptations in poverty.

All our ways are strewed with snares, and even our. own senses conspire against us.

Whither, O my GOD, shall our poor souls go, encompassed with a body so frail, and a world so corrupt Whither, but to thee, the Justifier of sinners; and to thy grace, the Sustainer of the weak

Thy grace instructs us what we ought to do, and breeds in us the will to endeavor what we know.

Thy grace enables us to perform our resolves; and when all is done, thy grace must give the success.

Govern us with thy grace, O Eternal Wisdom! and direct our steps in thy way.

Order every, seeming chance to prevent our falling; and still lead us on towards our happy end.

Give us the eye and wing of an eagle, to see our danger, and fly swiftly away.

If yet we must needs engage our enemy, and no means left to escape the encounter:

Strengthen us, O LORD, to persevere with courage; that we may never be wanting in our fidelity to thee.

Convince us, blessed JESUS, into this firm judgment, and make our memories faithfully retain it:

Whatever our senses say to deceive us; or the world to obscure so beauteous a truth:

That thyself alone art our Chief Good; and the sight of thy glory our supreme felicity.

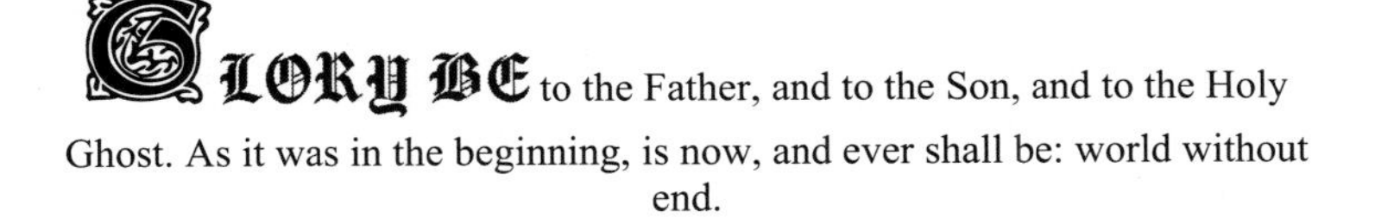

GLORY BE to the Father, and to the Son, and to the Holy Ghost. As it was in the beginning, is now, and ever shall be: world without end.

Amen.

PSALM 3.

HAPPY, O LORD, are they, who have so much employment, that there remains no room for idle thoughts.

Happy are they who have so little business, that they want no space to attend their souls.

Happy yet more are they, who, in the midst of their work, often think of the wages above.

Whom nothing diverts from their chief concern, of seeking to make their calling and election sure.

But while their backs are bowed down with labor, they freely raise up their minds to heaven.

And while they are tied to their beds with sickness, yet

move on to their eternal rest.

Often they rejoice with themselves alone, and silently say in their contented hearts:

Here we are narrowly confined; and our time entertained with trivial affairs.

But hereafter we expect an unbounded enlargement;

and the same glorious office with the blessed angels.

Here are we subject to a thousand miseries, and the

most prosperous life is vain and short

But hereafter we expect an infinity of joy, and the "solid pleasures of heaven for ever."

We too, O gracious LORD, who now adore thee, and in thy presence sing these holy words,

We humbly pray thee guide us in the middle path, that we never decline to any extreme.

Deliver us both from the stormy sea of business, and from the dead water of a slothful life:

Lest we be cast away by forgetting thee; or become corrupted by neglecting ourselves.

Make us recollect our thoughts, how much soever our condition distracts us.

Make us look up with confidence in our GOD, how low soever our afflictions depress us.

Make us look up to the eternal mountains, and feed our souls with this sweet hope:

The day will come, that, out of this dark world, we shall joyfully ascend to that beauteous light.

The day will come, and cannot be far off; when we shall rest for ever in the bosom of bliss.

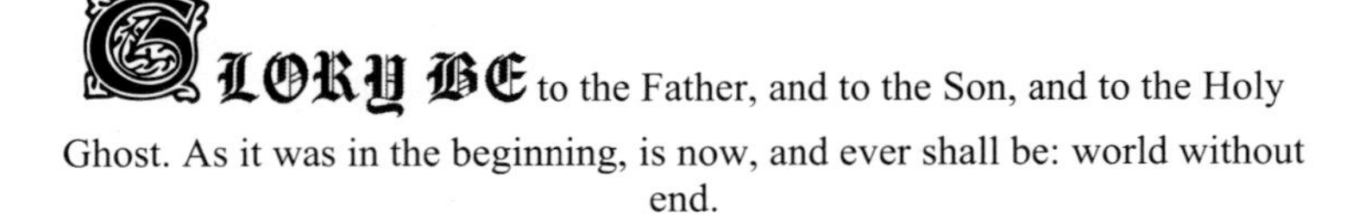

GLORY BE to the Father, and to the Son, and to the Holy Ghost. As it was in the beginning, is now, and ever shall be: world without end.

Amen.

PSALM 4.

HAPPIEST of all, O LORD, are they whose very business is thy service:

Who not only bestow an interrupted glance, but steadily and constantly fix their eyes on thee:

Who not only visit thy house sometimes, but night and day dwell in thy presence.

When the sun rises, it finds them at their prayers; and when it sets, leaves them at the same sweet task.

Every place is to them a church, and every day a holy sabbath.

Every object an occasion of piety; and every accident an exercise of virtue.

Do they behold the beauteous stars They presently adore their great Creator.

Do they look down on the fruitful earth They instantly begin to praise his bounty.

Let war or peace do what they will, and the unconstant world reel up and down,

They pass through all unconcerned, and smoothly go on in their regular course:

Looking still up to the glorious life above; and entertaining this in hope and solitude.

If they depart sometimes from their proper centre, and forsake awhile their beloved retirement,

It is to approach and give light to others, and inflame some cold or lukewarm heart.

While they are thus abroad, their minds are at home with thee; and nothing can divide them from thy presence.

Yet do they wisely make haste to return, and enjoy thee alone.

There you receivest them as familiar friends, and freely admittest them into thy secret sweetness.

You givest them a taste from thine own full board, and overflowest their hearts with the wine of gladness.

Often they feel a little beam from heaven strike gently, and fill their breast with light.

Often that gentle light is kindled into a flame, and chastely burns with pure desires;

Desires that still mount up and aim at thee, the supernatural centre of all their hopes.

Blessed Providence! who governest all things in perfect wisdom, and assignest to every one his proper place,

If you have pleased to dispose our lives, in circumstances less favorable than these,

'O let thy powerful hand supply our wants, and lead us on in our low path!

That, at least, afar off we may follow them who strive to tread so near thy steps.

So shall we, too, though slowly, arrive at the rich inheritance of that Holy Land.

So shall we gladly enter those blissful gates, and dwell for ever in the city of peace.

GLORY BE to the Father, and to the Son, and to the Holy Ghost. As it was in the beginning, is now, and ever shall be: world without end.

Amen.

GOD, *who seest and pitiest the infirmity of our nature, surrounded on every side with dangers and temptations, strengthen us, we beseech thee, with thy all powerful grace, to stand continually on our guard, resolved even to death, either warily to avoid, or stoutly break through all that offers to divert or stop the advancement of thy love in our hearts; and grant us so wisely to improve the talents of capacity, and means thy providence assigns us in this present life, that at the great day of account, we may every one be received with those precious words, "Well done, you good and faithful servant, enter you into the joy of thy MASTER;" through our LORD JESUS CHRIST, thy Son, who, with thee, and the HOLY GHOST, liveth and reigneth, one GOD, world without end.* Amen.

At Noon.

PSALM 5.

IF we rejoiced for ourselves in the sufferings of our LORD, let us now rejoice for him that his sufferings are ended.

Never again, O JESUS, shall those blessed eyes weep, nor thv holy soul be sorrowful to death.

Never shall thy precious life be subject any more to the bloody malice of ambitious hypocrites.

Never shall thy innocence any more be exposed to the barbarous fury of an ungrateful multitude.

But you shall live and reign for ever; and all created nature perpetually adore thee.

O happy end of well endured afflictions! O blessed fruits that spring from the cross of JESUS!

Look up, my soul, and see thy crucified LORD sit gloriously enthroned at the right hand of his FATHER.

Behold the ragged purple now turned into a robe of light, and the scornful reed into a royal sceptre.

The wreath of thorns is grown into a sparkling diadem, and all his scars polished into brightness.

The impenitent Jews are scattered over the world, to attest his truth and their own obdurate blindness.

But he himself is crowned with eternal triumphs, and

the souls he has redeemed shall sing his victories for ever. Live, glorious King of men and angels; live, happy

Conqueror of sin and death.

Our praises shall always attend thy cross, and our patience endeavor to bear our own.

Through fiercest dangers our faith shall follow thee, and "nothing wrest from us our hope at last to see thee.

We will fear no more the sting of death, nor be frighted at the darkness of the grave.

Since you have changed our grave into a bed of rest, and made death itself but a passage into life.

We will love no more the pleasures of vanity, nor set our hearts on unsatisfying riches;

Since you have opened Paradise again, and purchased for us the kingdom of heaven.

GLORY BE to the Father, and to the Son, and to the Holy Ghost. As it was in the beginning, is now, and ever shall be: world without end.

Amen.

PSALM 6.

BLESSED be thy name, O holy JESUS! and blessed be the mercy of thy providence.

Who have cast our lots in these times of grace, and designed our birth in the days of light,

When we may clearly see our ready way, and directly go on to our glorious end.

Till you appearedst, O you only Light of the world! our miserable earth lay covered with darkness.

Till you sufferedst, O sovereign LORD of life! our vile nature lay condemned in the shades of death.

The kingdom of heaven was shut up, and the entrances of Paradise were by sin made impassable.

But when You, O glorious Conqueror! hadst overcome death, you didst open the kingdom of heaven to all believers.

Soon as thine own afflictions were ended, you didst communicate thy joys to all the world;

To all that esteemed so blessed a sight, and stood prepared to entertain thy coming.

The hearts that love thee you fillest with gladness, and overflowest them with an ocean of heavenly delights.

Come, happy souls, to whom belongs so fair a title to all these mercies!

Come, let us now raise up our thoughts, and continually meditate on our future beatitude.

Let us comfort our labors with the hope of rest, and solace our sufferings with the expectance of a quick reward:

Now that the hand of our gracious LORD has unlocked the gates of everlasting bliss:

Now that they stand wide open to admit such as press on with their utmost strength:

Such as have wisely made choice of heaven, for the only end and business of their life:

Rejecting all these false allurements, to attend the pursuit of true felicity.

O blessed JESUS, our Hope, our Strength, and the full Rewarder of all thy servants!

As you have freely prepared for us ready wages; so, LORD, let thy grace enable us to work.

Make us direct our whole life to thee, and undervalue all things compared with thy love.

Seal you up our eyes to the illusions of the world, and open them upwards to thy solid glories.

That when our earthly tabernacle shall be dissolved, and this house of clay fall into the dust;

We may ascend to thee, and dwell above in that building not made with hands, eternal in the heavens.

GLORY BE to the Father, and to the Son, and to the Holy Ghost. As it was in the beginning, is now, and ever shall be: world without end.

Amen.

PSALM 7.

PRAISE our LORD, O ye children of men! Praise him as the Author of all your hopes!

Praise our Lora), O ye blessed of heaven! Praise him as the Finisher of all your joys!

Sing, O ye reverend Patriarchs and holy Prophets; sing hymns of glory to the great MESSIAS.

Sing and rejoice all ye ancient saints, who so long waited for his gracious appearance.

Sing and rejoice all ye souls of the righteous, who wait for a blessed resurrection:

Bring forth your best and purest incense, and humbly offer it at the throne of the LAMB;

The LAMB that was slain from the beginning, of the world, by the sprinkling of whose blood ye are all saved.

O still sing on the praises of the King of peace, and bless for ever his victorious mercy!

It is He who dissolved for you the power of darkness, and brake asunder the bars of death.

How did your glad eyes then sparkle with joy, to see your desired Redeemer!

How were your spirits transported with delights, to behold the splendors of his glorious presence!

His presence that can quickly turn the saddest night into a cheerful day. **Hallelujah**.

That can change a dungeon into a house of mirth.— **Hallelujah**.

And make every place a paradise. **Hallelujah**.

O glorious Presence! when shall our souls be filled with strong and constant desires of enjoying thee

When shall our desires be filled with the everlasting fruition of thy blessed self

Henceforth for thee, and for thy sacred love, O you great and only Comfort of our souls;

May all afflictions be welcome to us, as wholesome physic to correct our follies.

May the pleasures of the world be rejected by us; as dangerous fruits that fill us with diseases.

May we, by thy example, neither fear to die, nor refuse the labors of this life.

But while we live, obey thy grace; that when we die, we may enjoy thy glory.

GLORY BE to the Father, and to the Son, and to the Holy Ghost. As it was in the beginning, is now, and ever shall be: world without end.

Amen.

In the Afternoon.

PSALM 8.

WHY do we so eagerly pursue this world, and seek its fond enjoyments

A world of vanity and false deceits; a world of misery and sad disasters.

You art, O glorious JESUS, the beauty of angels, and the everlasting joy of all saints.

You art the very heaven of heavens, and in thy sight alone is the fullness of bliss.

All this you art and infinitely more; and yet, alas, how few esteem thee!

The world, we dearly know, too often has deceived us; and yet our rashness matters not to be undone by it again.

You never, O JESUS, has failed our hope, and yet our dullness fears to rely on thee.

The world distracts and embroils our spirits, and we delight in our misery.

You always, O JESUS, fillest our hearts with peace, and we are weary of thy happiness.

The world calls, and we faint in following it; you tallest, and we are still relieved by thee:

Yet is our nature so ungratefully perverse, we run after that which tires, and abandon that which refreshes.

Sometimes our lips speak gloriously of thee, O you living Fountain of eternal bliss!

Some happy times we relish thy sweetness, and decry aloud the poison of the world,

But we are soon enticed by its gilded cup; and easily forsake the waters of life.

O blessed JESUS, who tookest upon thee all our frailties; to bestow on us thine own perfections:

Teach us to prize the joys of heaven; and part with all things else to purchase thee.

Make all the pleasures of this life bitter to our taste, as they are indeed pernicious to our healths.

Let not their flatteries any more delude us, nor superfluous cares perplex our minds.

But may our chief delight be to think of thee, and all our study to grow great in thy love.

GLORY BE to the Father, and to the Son, and to the Holy Ghost. As it was in the beginning, is now, and ever shall be: world without end.

Amen.

PSALM 9.

ALL this is true, and yet the world is loved, and our nature inclines to affect its vanities.

It is loved, and so it justly deserves, did we rightly understand its real value.

Our life indeed seems mean and trivial, and all things about us seem troublesome and dangerous.

Yet, O my GOD, are their consequences excellent in this, that they are our only way of coming to thee.

This world, and this alone, is the womb that breeds us, and brings us forth to see thy light.

Whether we eat or drink, or whatsoever else an innocent hand can undertake;

If we regard our happy end, and order all to the improvement of our minds:

They instantly change their name, and become religious. Riches themselves, and imperious honor, have not so

perverse and fixed a malice:

But a prudent use converts them to piety, and makes them fit instruments of highest bliss.

Our very delights, (O the goodness of our God!) may be so tempered with a wise alloy;

That his mercy accounts them as parts of our duty, and fails not to give them their full reward:

While they are entertained for the health of our bodies, or the just refreshment of our wearied spirits:

And both our bodies and spirits constantly applied to gain new degrees of the love of heaven. Thus, gracious LORD, `every moment of our lives may still be climbing up towards thee.

Thus may we still proceed in thy service, even then when we most of all serve ourselves.

And then indeed we best serve ourselves, when we are busiest in thy service.

You sweetly vouchsafest to style that thy glory, which is nothing but our interest.

O blessed JESUS, King of clemency, and great. Reward every improved grace!

You who earnest down from heaven, not only to shed thy blood for us; but to show us a pattern; and madest us free, to work for our own profit!

Instruct our gratitude to consecrate all to thee; since all by thy bounty redounds to ourselves.

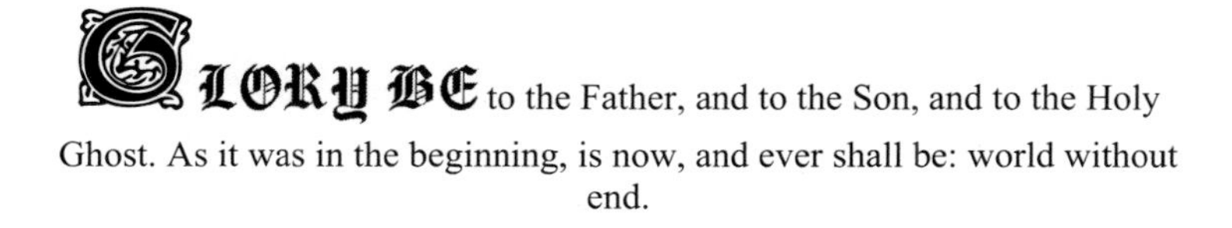

GLORY BE to the Father, and to the Son, and to the Holy Ghost. As it was in the beginning, is now, and ever shall be: world without end.

Amen.

PSALM 10.

THIS life indeed is the way we must walk, but this alone cannot bring us to our end.

Ere we arrive at our appointed home, we must be led through the gates of death.

Where we shall be absolutely stripped of all we have, and carry nothing with us but what we are.

Where we must not only quit the whole world, but leave behind us even a part of ourselves.

Have You, my soul, seen some neighbor die, and dost you remember those circumstances of sorrow

We are sure the case ere long will be our own, and are not sure but it may be very soon.

Have we ourselves been dangerously sick, and do we remember the thoughts we had then

How we resolved to correct our passions, and strive against the vices that so particularly endanger us

' It will come to this again, and no reprieve be found to stay one single minute the hand of death.

But he immediately will seize upon us, and bear us away to the region of spirits:

There to be ranged in our proper place, as the course of our life has qualified us here.

Nor is this all, to expire and die, and dwell for a time in a state of separation;

We most expect another day, a day of public accounts and restitution of all things;

When the archangel shall sound his trumpet, and proclaim aloud this universal summons:

"Arise, ye dead, and come to judgment; arise and appear before the throne of GOD."

Then shall the little heaps of dust immediately awake, and every soul put on her proper body.

Immediately all the children of ADAM shall be gathered together, from heaven, and hell, and every corner of the earth.

There they must stand, and all attend their doom; but, Oh! with how sad and fatal a difference!

The just shall look up with a cheerful confidence, and in their new white robes triumph and sing;

Hallelujah! let us rejoice, for the marriage of the LAMB is come, and his bride has prepared herself.

Let us rejoice, for the kingdom of the world is made our LORD'S and his CHRIST's; and he shall reign for ever and ever.

Let us rejoice, for now our Redeemer is nigh; behold he comes quickly, and his reward is with him.

Come, come, LORD JESUS, you long desire of hearts; come quickly, you full delight of our souls.

“Come, and declare to all the world thy glory; come, and reward before all the world thy servants."

Lo, where he comes aloft in power and majesty, attended with a train of innumerable angels.

Behold where he sits enthroned on the wings of cherubims, and takes at once a view of all mankind.

Soon he commands his angels to sever his sheep, and gather them together on his right hand.

First then to them he turns his glorious face, and shines upon them with these ravishing words:

"Come, ye blessed of my FATHER, possess the kingdom prepared for you from the beginning of the world."

O the joys their souls shall feel, when those heavenly words shall sound in their ears!

Joys which the wit of man cannot conceive; joys that the tongues of angels cannot express!

Let it suffice, themselves shall taste their own felicity, and feed on its sweetness for evermore.

But O! with what dejected eyes, and trembling hearts shall the wicked stand expecting their Judge

What shall they do, when, wherever they look, their eye can meet with nothing but despair

Above, the offended Judge, ready to condemn them; below, the bottomless pit ready to devour them.

Within, the worm of conscience gnawing their bowels; and round about all the world in flames.

What shall they do, when the terrible voice shall strike them down to the bottom of hell

"Depart, ye cursed, into everlasting fire, prepared for the Devil and his angels."

The day of man is past, when sinners did what they pleased, and GOD seemed to hold his peace.

It is now the day of GOD, when his wrath shall speak in thunder, and sinners suffer what their wickedness deserves.

Then shall they sink immediately into the pit of sorrows, and dwell in darkness and torments for ever.

Whilst the just shall go up in joy and triumph, and reign with our LORD in his kingdom for ever.

Thus shall the whole creation he finally disposed, and mercy and justice divide the world,

O my soul! who now art here below, and readest these dreadful truths as things afar off:

Know, you shall then be present, and see them with thine eyes, and be thyself concerned for all eternity.

Know, as you live, you art like to die; and as you diest, you art sure to be judged.

Think what you then wouldest give to have repented in time; think what you wouldest give for a little time to repent.

Watch therefore now, and continually pray; for we know not the hour when the Son of man will come.

O Son of GOD, and man! who tamest in mercy to save us; bring the same mercy with thee, when you comest to judge us.

Meanwhile assist us with thy heavenly grace, to stand perpetually with our accounts prepared,

That we may die in the peace of GOD, and of his holy church, and go to live with him and his saints for ever.

GLORY BE to the Father, and to the Son, and to the Holy Ghost. As it was in the beginning, is now, and ever shall be: world without end.

Amen.

In the Evening.

PSALM 11.

RETIRE, O my soul, into thine own bosom, and search what you aimest at in all thy thoughts.

Where dost you place thy chief felicity; and whither tend thy strongest desires

Go to the great and prudent of the world, and learn of them to choose thy interests.

Do they not there increase their estates, where they mean to spend most of their life

Do they project their mansion seat in a country through which they pass as travelers

No more, my soul, should we build our best hopes on the sandy foundation of this perishable earth.

Where we are sure we cannot stay long; and are not sure we shall stay a very little.

O you eternal Being, who changest not, yet art the cause and end of all our changes!

Who still remainest the same richfulness in thyself, the same bright glory to all thy blessed!

Teach us, O LORD, to use this transitory life as pilgrims returning to their beloved home:

That we may take what our journey requires, and not think of settling in a foreign country.

But wisely forecast our treasures so, as to be happy there, where we must always be.

GLORY BE to the Father, and to the Son, and to the Holy Ghost. As it was in the beginning, is now, and ever shall be: world without end.

Amen.

PSALM 12.

NOW you have found thy happy end, and found it the my good that lasts for ever.

Study, O my soul, to know still more, and still more value those immortal joys.

Strive for so glorious a prize with thy whole force, and the utmost strainings of all thy faculties.

Purchase at any rate that blessed inheritance, and wisely neglect all things else;

All that divert thee from thy holy course, or retard the speed of thy advancement.

For though the least in the kingdom of heaven be happy enough, where every vessel is filled to the brim;

Yet to enlarge our capacity to the least degree higher, deserves the busiest diligence of our whole life.

Shall the industrious bee endure no rest, but fly, and sing, and labor all the day

Shall the unwearied ant be running up and down, to fetch and carry a few grains of corn

And shall we, for whom all nature so faithfully works, and almost tires itself in a perpetual motion:

For whom the tender providence of GOD commands even his angels to watch and pray:

For whom the adored JESUS came down from heaven, and spent a whole life in continual labors:

Shall we sleep on in a drowsy sloth, and hardly stir a finger to help ourselves

O blessed hope, be you my chief delight, and the only treasure I covet t) lay up:

Be you the quickening life of all my actions, and sweet alloy of all my sufferings.

So shall I never refuse the meanest labors, whilst I look to receive such glorious wages.

So shall I never repine at any temporal loss, whilst I hope to gain such eternal rewards.

GLORY BE to the Father, and to the Son, and to the Holy Ghost. As it was in the beginning, is now, and ever shall be: world without end.

Amen.

PSALM 13.

BUT, Oh! it is not so much our sloth undoes us, as the imprudent choice in applying our diligence.

Many, alas! take pains enough; many perplex themselves too much.

See how the busy toilers of the world are chained perpetually like slaves to their work.

How early they rise, and late go to sleep, and eat the bread of care and sorrow.

See how the hardy soldiers follow their Prince through a thousand difficulties and dangers.

See how the venturous mariners expose their lives over stormy seas, into barbarous nations,

To gain.a few pence, or some petty honor, which others have more share in than themselves.

O bounteous LORD, how easy are thy commands; how cheap have you made the purchase of heaven!

Half these pains will make us saints; half these sufferings canonize us for martyrs:

Were they devoutly undertaken for thee, and the higher enjoyment of thy glorious promises.

You dost not bid us freeze under the Polar Star, or burn in the heats of the Torrid Zone;

But proposest a sweet and gentle rule, and such as our nature itself would choose,

Did not our passions strongly mislead us, and the world about us distract our reason.

You biddest us but wisely love ourselves, and attend, above all things, our own true happiness.

You biddest us value even this world as much as it deserves, since it is the school that breeds us up to the other.

Only we are forbidden to be willful fools, and prefer a short vanity before eternal felicity.

O the mild government of the King of heaven! this we can do, whatever else we are doing.

This we can do, even whilst we sit still, and only move our thoughts towards thee.

Nay, then we best perform this best of works, when all our powers are quiet in thee.

O make us to love thee so much the more, as you more discoverest the excess of thy love.

GLORY BE to the Father, and to the Son, and to the Holy Ghost. As it was in the beginning, is now, and ever shall be: world without end.

Amen.

O GOD, *whose eternal providence has embarked our souls in the ship of our bodies, not to expect any port of anchorage on the sea of this world, but to steer directly through it to thy glorious kingdom: Grant us, we beseech thee, that daily reflecting with what care and unwearied diligence the wretched adventurers for all sorts of vanities pursue round about us their desperate courses, we may heartily feel ourselves confounded with just reproach, who knowing our engagements on so important a voyage, yet take so little pains to perform it. Preserve us, O LORD, from the dangers that on all sides assault us, and keep our affections still fitly disposed to receive thy holy inspirations; that being carried sweetly and strongly forward by thy HOLY SPIRIT, we may happily arrive at last in the haven of eternal salvation, through our LORD JESUS CHRIST.*

The Office of our Blessed Savior.

This may be said on all the Feasts of our Savior, as CHRISTMAS, NEWYEAR'S DAY, and on other occasional Commemorations of the great benefits we receive by Him, according as any one's particular devotion may direct.

Morning Prayer.

Antiphon

Come, let us adore our GOD that redeemed us.

PSALM 1.

BRING TO OUR LORD, all you his servants, bring to our LORD, the sacrifice of praise; bring to our LORD, all ye nations of the earth, bring hymns of glory to his great name.

Come let us adore our GOD that redeemed us.

He is our GOD and we his people, created by his goodness to be happy for ever; he is our Redeemer, and we his purchase, restored by his death to a better eternity.

Today let us adore our GOD that redeemed us.

Let us learn of him, and he will teach us his ways; let us follow him, and we shall walk in the light; for the law and its types were given by Moses, but grace and truth came by JESUS CHRIST.

Today let us adore our GOD that redeemed us.

Come let us ascend to the house of our LORD, where he is truly worshipped, and celebrated this day with a holy joy, imploring his mercies for all we need, and blessing his bounty for all we have.

Today let us adore our GOD that redeemed us:

GLORY BE to the Father, and to the Son, and to the Holy Ghost. As it was in the beginning, is now, and ever shall be: world without end.

Amen.

HYMN 1

JESUS, who from thy FATHER'S throne to this low vale of tears came down,
In our poor nature dressed!
O may the charms of that sweet love, Draw up our souls to thee above,
And fix them there to rest. JESU, whose high and humble birth, In heaven the angels, and on earth
The faithful shepherds sing;
O may our hymns, which here run low, Shoot up aloft, and fruitful grow,
In the eternal spring.
JESUS, who took'st that heavenly name, Thy blessed purpose to proclaim,
Of saving lost mankind!
O may we bow our heart and knee, Bright King of Names, to glorious thee,
And thy hid sweetness find Jesus, who thus began our bliss, You carried'st on our happiness!
To thee all praise be paid.
O may the great mysterious Three, For ever live, and ever be,
Ador'd, belov'd, obey'd. Amen.

PSALM II.

COME now, and hear, ye that fear the LORD, and I will tell you what he has done for my soul.

Hear, and I will tell you what he has done for yours; and the wonders of his bounty to all the world.

When we lay asleep in the shades of darkness, of nothing, his mighty hand awaked us into being:

Not that of stones, or plants, or beasts, over which he has made us absolute lords:

But of an accomplished body and immortal spirit, little inferior to his glorious angels.

He printed on our souls his own similitude, and promised to our obedience his own felicity.

He endued us with appetites to live happily; and furnished us with means to satisfy those appetites.

Creating a whole world to serve us here, and providing a heaven, the purchase of his own merits, to glorify us hereafter.

Thus didst you favor us, O infinite Goodness! but we, what return did we make unto thee

Blush, O my soul, for shame, at so strange a weakness; and weep for grief at so extreme an ingratitude.

We fondly embraced a little present satisfaction, before the pleasure of Paradise and the eternity of heaven.

Behold the unhappy source of all our miseries, which still increased its streams as they went further on;

Till at last they exacted a deluge of justice, to drown their deluge of iniquity.

And here, alas, had been an end of man; a sad and fatal end of the whole world:

Had not our wise Creator foreseen the danger, and in time prevented the extremity of the ruin:

Reserving for himself a few choice plants to replenish the earth with more hopeful fruit.

Yet they quickly grew wild, and brought forth sour grapes, and their children's teeth were set on edge.

Quickly they aspired to an intolerable pride of fortifying their wickedness against the power of Heaven.

Justice was now provoked to a second deluge, and to bring again a cloud over the earth.

But mercy discovered a bow in the cloud, and our faithful GOD remembered his promise:

Allaying their punishment with a milder sentence; only catering.; them from the place of their conspiracy:

Which yet his providence turned into a blessing, by making it an occasion of peopling the world.

Still their rebellious nature disobeyed again, and neither feared his judgments, nor valued his mercies.

Then he selected a private family, and increased and governed them with a particular tenderness.

Giving them a law by the hand of angels, and engaging their obedience by a thousand favors.

But they neglected too their GOD, and heaven, and fell in love with the ways of death.

When you hadst thus, O LORD, tried every remedy, and found our disease beyond all cure:

When the light of nature proved too weak a guide, and the general flood too mild a correction:

When the miracles of MOSES could not soften their hearts, nor the law'of angels bring any to perfection:

When all was reduced to this desperate state and no imaginable hope left to recover us:

Behold the eternal Wisdom finds a strange expedient of salvation, the last and highest instance of almighty love.

Himself he resolves to clothe with our flesh, and come down among us to die a cursed death, and bear our sins in his body on the tree.

Wonder, O my soul, at the mercies of thy LORD, how infinitely transcending even our utmost wishes.

Wonder at the admirable providence of his counsels, how exactly fitted to their great design.

Had he been less than GOD, we could never have believed the sublime mysteries of his heavenly doctrine, especially those of his incarnation, and our redemption.

Had he been other than man, we must have wanted a suffering Redeemer, as well as the powerful motive of his holy example.

Had he been only GOD, he could never have died upon the cross, or suffered the least of those afflictions he so gloriously overcame.

Had he been merely man, his sufferings had wanted their infinite merit, and he could never have overcome those infinite afflictions he so patiently suffered, to accomplish our redemption.

O blessed JESUS! both these you art in thyself; be you both these to us.

Be you our GOD, and make us adore thee; be you our leader, and make us follow thee.

GLORY BE to the Father, and to the Son, and to the Holy Ghost. As it was in the beginning, is now, and ever shall be: world without end.

Amen.

PSALM 3.

SOON as the blessed decree was made of sending the SON of GOD to redeem mankind;

Immediately his goodness was ready to come amongst us, had the world been ready to receive him.

But we are as yet too gross and sensual, and utterly uncapable of so pure a law.

We are immersed in cares and pleasures, and wholly indisposed for so fair an obedience.

While we were thus unfit for thee, O you GOD of pure and perfect holiness

You graciously wert pleased to stay for us; and all that time prepare us for thy presence:

From the beginning entertaining us with hope; and through every age confirming our faith.

How early, O my GOD, didst you engage to relieve us; “The seed of the woman shall bruise the serpent's head.”

How often didst you repeat thy promise to ABRAHAM, "In thy seed shall all the nations of the earth be blessed!"

How many ways did thy mercy invent, by unquestionable tokens to give notice of thy coming!

> “Behold a virgin shall conceive, and bear a son, and his name shall be called IMMANUEL.”
>
> “There shall come forth a rod out of the stem of JESSE, and a branch shall grow out of his roots, And the SPIRIT of the LORD shall rest upon him; the SPIRIT of wisdom and understanding; The SPIRIT of counsel and might; the SPIRIT of knowledge, and the fear of the LORD.”

> "The LORD thy GOD shall raise up unto thee a Prophet of thy brethren, like unto me; unto him shall ye hearken."

Hark how the Almighty FATHER introduces his SON, commanding first "all the angels of GOD to worship him:"

> "You art my SON, my dearly beloved SON; this day have I begotten thee: You art my Son, and I will be thy FATHER."
>
> "I will give thee the Heathen for thine inheritance; and the uttermost parts of the earth for thy possession."
>
> "And is it a light thing that you should be my servant to raise up the tribes of JACOB, and restore the preserved of ISRAEL"
>
> "I will give thee for a light to the Gentiles, that you may be my salvation to the ends of the earth."

Hark how the ancient Prophets rejoice in the Messiah, and in soft and gentle words foretell his sweetness:

> "He shall come down as rain into a fleece of wool, and as drops of dew distilling on the earth."
>
> "He shall feed his flocks like a shepherd; and gently lead those that are with young."
>
> "He shall gather the lambs with his arms, and carry them in his bosom."
>
> "The bruised reed shall he not break, nor quench the smoking flax."
>
> "Righteousness and peace shall flourish in his days; and of his kingdom there shall be no end."
>
> "Then shall the eyes of the blind be opened, and the ears of the deaf be made to hear."
>
> "Then shall the tongues of the dumb be loosened; and the lame shall leap as a hart."

Thus did thy holy Prophets prophesy of thee; thus did their children sing thy praises.

> "Blessed be the LORD our GOD, who only does wondrous things; and blessed be the name of his Majesty for ever,"
>
> "His dominion shall reach from the one sea to the other, and from the river to the ends of the world."
>
> "They who dwell in the wilderness shall kneel before him; his enemies shall lick the dust."
>
> "The Kings of Tarshish, and of the isles, shall bring presents; the Kings of Sheba and Saba shall offer gifts."
>
> "Yea, all Kings shall fall down before him; all nations shall serve him."
>
> "He shall spare the simple and needy when he cries; the poor also, and him that has no helper."
>
> "He shall redeem their soul from deceit and violence and precious shall their blood be in his sight."

O you eternal King of heaven, make good to thy servants these happy predictions.

So rule us here, that we may obey thy grace; so favor us hereafter, that we may enjoy thy glory.

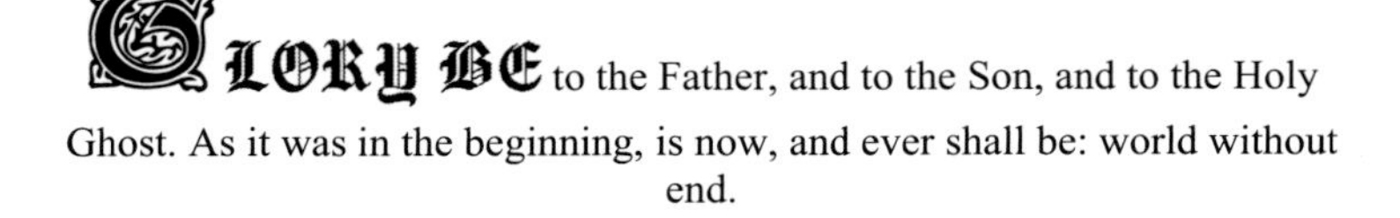

GLORY BE to the Father, and to the Son, and to the Holy Ghost. As it was in the beginning, is now, and ever shall be: world without end.

Amen.

PSALM 5.

IT was not thy joys alone, O dearest LORD, that thou inspiredst into thy holy Prophets:

But you revealedst to them thy sorrows too, and commandedst to publish them with tender care:

That they, not only should speak thy words, but, the more to affect us, put on thy person.

O let our eyes run down with water, and our hearts faint away with grief;

While we remember the sufferings of our LORD, and hear his sad complaints.

> "I gave my back to the smiters, and my cheeks to them that plucked off the hair; I hid not my face from spitting."
>
> "My enemies whisper together against me, and say, When shall he die and his name perish."
>
> "My familiar friend, that did eat of my bread, has lifted up his heel against me."
>
> "But you upholdest me, O LORD, and settest me before thy face for ever."
>
> "Behold, I am poured forth like water; I am taken away as a shadow when it declineth:"
>
> "My heart within me is as melted wax, and all my bones are out of joint:"
>
> "My strength is dried up like a potsherd; and my tongue cleaveth unto the roof of my mouth."
>
> "I expected some to pity me, and behold there was none; I looked for comforters, but I found not one."
>
> "My GOD, my GOD, how far have you forsaken me! You have even brought me to the dust of death. "Our

> fathers called to thee, and were delivered; they trusted in thee, and were not forsaken."
>
> "But I am a worm, and no man; a reproach of men, and despised of the people. All that see me, laugh me to scorn; they shoot out their lips, they shake the head, saying: He trusted in the Lone, let him deliver him; let him deliver him, seeing he delighted in him."
>
> "Be not far from me, for trouble is near; for there is none to help me."
>
> "The assembly of the wicked have enclosed me, and pierced my hands and my feet. I may tell my bones; they look and stare at me. They parted my garments among them, and cast lots upon my vesture. They gave me gall for my meat, and in my thirst they gave me vinegar to drink."

All these sad things, O LORD, thy Prophets foretold, to prepare our faith for such incredible truths.

All these, indeed, they expressly foretold; but, ah! could there be found such wretches, as would ever ant them

Yes, O my LORD! Thine own nation conspired against thee, and with innumerable affronts most barbrously murdered thee.

This too, even this thy cruel' death you plainly foreshewedst: "The inhabitants of Jerusalem shall look upon me, whom they have pierced."

But, O ye holy Prophets! what was the dismal cause that shed the blood of this spotless lamb

> "He had," they quickly answer, "done no iniquity, nor could any guile be found in his mouth."
>
> "But he was smitten for the sins of, the people, and taken away from the land of the living".
>
> "He delivered himself up unto death, and was numbered with the wicked;"

He bore the sins of many, and prayed for his persecutors.

> "He was wounded for our transgressions, he was bruised for our iniquities, the chastisement of our peace was upon him, and with his stripes we are healed."

O blessed JESUS, who tookest upon thee our infirmities, to, bestow on us thine own perfections!

Heal us, you great Physician of our souls, and let us sin no more, lest a worse thing come upon us.

Heal us, by the mystery of thy holy incarnation, and the meekness of thy humble birth.

Heal us, by the precious blood of thy circumcision, and the sweet and everblessed name of JESUS.

Heal us by thy gracious manifestation to the Gentiles, and the powerful influence of all thy miracles.

Heal us by the exemplary obedience of thy presentation in the temple; heal us by the sovereign balsam of thy passion.

Heal us by the joys of thy victorious resurrection, and the triumph of thy glorious ascension.

Heal us by the memory of thy blessings; heal us by the memory of this day's mercy.

Heal us, you great Physician of our souls, and let us sin no more, let a worse thing befall us.

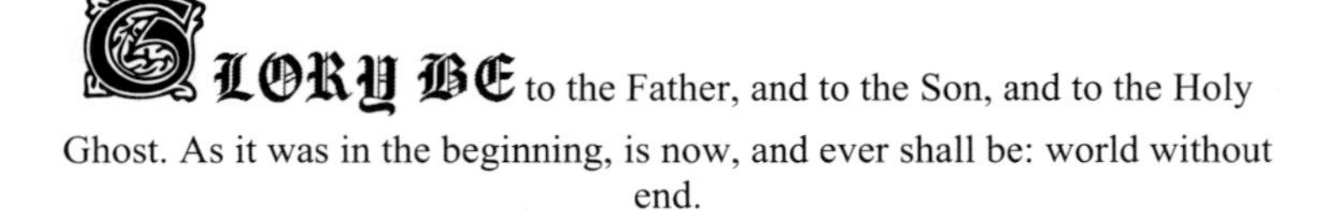

GLORY BE to the Father, and to the Son, and to the Holy Ghost. As it was in the beginning, is now, and ever shall be: world without end.

Amen.

At Noon.

PSALM 5.

PRAISE the LORD, all ye nations of the earth; praise him with the voice of joy and thanksgiving.

Praise him with the well tuned strings of your heart, praise him with the sweetest instrument, obedience.

Let every one that pretends to felicity sing immortal praises to the GOD of our salvation.

He is our full and all sufficient Redeemer: He has perfectly finished what he graciously undertook.

For all our trespasses he made satisfaction: For all our forfeitures he has paid the ransom.

We by disobedience were banished from paradise, and he has received us to his own kingdom.

We wandered up and down in the wilderness of error, and he has guided us into the ways of truth.

We were by nature children of wrath, and he has mediated our peace with his offended FATHER.

We were become the slaves of sin, and he has bought our freedom with his own blood.

We were in bondage to the dominion of SATAN, and he has overcome him, and confined his power.

We were in danger of sinking to hell, and he has saved us from that bottomless pit.

The gates of heaven were shut against us, and he went up himself and opened them to all believers:

Dissolving for ever the terrors of death, and rendering it now but a passage into life.

O gracious LORD, who madest us when we were not, and restoredst us again when we had undone ourselves,

Who wouldest at any rate redeem us from misery, at any rate procure our felicity,

How came we wretches to be so considered How came we sinners to obtain such favor

That from thy throne of glory, where Seraphims adored thee, you should descend on our earth, where slaves affronted thee.

That you should lead a life of poverty and labor, and die a,death with shame and sorrow.

That you should do all this for such worms as we, without the least concern or benefit to thyself.

Only to raise us up from our humble dust, and to set us to shine with thy glorious angels.

O infinite Goodness, the bounteous Author of all our hopes, and strong Deliverer of us from all our fears!

What shall we say to this thy excessive love What shall we render for these thy unspeakable mercies

We search over all we have, and find nothing to return thee, but what thyself has freely given us.

We search over all you have given us, and find nothing you expectest; but that we use thy gifts to make ourselves happy.

O may our souls perpetually bless thee; and every minute of our time be spent in thy service.

Let us not live, O LORD, but to love thee; nor breathe, but to speak thy praise; nor be at all, but to be all thine.

GLORY BE to the Father, and to the Son, and to the Holy Ghost. As it was in the beginning, is now, and ever shall be: world without end.

Amen.

PSALM 6.

SING on, my soul, the praises of thy LORD, sing on the mercies of thy GOD:

Whose wisdom has contrived so compendious a method, to redeem mankind by one short word.

He saw, the only cause of all our ruin was our love misplaced on this present world.

He saw, the only remedy of all our misery was to fix our love on the world to come.

This therefore was his great intent, and in this concentered he all his merits;

To change the bias of our wrongset hearts, by establishing amongst us new motives of love:

By revealing to us the mystery of his sufferings, and thence discovering the highest motives of love.

Such as might strongly incline our affections, and efficaciously draw us to love our true good:

Such as might gain by degrees upon all mankind, and render salvation easy and universal.

For this he came down from his FATHER'S bosom, to show us the rules of eternal life, the purchase of his blood:

That we might firmly believe those sacred truths, which GOD himself with his own mouth had told us.

For this he also conversed so long on our earth, to encourage and provoke us by his own example;

That we might confidently embrace those unquestionable virtues, which GOD himself, in his own person, had practiced.

For this he endured those sharp and many afflictions, and became at last obedient even to death; so making atonement for our sins:

That we might patiently hence suffer whatever should befall us, when GOD himself was so treated by his creature.

For this he often preached the joys of heaven, and set them before us in so clear a light;

That seeing so rich a prize hang at the race's end, we might run, and strain our utmost force to gain it.

For this he ordained the mysteries of grace, and left us a sacrifice made up of mercies:

That he might breed, and nourish us in the life of love,

and ravish our hearts with the sweetness of his presence.. For this he established a perpetual church, and sent the HOLY GHOST to inspire, and govern it:

That it might flourish for ever in truth, and sanctity, and plant the same heavenly seed over all the world.

For this he assumed those strange endearing names of Friend, and Brother, and Spouse to us wretches:

Doing far more for us than all those names import, far more than all our hearts can wish.

Blessed, O glorious Jesus!' be the wisdom of thy mercy, that has found so sweet and short a way for us (though painful to thee) to save us.

You art, O LORD, the cause of our love, and love the cause of our happiness.

By love we fulfil all thy commands, and by making us love you fulfillest all thy FATHER'S.

By love we are reconciled from enemies to friends, by love we are translated from death to life.

By love we are delivered from the fear of hell, by love we are adopted to be heirs of heaven.

By love we are disposed for that blissful vision, by love we are secured of the enjoyment of our GOD:

Who by the sole perfection of his own free goodness, would never deny himself to any that love him.

Else would their very loving him be the cause of their misery, since the misery of a soul is the want of what it loves.

Thus, LORD, whatever thy holy books record of thee, in expressions suited to our low capacities,

Whatever they say of thy wonderful conception and birth; whatever they relate of thy holy life or meritorious death;

Whatever they tell of thy glorious resurrection, or triumphant ascension into heaven;

Whatever they teach of the corruption of our sinful nature and of the new principle of life, by the inspiration of thy HOLY SPIRIT;

Whatever they speak of thy intercession for us at thy FATHER'S right hand, and of the heavenly sanctuary and altar;

Whatever we read in them of the resurrection of the dead, of the judgment to come, and of thy kingdom both in heaven and earth:

Lastly, whatever they say of thy restoring all things, and repairing again the ruins of mankind:

All is exactly verified by this one line, which may our thankful hearts repeat with joy:

"Heaven is attained by love alone, and love alone by thee."

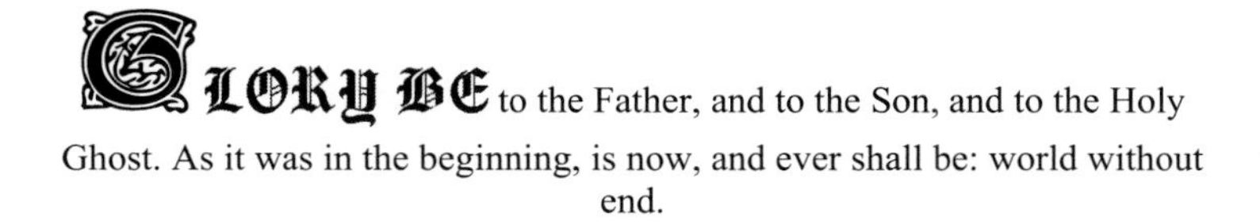

GLORY BE to the Father, and to the Son, and to the Holy Ghost. As it was in the beginning, is now, and ever shall be: world without end.

Amen.

PSALM 7.

STILL, O my soul, let us sing to him, whose mercies are no fewer than infinite:

To him, whose pity took us by the hand, and kindly led us into his own light:

To thee, O blessed JESUS, our LORD and our GOD! who alone art the Source of all our happiness.

The world, till you earnest, sat wrapt in darkness, and few discerned so much as a shadow of thee.

They followed their appetite, sense, and humor, and placed their felicity in being prosperous here:

Little considering the life to come; but less the joys that entertain that life.

This was, alas! their miserable state; and, worse than this,. they had no power to help it.

How could they believe what they never heard, or love what they never believed

How could they desire what they never loved, or be glad to receive what they never desired

It was You, O LORD, first taughtest us our true end, the blissful vision of the eternal Deity.

It was you first taughtest us the true means to attain that end, by a hearty love, and desire to attain it.

O the blessed changes which thy hand has wrought! O the happy improvements which thy coming has produced!

Now every woman and illiterate man can discourse familiarly of the highest truths:

The creation of the world, and the fall of Adam, the incarnation of GOD, and the redemption of man:

The mystery of the Trinity, and the miracle of the resurrection, the day of judgment, and the state of eternity.

All these we know; but it was You, O LORD, who taughtest us, and didst, by thy holy Church and word, first spread them over the world.

Now you have opened our eyes, we plainly see what unassisted nature could never have reached.

We see the framing right our affections here, is the measure of our happiness hereafter.

If we supremely esteem the goods of the future life, we shall find them there, and be happy.

If we love heaven with our whole soul, and press on strongly with all our force:

We shall enter into its glories with a surprising delight, and possess them for ever in a perpetual ecstasy.

We see our souls are made to know, and perfect themselves by the worthiest object.

We see their nature is free and unconfined, and nothing can fill them but that which is infinite.

All other knowledge enlarges our faculties, and breeds new desires to know still more,

Which, if unsatisfied, we yet are miserable, since none can be happy who want their desire.

Only the sight of GOD fills us to the brim, and infinitely overflows our utmost capacities.

It fills and overflows all the powers of our souls with joy and wonder, and inconceivable sweetness.

O blessed and glorious sight! when will the happy day appear, and open to my soul that beauteous prospect! You art my full and high felicity, and alone sufficient for me.

O make me ardently love thee, that I may eagerly desire thee; and eagerly desire thee, that I may enjoy thee in all the transports of divine love.

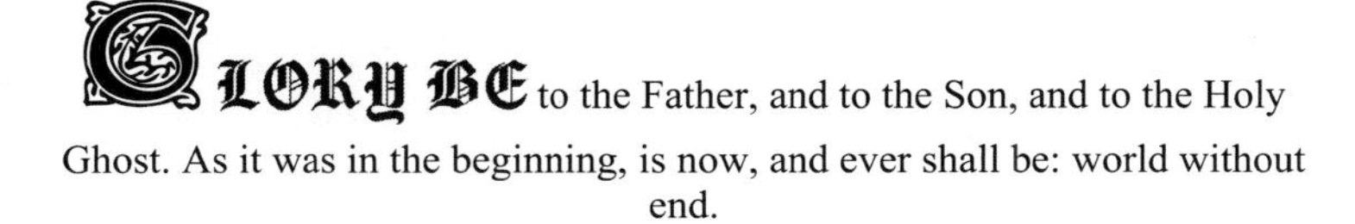

GLORY BE to the Father, and to the Son, and to the Holy Ghost. As it was in the beginning, is now, and ever shall be: world without end.

Amen.

HYMN 2.

SWEET JESUS! why, why dost you love Such worthless things as we
Why is thy heart so much towards us, Who seldom think on thee
Thy bounty gives us all we have; And we thy gifts abuse:
Thy bounty gives us even thyself; And we thyself refuse.
And why, my soul, why do we love
Such wretched things as these; These that withdraw us from the LORD,
And his pure eyes displease
Break off, and raise thy manly eye Up to those joys above:
Behold all those thy LORD prepares, To woo and crown thy love.
Alas, dear LORD! I cannot love, Unless you draw my heart;
You who so kindly makes me know, O make me do my part.
Still do you love me, O my LORD,
That I may still love thee:
Still make me love thee, O my GOD,
That you mayst still love me.
To thee, great GOD, to thee alone,
One coeternal Three,

All power and praise, all joy and bliss,
Now, and for ever be.

BLESSED be thy holy name, O glorious Son of God! and blessed be thy mercy for ever: You have perfectly fulfilled all thy Prophets foretold, and infinitely transcended all the wonders they admired: You have done enough to convince us into faith, and suffered abundantly to inflame us with thy love. Most gracious LORD, who have so loved the world, that you gayest thyself to redeem it, and humbly tookest upon thee our nature, that you might suffer as man for the sins of men, and in it familiarly teach us the truth of our salvation; and might invincibly also fortify us against all persecutions, and efficaciously draw us after thee into thine own kingdom, by thy holy life, and precious death, and, glorious resurrection: Do you fill our souls with a sense of this wonderful love, that we may live in thy obedience, die in thy favor, and rise again to rejoice with thee for ever in thy glory: Who, with the FATHER and the HOLY GHOST, live and reignest, GOD and King, world without end. Amen.

In the Afternoon.

PSALM 8.

LIFT up thy voice, O Jerusalem, and be not afraid; say unto the cities of Judah, Behold your GOD.

Behold the LORD your GOD is come with a strong hand, his reward is with him, and his work before him.

He is come to bring redemption to all the world, and graciously offers it first to you his people.

But ye refused the Holy One, and the Just, and desired a murderer to be granted unto you.

Hark, with how sweet compassion thy kind Redeemer complains of thy ingratitude

> "O Jerusalem, Jerusalem, you that killest the prophets, and stonest them who are sent unto thee!"
>
> "How often would I have gathered thy children together, as a hen does her chickens under her wings, and you wouldest not."

Hark with how tender a reproof thy LORD unwillingly withdraws from thee his favor:

> "O hadst you known, even You, at least in that thy day, the things which belonged unto thy peace! but now they are hid from thine eyes."

Hearken, however, once more; and if his kindness cannot move thy love, let his anger work upon thy fear.

Gird thee with sackcloth, O Jerusalem, and he down in ashes; cover thee with mourning, and bitterly lament:

> "For the day shall come upon thee, that thine enemies shall cast a trench about thee, and shall compass thee round, and keep thee in on every side:"
>
> "And shall lay thee even with the ground, and thy children within thee, and they shall not leave in thee one stone upon another, because you knewest not the time of thy visitation."

But how long, LORD, holy and merciful, how long wilt you be angry with them For ever

Have you not said, He that scattereth Israel shall gather them again, and keep them as a shepherd does his flock

Remember thy ancient promises, O LORD, and save the remnant of thy once loved Israel.

Let them yet have hope in thee, for with thee is mercy, and with thee is plenteous redemption. O LORD, redeem Israel from all their iniquities.

Takeaway the veil from before their eyes, that they may see thy truth and embrace it.

Take away the hardness of their stony hearts, that they again may be thy people, and you again their GOD.

The kingdom we expected deserves not that name, a short, a vain, a troublesome prosperity.

Thy dominion, O LORD, is holiness and peace, and of thy kingdom there shall be no end.

Such was the kingdom you promisedst to David, "They shall live and reign with thee for ever."

O make us love, dear LORD, this eternal kingdom, and all things else shall be added unto it.

GLORY BE to the Father, and to the Son, and to the Holy Ghost. As it was in the beginning, is now, and ever shall be: world without end.

Amen.

PSALM 9.

RISE, holy spouse of the Son of God! rise, and put on the robes of joy.

Arise, shine, for thy light is come, and the glory of the LORD is risen upon thee.

The Gentiles shall come to thy light, and Kings to the brightness of thy rising.

Lift up your eyes round about, and see, they all gather themselves together, they come to thee.

Thy sons come from far, and thy daughters shall be nursed at thy side.

Then shall you see, and How in abundance; thy hearts shall wonder, and be enlarged with gladness.

When the multitude of the islands shall be converted to thee, and the strength of the Gentiles submit to thy laws. The sons of strangers shall build up thy walls, and their Kings shall minister unto thee.

For in my wrath I smote thee, but in my favor I had mercy on thee. .

Therefore thy gates shall be open continually, they shall not be shut day nor night.

And they shall call upon thee, the city of the LORD, the Son of the Holy One of Israel.

For our LORD shall he thy everlasting light, and the days of thy mourning shall end in glory.

Thy foundation shall be laid on a firm rock, and the gates of hell shall not prevail against thee.

With thee shall be the tabernacle of GOD, and he will dwell with thee, and the gates of thy city shall not be shut at all by day.

Thy rock cannot be shaken, thy light can never be extinguished, and even the blind eyes shall be made to behold it.

And the earth shall be filled with the knowledge of the LORD, as the waters cover the sea.

All this we read, all this we firmly believe, for the mouth of the LORD has spoken it.

Heaven and earth shall pass away, but not one tittle of his word shall pass away, till all be fulfilled.

Many of the sacred prophecies are already fulfilled, abundantly sufficient to assure us of the rest.

Already a virgin has brought forth a son, and given him the gracious name of JESUS.

The wise men of the East have been led to him by a star, and offered him gold, and frankincense, and myrrh.

His holy parents have presented him in the temple, and the devout SIMEON was overjoyed to see him.

He confirmed his doctrine with innumerable miracles, and defended the truth to the last drop of his blood.

He rose again victoriously from the grave, and ascended in triumph to the right hand of his FATHER.

And there, O glorious JESU, may you sit and reign, till all thy enemies become thy footstool!

Nor has thy judgment slept, O dreadful LORD! but with a swift and terrible vengeance crushed them into ruin.

Jerusalem was long since made a heap of stones; and the children of thy crucifiers ran wandering over the world.

Nevertheless whilst you art thus severe in the predictions of thy justice, you have not forgotten those of thy mercy.

Thousands of that ungrateful people have acknowledged thee their LORD, thousands of that perverse generation have submitted to thy sceptre.

Whole nations of the Gentiles have embraced the faith, and remotest islands received thy law.

Blessed for ever be thy name, O LORD! and blessed he the sweetness of thy mercy;

Who revealest thyself to those that knew thee not, and art found of those that sought thee not;

Who often followest those that flee from thee, and never refusest any that come unto thee.

O you in whom, while we remain, we live, and from whom divided we instantly die!

Curse not, we humbly beg, these fruitless branches, lest they wither away and be cast into the fire.

Pronounce not against us that dreadful sentence, Cut them down, why cumber they the ground

But mercifully cut them off from their wild stock, and graft them into thyself, the only true Vine.

Water, O LORD, our weeds with the dew of heaven, and bless our low shrubs with thy powerful influence.

So grapes shall grow on thorns, and figs be gathered on thistles.

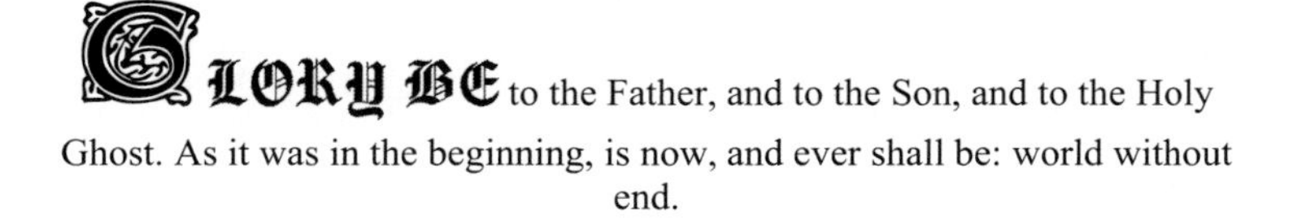

GLORY BE to the Father, and to the Son, and to the Holy Ghost. As it was in the beginning, is now, and ever shall be: world without end.

Amen.

PSALM 10

REJOICE in the LORD, all ye children of ADAM; rejoice in the bounty of his free grace;

No longer now confined to a few choice favorites; and the narrow compass of a private family.

He has thrown down the partition wall, and opened the way of life to all mankind:

That all may believe, and love him here; and all enjoy and be happy in him hereafter.

But, O my GOD, what do we see; when we look abroad into the wide world

We see the sad effects, but cannot see the cause, why so many kingdoms he miserably waste, sitting still in the shadow of death.

We know, O LORD, thy ways are in the deep abyss; and humbly we adore thy secret counsels.

Only we cannot think of their lamentable condition, without pitying their misery, and imploring thy mercy.

Some have not yet so much as heard of thee; and others who have heard, refuse to entertain thee.

Some who have once acknowledged thee, have quite fallen away; and others reject what they list, and obey by halves.

Many of those who believe the truth, abuse their holy faith by a wicked life.

Thus the far greatest part of wretched mankind, whom thy goodness created in thine own similitude:

Whom thy SON redeemed with his precious blood, and designed to so great and lasting a happiness:

Still fail of their true end, and die in their sins.

Look down, O LORD, and behold from heaven; behold from the habitation of thy holiness.

Where is thy zeal, and the sounding of thy bowels Where are thy promises to thy beloved Son

Have you not said, All nations shall adore him; and all the people upon earth shall be blessed in him

Have you not said thyself, O glorious JESUS! "When I am exalted, I will draw all men unto me."

Have you not given thy disciples express commission, to "go into all the world, and preach the Gospel to every creature."

Remember, O you GOD of everlasting truth! Remember, O you Author and Finisher of our faith!

Remember these thy dear engagements; and graciously accomplish what you have mercifully begun.

Visit, O LORD, thine own house first; and thoroughly redress what you findest amiss.

Make our lives holy according to our faith, and perfectly unite us in the bonds of love.

Kindle in the hearts of Kings, and the great ones of the world, an heroic spirit to advance thy glory.

Inflame the hearts of the Prelates, and Priests of thy church, with a generous zeal for the conversion of souls.

Convince them all, that it is the end and duty of their place, to improve mankind in virtue and religion.

One mercy more we humbly beg; which, O! may thy providence favorably supply:

Prepare, O LORD, the hearts of those that err, and make them apt to receive the truth.

Then choose thy burning and thy shining lights, and send them forth over all the world.

Send them, O GOD of infinite love! but send them not alone; lest they faint by the way, and miscarry in the end.

Go with them thyself, and guide them by thy grace, and crown their labors with thy powerful blessing.

So shall the humble valleys be raised up, and the stubborn mountains be brought low.

So shall the crooked paths be made straight, and the rough ways smooth and plain.

So shall the glory of GOD be every where revealed, and all flesh shall see it together.

Happy the times when this shall come to pass; happy the eyes that shall see these times.

Come glorious days, wherein that Sun shall shine; which enlightens at once both hemispheres.

Come, holy JESUS, and make those glorious days, and let no cloud overcast them for ever.

Come, and in the largest sense maintain thy title, and be effectually the Savior of the universal world.

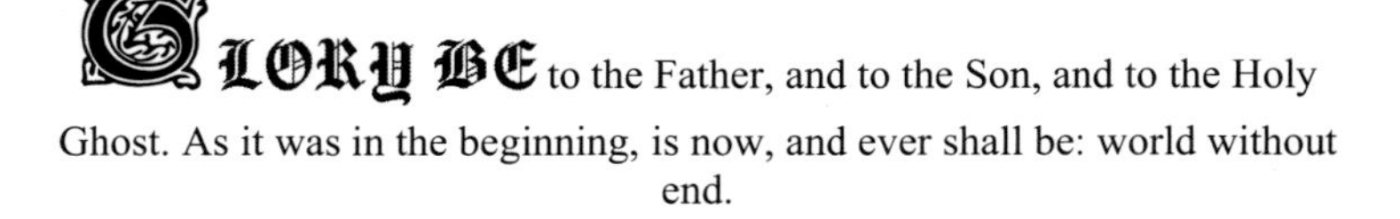

GLORY BE to the Father, and to the Son, and to the Holy Ghost. As it was in the beginning, is now, and ever shall be: world without end.

Amen.

. Hallelujah.

HYMN 3.

JESUS! Whose grace inspires thy Priests,
To keep alive by solemn feasts,
The memory of thy love:
O may we here so pass thy days, That they at last our souls may raise,

To feast with thee above. JESU! Behold the wise from far, Led to the cradle by a star,
Bring gifts to thee their King;
O guide us by thy light, that we The way may find, and so to thee,
Ourselves for tribute bring.
JESUS, the pure, and spotless Lamb, Who to the Temple humbly came,
Those legal rites to pay!
O make our proud, and stubborn will, Thine, and thy Church's laws fulfill;
Whatever fond nature say. JESUS, who on the fatal wood,
Pour'dst forth thy life's last drop of blood,
Nail'd to a shameful cross!
O may we bless thy love, and be Ready, dear LORD, to bear for thee
All grief, all pain, all loss.
JESUS, who, by thine own love slain, By thine own power tookst life again,
And from the grave didst rise!
O may thy death our spirits revive, And at our death a new life give,
A life that never dies.
JESU, who to thy heaven again Return'dst in triumph there to reign,
Of men and angels, King!
O may our parting souls take flight, Up to that land of joy and light,
And there for ever sing.
All glory to the sacred Three, One undivided Deity;
All honor, power, and praise:
O may thy blessed name shine bright, Crown'd with those beams of beauteous light,
Its own eternal rays.

HOLY *and everblessed JESUS, who, being the eternal SON of GOD, and most high in the glory of GOD the FATHER, didst vouchsafe for us sinners to be born of an humble virgin, and suffer intolerable persecutions, even to death upon the cross; work in us, we beseech thee, a due sense of thy infinite love, that adoring, and believing in thee as our LORD and Savior, we may trust in thy infinite merits, imitate thy holy*

example, obey thy commands, and finally enjoy thy promises, living and reigning with thee, who, with the FATHER and the HOLY GHOST, live and reignest, GOD blessed for ever, world without end. Amen.

In the Evening.

PSALM 11.

RETIRE NOW, O my soul, from thy common thoughts, permitted to entertain thy less serious hours.

Retire, and call thy wandering thoughts home, and speedily range them into peace and order;

That so you may be prepared to hear thy Loral invite thee, among the rest, to taste his sweetness.

> "Come unto me," says he, "all ye that labor, and are heavy laden, and I will give you rest."
>
> "Take my yoke upon you, and learn of me, for I am meek, and lowly in heart; and ye shall find rest unto your souls."
>
> "For my yoke is easy, and my burden light."

Enough, dear LORD, enough is said, to draw all the world to thy holy discipline.

What can be offered so agreeable to our natures, too much, alas! inclined to pleasure and profit

What can be offered so powerfully attractive, as to make our work delightful, and then reward it

Whither, O my GOD, should we go, but unto thee You have the words of eternal life.

You art our wisest Instructor to know what to do, and our only Enabler to do what we know.

You art the free Bestower of all we have, and faithful Promiser of all we hope.

You kindly tallest us; O make us gladly hear thy voice, and constantly follow it till we come to thee.

Suffer us no longer to go astray like lost sheep, wandering up and down in our byways.

Suffer us no longer to be distracted about many things, from thee, O Lord, who art but one.

But gather us up from the world into ourselves; then take us from ourselves into thee;

There to be ravished with thy holy embraces; there to be feasted with the antepasts of heaven.

O how unspeakable are thy sweetnesses, O LORD, which you have hid for those that fear thee;

Which you have partly revealed to those that love thee, and keep themselves uncorrupted with the world.

But, O what are they then to those that see thee; and, in that sight, see all things else!

To those who rejoice perpetually before thee; and, in • that joy, find all joys else!

O beauteous Truth, which known, enforces love; and loved, begets felicity!

Live you for ever in my faithful memory, and be my constant guide in all my ways.

Still let me think on those joys above, and undervalue all things compared to my salvation.

Still let me think on my Savior's love, that purchased for me all those joys.

O You, my adored Redeemer, be you the wish of my heart, the scope and end of all my time.

Soon as I awake, let me look up to thee; and when I arise, first lowly bow to thee.

Often in the day let me call in my thoughts to thee; and when I go to rest, close up mine eyes in thee.

So shall my time be governed by thy grace, and my eternity crowned with thy glory.

GLORY BE to the Father, and to the Son, and to the Holy Ghost. As it was in the beginning, is now, and ever shall be: world without end.

Amen.

PSALM 12.

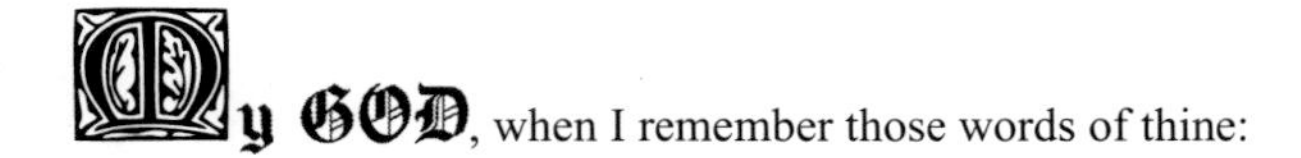

My GOD, when I remember those words of thine:

"Repent, for the kingdom of heaven is at hand:"

Make me apply those searching words unto myself, and bind them fast on my own soul.

Repent, O my soul, for the kingdom of heaven is at hand; repent, for the kingdom of heaven depends upon thy repentance.

I cannot repent without the grace of GOD; nor obtain his grace without his own free gift.

O my Savior, who earnest not to call the righteous, but, such as I am, sinners to repentance!

Make me heartily sorry for what I have done amiss; and let me not do again what will make me sorry.

Deliver me, O LORD, from the punishments I deserve; deliver me from the sin that deserves those punishments.

Teach me that safe and easy method of censuring myself; to be acquitted by thee.

Every night let me sit as an impartial judge, and call before me all my day.

Let me severely examine every thought and word, and strictly search every deed and omission:

Imploring for the past the mercy of Heaven; and for the time to come the same unbounded mercy.

If I, perhaps, find some little things well done, when weighed with the allowances you makest,

Let me return all the glory to my GOD, and beg his grace to continue and improve it.

His is the hand that sows the seed; his is the blessing that gives the increase.

Thus let me, once a day at least, look home, and seriously inquire into the state of my soul.

Let not the sun go down upon my wrath, nor on any unrepented sin.

Still let me write at the foot of my account: " Reconciled to my GOD, and in charity with all the world."

Then go to bed with a quiet conscience, and full in peace and hope.

GLORY BE to the Father, and to the Son, and to the Holy Ghost. As it was in the beginning, is now, and ever shall be: world without end.

Amen.

PSALM 13.

HARK, how he tells us this new and glorious secret: " We shall be hereafter like the angels in heaven."

O sweet and precious word to them that relish it, and thoroughly digest its strong nourishment;

To them that feed on it often as their daily bread: c We shall be hereafter like the angels in heaven."

And what, O LORD, are these blessed angels, but spirits, that know, and love, and delight in thee for ever

Such, O my soul, we shall be, and such a life we shall lead; we shall be, and live, like the angels in heaven.

We shall know all that is true, and love all that is good; and shall delight in that knowledge and love for ever.

No ignorance shall darken, nor error deceive us; we shall be like the angels in heaven.

No cares shall perplex us, nor crosses afflict us; we shall be like the angels in heaven.

Our joys shall be full, and pure, and everlasting; we shall be like the angels in heaven.

Cheer thee, O my soul, and bless thy bounteous LORD; it is by him we shall be like the angels in heaven.

Cheer thee, and raise thy hopes yet gloriously higher; we shall be like himself, for we shall see him as he is.

GLORY BE to the Father, and to the Son, and to the Holy Ghost. As it was in the beginning, is now, and ever shall be: world without end.

Amen.

GRANT *us, O LORD JESUS, SO frequently to renew the memory of thy grave, that we may be always prepared for our own; and so seriously to reflect on the consequences of an holy death, that every day we may grow less affected to this transitory life, and more in love with thy eternal joys.*

NOW *our LORD JESUS CHRIST himself, and GOD even our FATHER, who has loved us, and has given us everlasting consolation and good hope through grace, comfort our hearts, and establish us in every good word and work.* Amen.

THE *blessing of GOD ALMIGHTY, the FATHER,* ✠ *the Son, and the HOLY GHOST, be with us this night, the rest of our lives, and evermore.* Amen.

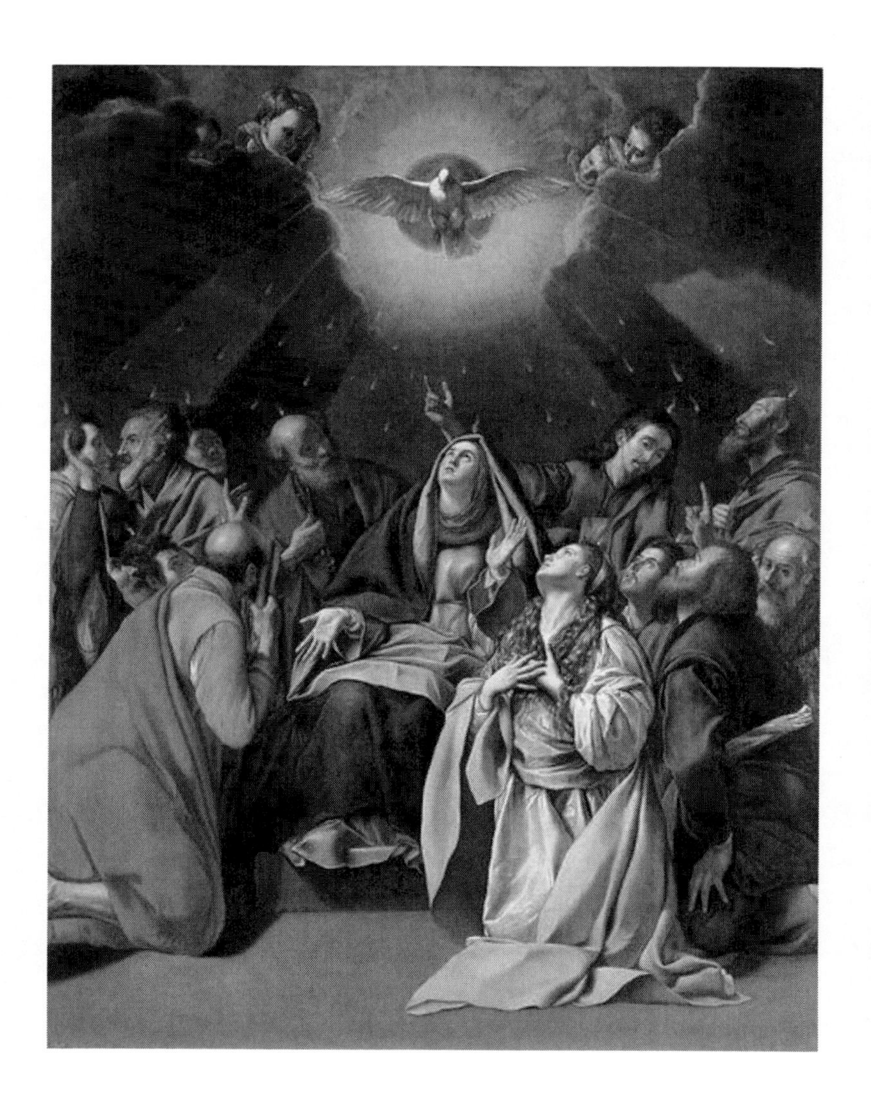

The Office of the Holy Ghost.

Morning Prayer.

Antiphon

Come, let us adore our GOD that sanctifies us.

PSALM 1.

COME, let us humbly implore his grace, to make us worthy to adore our SANCTIFIER, who from the FATHER and the SON eternally proceeds, and with the FATHER and the SON together is worshipped and glorified.

Come, let us adore our GOD that sanctifies us.

He infuses into us the breath of life, and brings us forth in our second birth; a birth that makes us heirs of heaven, and gives us a title to everlasting happiness.

Come, let us adore our GOD that sanctifies us.

Let us prepare our understandings to assent to his truths, and our wills to follow his Divine inspirations; let us fill our memories with his innumerable mercies, and our whole souls with the glory of his attributes.

Come, let us adore our GOD that sanctifies us.

Let us confidently address to him our petitions, who promises to help the infirmities of our prayers; let us not doubt the bounty of his goodness, but hope he will grant what himself inspires to ask.

Come, let us adore our GOD that sanctifies us.

GLORY BE to the Father, and to the Son, and to the Holy Ghost. As it was in the beginning, is now, and ever shall be: world without end.

Amen.

PSALM 2.

LORD, with how sweet and natural a conduct does thy providence govern the children of men!

Leading them from one degree to another, till you have brought them up to their highest perfection!

You puttest them to learn in the school of virtue, and disposest their capacities into several forms.

In the first ages, when the world was young, you gayest them for their guide the book of nature.

There thy divine assistance helped them to read some few plain lessons of their duty to thee.

They saw this admirable frame of creatures; and as far as they could argue, they could conclude:

> "There is a GOD, the Cause of all things; there is a Providence, the Disposer of all things."
>
> "He must be powerful, that made so vast a world; he must be wise, that contrived such excellent works."
>
> "He must be goodness itself that did all this for us; and we must be ungrateful wretches, if we do nothing for him."

After this, you gayest thy people a written rule, which trained them up in a set form of discipline,

Which grew and spread into a public religion, and was uniformly professed by a whole nation.

They had some weak conception indeed of the kingdom of heaven, and some imperfect means to bring them thither.

But as to those high supernatural mysteries, that so gloriously exalt the Christian faith:

They all, alas! were blind, or in the dark, while the veil was before their eyes,

And were often exposed to the effects of their ignorance, wanting those clear instructions to know their end, wanting those powerful motives to love their GOD:

Yet this prepared them for the times of grace, to which thy mercy, LORD, reserved far greater favors:

To which you have promised, by thy holy Prophets, an effusion of blessings:

> "I will put my laws into their mind, and write them in their hearts; and I will be to them a GOD, and they shall be to me a people."
>
> "I will pour out my SPIRIT on all flesh, and your sons and your daughters shall prophesy."
>
> "They shall no more teach every one his neighbor; for all shall know me from the least to the greatest."

O merciful LORD, who have loved us from the beginning, be graciously pleased to love us to the end.

Pity the unhappy state of fallen mankind, which neither nature nor law could bring to perfection.

If any riper souls came forward to the birth, there wanted Spirit to bring them forth.

But O send out thy SPIRIT, and they shall be created; and from their nothing of sin, even a darkness deeper than nothing, be raised to the life and light of holiness.

Send out thy SPIRIT, and renew the face of the earth; and our weeds and our thorns shall be turned into a Paradise.

GLORY BE to the Father, and to the Son, and to the Holy Ghost. As it was in the beginning, is now, and ever shall be: world without end.

Amen.

PSALM 3.

LOOK up, O languishing world, look up and see how punctually thy faithful LORD performs his word..

When he had finished here that glorious work, which his goodness undertook for our redemption:

When he had told us what we ought to do, and what to suffer for the kingdom of heaven:

When he himself had done more than he required of us, and suffered more than our boldest hopes could expect from him:

He first prepares the hearts of his disciples, and comforts their sorrows with these sweet words:

> "Children, I will not leave you comfortless; but will pray to my FATHER, and he shall give you another Comforter;"
>
> "Even the SPIRIT of truth, and he shall teach you all things, and bring to your remembrance whatsoever I have said unto you."

> "Peace I leave with you, my peace I give to you: Let not your hearts be troubled, neither let it be afraid."

> "I go to my FATHER, and to your FATHER; to Thy GOD, and your GOD."

> "I go to prepare a place for you, that where I am, there ye may be also."

This said, he led them forth together, and gave them his blessing; and parting from them, went away into heaven.

When the appointed time was come, as all the works of GOD go forth in their fittest season:

When his disciples were gathered together in one mind and place, and so ready for the visits of heaven:

When they had long continued in ardent prayer, and wrought their affections to the highest point of desire:

Suddenly there was a sound from heaven, whence every good and perfect gift descends;

A vehement rushing wind filled the whole house; for the grace of GOD is strong and liberal.

Behold, on the head of each sat a tongue, as of fire. While they were all illuminated with a pure light, and inflamed with a fervent heat:

And to communicate both these to every nation, they were all endued with the gift of languages.

Thus was the promise of our LORD fulfilled; and thus the messengers of everlasting peace prepared:

Miraculously baptized with the HOLY GHOST and with fire, and perfectly qualified for their great commission.

To preach to every creature this happy Gospel: " He that believeth and is baptized, shall be saved."

GLORY BE to the Father, and to the Son, and to the Holy Ghost. As it was in the beginning, is now, and ever shall be: world without end.

Amen.

PSALM 5.

HOW glorious is thy grace, O LORD, over all the world! How admirable the influence of thy HOLY SPIRIT!

They that through dullness so slowly understood the oft repeated lessons of their Divine Master,

Now with the first swift glance see through all, and no mystery can pose them.

They, who through fear forsook their LORD, and fled away from the danger of being his,

Now rejoice in suffering for his name, and neither life nor death can forbid them to confess him.

They, who even after their SAVIOR'S resurrection shut fast the doors for fear of the Jews,

Now, in the open streets and public synagogues, confidently proclaim the name of JESUS.

O! were there now such tongues of fire, to kindle in the world such divine flames!

O! were there now such hearts in the world, to receive the holy sparks that fall from heaven!

The great Apostle preached but one sermon, and converted three thousand souls.

He preached again, and wrought but one miracle, and five thousand were added to the Church.

Thus every day they increased in their number, and their number increased in virtue and piety.

They sold all they had, and brought the price and laid it down at the Apostles' feet.

They lived in common, they called nothing their own, enjoying a blessed communion in all things, spiritual and temporal.

Even in their will and understanding they were all united; they being all, after the heavenly image, of one heart and one mind.

Every one had enough, and that is to be rich; none had too much, and that is to be free:

Free from the cares that perplex the wealthy; free from the temptations that wait on superfluity.

They prayed, and mingled with their prayers their tears; they wept, and mingled with their tears their complaints.

Ah, dearest LORD! why were we not so happy, to be converted by thee, while you dwelledst amongst us.

Why not to entertain salvation when you broughtest it to our homes, and preferredst our little nation before all the world.

You didst cleanse the leprous, and heal all manner of diseases; you didst raise the dead, and cast out devils by thy word.

Yet we, alas! how many of us blasphemed thy name!

How many conspired with thy bloody crucifiers!

Spare us, O LORD! Have mercy upon us, O JESUS! for we knew thee not to be the LORD of glory.

Blessed be thy HOLY SPIRIT, who has opened our eyes, and made us see through the veil that eclipsed us. Now we believe thee to be the Messias we expected; now we acknowledge thee to be the King of Israel.

Such were the favors of those happy times; and O how happy were our times had we those favors!

Ours are become miserable by the unfruitful lives and scandalous examples of too many Christians.

Too many, alas! Yet even the gates of hell can never prevail against the power of GOD.

Still the same SPIRIT governs the world, and keeps alive the same primitive fire.

Still there are hearts full of the HOLY GHOST, full of that ravishing wine of Divine love.

Still there are souls who renounce all they have, and take p their cross and follow our LORD.

Still there are fiery tongues kindled by the breath of Heaven, who carry their sacred flames into every nation.

GLORY BE to the Father, and to the Son, and to the Holy Ghost. As it was in the beginning, is now, and ever shall be: world without end.

Amen.

At Noon.

Antiphon

Kindle in our hearts; O LORD, thy holy fire; that we may offer to thee the incense of praise. Hallelujah.

PSALM 5.

CONSIDER, my soul, the mercies of thy GOD; consider the wonders he has wrought for the children of men.

The eternal FATHER created us of nothing, and estrus in the way to everlasting happiness.

The eternal Son came down from heaven to seek us, and restored us again when we had lost ourselves.

The eternal SPIRIT sends and brings his grace to sanctify us, and give us strength to walk that holy way.

Thus every Person of the Sacred Trinity has freely contributed his particular blessing:

And all together, as one co-infinite Goodness, have graciously agreed to complete our felicity.

But, O ungrateful we! was it not enough to receive of GOD all we have and are

Was it not enough that the SON of GOD should come down, and live to teach us, and die to redeem us

Was not all this enough to make us love And love is all he aimed at, and love is all we needed.

Let us confess to thee, O merciful LORD! let us confess unto thee our miserable condition.

Such, alas! was the corruption of our nature, and so many and strong the temptations that surround us;

That without this thy last miraculous favor, sending the HOLY GHOST to guide and quicken us,

We should quite have forgotten our GOD that made us, and neglected the service of our LORD that bought us;

Had not thy fullness been furnished with one blessing more to bestow on thy children:

Hadst you not providently reserved a better blessing than the dew of the clouds and the fatness of the earth.

These were the rewards of the old law; but behold far greater than these are here:

Divine refreshment from the heaven of heavens, and the fruits of the HOLY GHOST;

Meekness, and peace, and joy diffused in our breasts; strength and courage kindled in our hearts;

A thousand embraces of the Bridegroom of souls; a thousand pledges of his everlasting love.

These are the great rewards of the law of grace, and given to prepare us for the kingdom of glory.

O blessed SPIRIT, who bestowest thy favors as thou pleasest; and the more you have given, still the more you givest:

Dispose thy servants first to entertain thee; then graciously vouchsafe to descend into our hearts.

Fill us, O HOLY GHOST, and our little vessels; and as you Iffiest us, enlarge our capacities.

Make us, the more we receive of thee, still to grow in desire of receiving more; Till we ascend at length to those joys above, where all our faculties shall be stretched to the utmost.

Where they shall be filled to the brim; and overflowed with a torrent of pleasure for ever. **Hallelujah**.

GLORY BE to the Father, and to the Son, and to the Holy Ghost. As it was in the beginning, is now, and ever shall be: world without end.

Amen.

PSALM 6.

BLESSED be thy name, O Holds SPIRIT, and blessed be the bounty of thy goodness.

When the eternal FATHER, by creating the world, had declared himself and his almighty power:

When the untreated WORD, by redeeming mankind, had revealed himself and his infinite wisdom;

Behold a strange condescension to our weak nature, the invisible SPIRIT visibly appears.

He descends from heaven in the shape of a dove, and gently descends on the Prince of Peace.

Again, he descends in the likeness of fire, and miraculously sits upon the heads of his disciples:

Mingling thus together in one, those chief ingredients of excellent virtue;

Mildness to allay the heat of zeal, and zeal to quicken that mildness;

Innocency to adorn the light of knowledge, and knowledge to direct the simplicity of innocence.

O blessed and admirable Teacher, who can instruct like the SPIRIT of God lie needs no years to finish his course, but with a swift and efficacious touch consummates all things:

He by one lesson perfected the Disciples, and polished rude fishermen into eloquent Preachers.

All this you have done, O infinite Goodness, and all we do is wrought in us by thee.

By thee we are regenerated at first, by thee confirmed by the imposition of hands:

By thee thy servants are consecrated into Priests; by thee our marriages are sanctified into blessings:

By thee our souls are comforted on the bed of sickness,

and by thy holy unction all our life is wisely governed.

If in the Church there be any wisdom or knowledge,

if any real sanctity or decent order,

If any faith in the mysteries of religion, if any hope of everlasting salvation,

If any love of GOD as our sovereign bliss, if any charity one towards another,

All flows from thee and thy free grace, O you boundless Ocean of eternal mercies!

cc All flows from thee;" and may we all return our little streams in tribute to thy bounty:

May every favor you offerest be thankfully received; and every talent you bestowest, diligently improved.

So shall we faithfully perform our duty, and render to thy grace its just glory:

While whatever we have we acknowledge from thee, and whatever you givest us is not in vain, but is powerful and glorious.

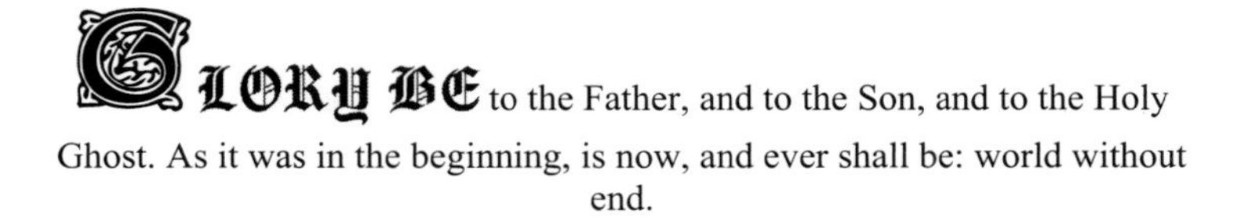
GLORY BE to the Father, and to the Son, and to the Holy Ghost. As it was in the beginning, is now, and ever shall be: world without end.

Amen.

PSALM 7.

STILL let us sing, O blessed SPIRIT! to thee let us sing these few lines more:

To thee, the eternal Love of the FATHER and the SON, and glorious Finisher of that sacred mystery:

To thee, the quickening SPIRIT of regenerated souls, in whom they live, and move, and have their being:

To thee, the sovereign Balsam of our wounds, and only Comfort of all our sorrows:

To thee, our Refuge in this place of banishment, and faithful Guide in this wandering pilgrimage:

To thee, the sacred Pledge of our free adoption, and ensuring Seal of our eternal salvation.

What do we say, O you adorable SPIRIT of GOD! what do we say, when we utter such words as these

We say what we can in our low capacities; but, alas, how short of thy unspeakable excellences!

O that we had the tongues of saints and angels! O that we had thine own miraculous tongues!

Those which sat flaming on the heads of the Apostles, and made them speak thy wonders in every language.

Still all our praises would be poor and narrow; still infinitely less than thy infinite perfections.

But if we cannot speak as our GOD deserves, shall we hold our peace, which our GOD forbids

Woe be to them, O LORD, who are silent of thee, and spend the breath you givest them on any but thyself.

O you that openest the mouths of the dumb, and makest the tongues of children eloquent!

Inspire thy servants, if not with expressions suitable to thee, at least with such as are profitable to us;

Such as may instruct us what we ought to do; such as may move us to do what we say.

And when we have tried our best endeavors, and taken measure of our own defects,

Let us heartily join in communion with the blessed above; that they, taught by Him, and made perfect, may supply our weakness with their worthier hymns.

Praise the eternal SPIRIT, by whom the world's Redeemer was conceived in the womb of a virgin, O all ye works of the LORD.

Praise him, by whom this virgin, in all generations blessed, was made the mother of the SON of GOD.

Praise him, O ye choirs of rejoicing angels, whose grace confirmed you in glory.

Praise him, O ye reverend Patriarchs, whose ways he governed, and by particular providence led you to felicity.

Praise him, ye ancients Prophets, whose souls he inspired, to teach his chosen people the mind of Heaven. Praise him, ye glorious Apostles, whom he empowered

to be ambassadors of peace between heaven and earth. Praise him, ye generous Martyrs, whose spirits he encouraged, and gave you victory over the terrors of death.

Praise him, ye blessed Confessors, whose lives he sanctified, and gave you victory over the world and yourselves.

Praise him, ye holy virgins, whose souls he espoused, and consecrated your chaste bodies into temples for himself.

Praise him, all you that live in his grace; praise him, all you that hope for his glory.

Praise him, all ye spirits and souls of the faithful, whom he has sealed against the terrible day, and whose hope he sustains even in the valley of the shadow of death.

Praise him, all ye churches of the saints; praise him, all ye nations and tribes of the earth.

Let every thing that has breath give glory to him, in the new creation; let every thing that has spirit praise the SPIRIT of our LORD, in the glorious restitution of all things.

Praise him, O my soul, for his mercies to thee; praise him for his goodness to all the world.

Praise him on thy choicest instrument, thy heart; praise him in thy best words, those of the church.

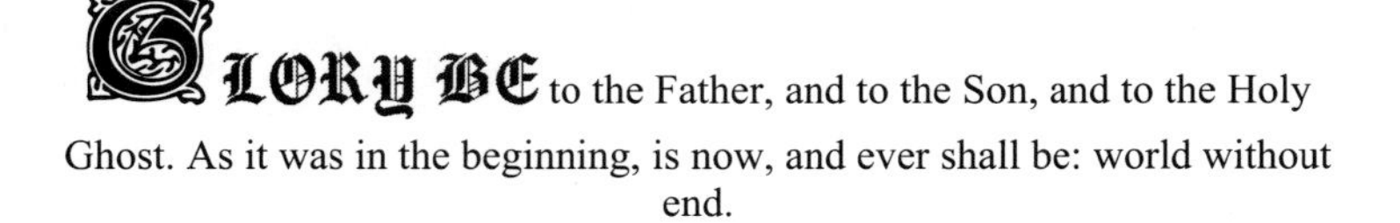

GLORY BE to the Father, and to the Son, and to the Holy Ghost. As it was in the beginning, is now, and ever shall be: world without end.

Amen.

In the Afternoon.

Antiphon

We are not our own, but the temples of the HOLY GHOST; let us dedicate ourselves entirely to his service.

PSALM 8.

COME, let us again prepare our hearts, and humbly offer this our sacrifice.

Let us remember, our GOD is a pure Spirit, and delights to dwell in a calm tabernacle.

He will not enter into a soul which is subject to sin, nor stay where he finds his grace neglected.

If he vouchsafes us the blessing of a visit; (and O how heavenly, sweet, and ravishing is his presence!)

Let us open wide our bosoms to receive him, and summon all our powers to entertain him.

Come, my understanding, and bring all that you knows; yea, bring all that enlightens thee in the way to felicity.

Come, my will, and call in all thy loves; and contract them into one, and settle this one here for ever.

Come, my memory, with all thy multitudes and swarms of notions; and forget them all, but what concerns eternity.

Come, my whole soul, with these thy faculties about thee; come, and, prostrate, adore the eternal SPIRIT.

Behold, he is now with us, and sits in our hearts, as on his throne, to receive our petitions, and give us his blessings.

He never will forsake us, if we chase him not away; but will guide and comfort us with his holy inspirations.

Come then, and with devoutest reverence attend; and let us hear what the LORD our GOD will say in us.

He leads us thus into retirement and silence, and there familiarly speaks to our hearts.

O you our merciful, though offended God! behold, thus low, we bow our heads:

Blushing for shame to see our folly, and so much the more, because we see our duty.

Happy were we, if we could be still thinking of thee, and raise all those thoughts into desires to be with thee.

Happy were we, could we always feel those fervors, which sometimes you inspirest.

O were that spark kindled into a fire, and that fire blown up into a continual flame!

Cure us, O you great Physician of souls; cure us of all our sinful distempers.

Cure us of this intermitting piety, and fix it into an even and a constant holiness.

O make us use religion as our regular diet, and not only as a medicine in necessity.

Make us enter into a course of hearty repentance, and practice virtue as our daily exercise.

So shall our souls be endued with perfect health, and disposed for a long, even for an everlasting life.

GLORY BE to the Father, and to the Son, and to the Holy Ghost. As it was in the beginning, is now, and ever shall be: world without end.

Amen.

Antiphon

Quicken us by thy grace, O LORD, and give us thy HOLY SPIRIT, that we may throughly mortify the works of the flesh.

PSALM 9.

NOW we have begun, permit us, mighty LORD, to speak once more, who are but dust and ashes.

Let us go on, and confess to thee, and open before thee all our miseries.

Such an occasion often endangers us; such a temptation too often overcomes us.

Our own infirmities are too strong for us, and our ill customs prevail against us.

Have mercy upon us, O GOD of infinite compassion! Have mercy upon us, O you Comforter of afflicted minds!

Have mercy upon us, and pardon what is past; have mercy upon us, and prevent what is to come.

Whenever you seest us unhappily engaged, and blindly running on in the ways of death,

O send thy holy grace to check our speed, and make us stay and look before us.

Show us the horrid downfall into that bottomless pit, where impenitent sinners are swallowed up for ever.

Strike our regardless souls with fear and trembling, at the dreadful sight of so sad a ruin.

Then turn our eyes; and kindly set before them the beauteous prospect of a pious life.

Make us look long and steadily upon it, and make us look through and see beyond it.

Give us, O gracious LORD, you free Beginner and perfect Finisher of all virtuous actions!

Give us a right spirit to guide our intentions, that we may aim directly at our true end.

Give us a faithful spirit to maintain our resolutions, that what we wisely resolve on, we may steadfastly adhere to.

Give us an holy spirit to sanctify our affections, that what we rightly design, we may piously pursue.

Suffer not the flesh to deceive us any more, but fortify our spirit against all its assaults.

Away flesh and blood, away deceitful world; you cannot enter into the kingdom of heaven.

You were created only to serve us in the way, and set us down at our journey's end.

Away with all your fond deluding dreams; be banished for ever from our awakened souls.

Come, you blessed SPIRIT of faith, and govern our lives with thy holy maxims.

Subdue our sense to the dictates of reason, and perfect our reason with the mysteries of religion.

Teach us to love and fear what we see not now, as at too great a distance for our short sight:

But what we are sure will hereafter be our bliss or our misery for ever.

GLORY BE to the Father, and to the Son, and to the Holy Ghost. As it was in the beginning, is now, and ever shall be: world without end.

Amen.

PSALM 10.

LET not our LORD be angry, and we will speak yet once; for we have much to ask, and he has infinite to give.

We have much to ask for ourselves and all the world, who depend entirely on his free goodness.

Many, O LORD, are the graces we want, and none can give them but thy bounty.

Many are the sins and miseries we are exposed to, and none can deliver us but thy providence.

Deliver us, O LORD, from what you knows is against.

us; deliver us from what we know ourselves will undo us.

Deliver us from the spirit of profaneness and infidelity; from the spirit of error, and schism, and heresy.

Deliver us from the spirit of pride and avarice; from the spirit of anger, and sloth, and envy.

Deliver us from the spirit of drunkenness and gluttony; from the spirit of lust and impurity.

Deliver us, O gracious GOD, from every evil spirit, and vouchsafe to give us of thine own good SPIRIT.

Vouchsafe to give us the spirit of fortitude; the spirit of temperance, and justice, and prudence;

The spirit of wisdom, and understanding, and counsel; the spirit of knowledge, and piety, and fear of thee;

The spirit of peace, and patience, and benignity; the spirit of humility, sobriety, and chastity.

O You, who never deniest thy favors, except we first deny our obedience!

You who art often near us, when we are far from thee;, often ready to grant, when we are unmindful to ask!

Refuse not, O LORD, to hear us, now we call upon thee; and make us still hear thee, when you tallest to us.

Fill our understandings with the knowledge of such truths, as may fix them on thee, the eternal Verity.

Inure our wills to embrace such objects, as may unite them unto thee, the Sovereign Goodness.

Show us the narrow way that leads to life; the way that few can find, and fewer follow.

Let not our faith grow wild with superfluous branches, nor be stripped into a naked and fruitless trunk.

Let not our hope swell up to rash presumption, nor shrink away into a faint despair.

Let not our love be cooled into a careless indifferency, nor heated into a furious zeal.

Suffer us not obstinately to persist in any known wickedness, nor maliciously to impugn any known truth. Suffer us not to die in our sins, without repentance; but have mercy upon us at that serious hour, and inspire us with thy grace now and always.

Have mercy upon us, and govern us in our life; have mercy upon us, and save us in our death.

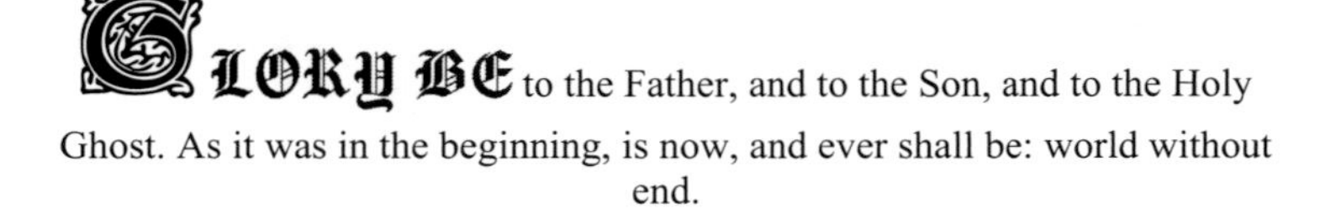

GLORY BE to the Father, and to the Son, and to the Holy Ghost. As it was in the beginning, is now, and ever shall be: world without end.

Amen.

HYMN 1.

COME, HOLY SPIRIT, send down those beams, Which gently flow in silent streams,
From thy bright throne above; Come, you Enricher of the poor, And bounteous Source of all our store,
Come, fill us with thy love.
Come You, our soul's delicious Guest, The wearied pilgrim's sweetest Rest,
The sufferer's best Relief: Come You, our passions' cool Allay, Whose comfort wipes all tears away,
And turns to joy all grief.
All glory to the sacred Three,
One everliving Deity,
All power, and bliss, and praise; As at the first when time begun,
May the same homage still be done, Till time itself decays.

BLESSED be thy name, O HOLY SPIRIT of GOD, who dividest thy gifts to every one as you pleasest, and workest all in all! In thee our sorrows have a Comforter to allay them, and our sins an Advocate to plead for them; in thee our ignorances have a Guide to direct them, and our frailties a Confirmer to strengthen them, and all our wants a GOD to relieve them. **Hallelujah**.

 GOD, who by thy HOLY SPIRIT didst at first establish a church, and who sanctifying it by the same SPURT, dost still preserve and govern it; hear, we beseech thee, the prayers of thy servants, and mercifully grant us the perpetual assistance of thy grace, that we may never be deceived by any false spirit, nor overcome by the suggestions of flesh and blood, but in all our doubts may be directed in the ways of truth, and in all our actions guided by this thy HOLY SPIRIT; who, with thee, and thy eternal Son, liveth and reigneth, one GOD, world without end. Amen.

In the Evening.

PSALM 11.

COME, my soul, consider again who this is, yea, who the SPIRIT of the LORD is; that we may give unto him the glory that is due unto his name.

For holy and reverend is his name; therefore let us fear before him, and let him be glorified iii himself, and glorified in all his saints.

Glorify him all ye saints, with the utmost powers he has given you; glorify him with your whole spirits, which he has formed and renewed in you.

Glorify him, who is the LORD and Giver of your life; glorify him, by whom ye are transformed into the very image and express portraiture of GOD.

Glorify him, who is to you the Renewer of nature; glorify him, who is to you the SPIRIT of glory.

HOLY FATHER, for ever hallowed be thy name in us, by thine own SPIRIT, whereby you adoptedst us to be thy children:

That we may live before thee, as an holy generation, and may do the work which you have given us to do HOLY LORD, SON of the FATHER, let thy kingdom,

which is a kingdom of holiness and peace, come into our hearts by the SPIRIT of holiness;

Which you sendest unto us from the FATHER, to prepare a throne for thee in us, even a throne of peace.

HOLY SPIRIT, let thy will be done in us, which is our sanctification, and is the will also of the FATHER, and of the Son.

O let it be done by the powerful operation of thine own living energy in our souls!

O let it be done by thy holy inspiration, gently moving and warming our hearts!

Send forth thy SPIRIT, O GOD; SO shall we be quickened:

And let thy glory be revealed within us; so shall we both know and do thy will, and thy name shall thence be glorified.

Come then, HOLY SPIRIT, come, and abide with us; that we, in thee, may glorify both the FATHER and the Son:

By doing the divine will on earth, as it is done in heaven; by living the life of angels:

Yea, living the life of CHRIST, not of angels only, and honoring the FATHER, as the Son did honor him, saying,

" Lo, a body you have for us prepared, and a spirit have you inspired, wherewith to do thy will, O LORD!" The SPIRIT of the LORD iS glorious, and perfects the

soul; and the inspiration of the ALMIGHTY gives understanding, and wisdom, and power:

That the kingdom of heaven may be represented on earth, and the will of GOD done by us below, as it is by those blessed spirits above.

Therefore we thirst after thee, the fountain of spiritual life; and as the hart pants after the water brooks, so do our souls pant after thee, O GOD.

O when shall we be satisfied with the living streams from the throne of our GOD! O when shall we come to draw freely from the wells of salvation!

O when shall a fountain be opened within us, as of water mingled with fire, perpetually springing up into eternal life! Behold, this is the SPIRIT of the LORD, whereof all his saints are made partakers; the fountain opened in Jerusalem for all the faithful to drink of, that they may be filled with light and joy.

Come, let us rejoice before our GOD, whose SPIRIT has made us; come, let us rejoice before our GOD, whose SPIRIT Both sanctify us.

GLORY BE to the Father, and to the Son, and to the Holy Ghost. As it was in the beginning, is now, and ever shall be: world without end.

Amen.

PSALM 12.

BUT while we rejoice in the SPIRIT of our LORD, we will humble ourselves before his footstool, and will mingle tears both of joy and grief with the bread which he gives us.

For we have sinned, and done perversely, and have been more ready to follow our devices and inclinations than his holy inspirations and motions.

Sorrow is therefore with us for a night, but joy comes in the morning; when the cheering light of the SPIRIT breaks in upon us.

And trouble we may also have in the world, but in him is sure consolation, and such a joy as none know but they that feel it. Wherefore blessed are they that mourn for their sins, and for the sins of the world; for they shall be comforted.

The SPIRIT of joy and peace shall flow into them from the presence of the LORD, and they shall be filled with his consolation,, though this be sown in bitterness and anguish of soul.

Yea, blessed are they that sow in tears; for our LORD shall rain salvation upon them, and they shall reap of the fruits of the SPIRIT with abundant gladness.

Come, let us rejoice before him, who has given us a new life; let us bless his name, who after a short heaviness fills our mouth with laughter, and our tongue with singing.

Great is the SPIRIT of our LORD, and of great power; his understanding is infinite, and out of darkness he brings forth marvelous light, to the joyful surprise of our souls.

He heals the broken in heart of a sudden, binds up their wounds, and wipes away their tears, making all things new.

He sends forth his breath into us, and we are presently revived; He gives medicine to heal our sickness, and we are healed from our sins, and a song of rejoicing is put by him into our mouths.

For his breath is life indeed, and in his light there is ecstacy of joy; and by his unction we are made whole, and the shadow of death driven away.

Come, let us rejoice in him, who has thus given us a new life; let us rejoice in him, who looses the prisoners of death, and turns again our captivity, as the streams in the South.

Let nothing now make us afraid; for it is no matter what the enemy threatens us; O let not our hearts be troubled!

Yea, let us not be moved, though hell should be moved against us; but let us be comforted still in the power of the HOLY GHOST, and under the overshadowing of his wings let our rest for ever abide.

Let us take comfort in him, notwithstanding our sins, yea, let us be never so sad.

For sin does not make us incapable of comfort, though want of repentance for sin does.

So we always carry away so much comfort of the HOLY GHOST, as we have of true contrition for our sins.

Wherefore deliver us, good LORD, from all those sins that exclude this divine Comforter.

Deliver us, O LORD, both from presumption, and from despair.

For presumption takes away the fear of thee, O GOD; and despair the love of thee for thy goodness.

Deliver us, and all that are called by thy name, from all impenitence, and from hardness of heart.

For impenitence excludes all sorrow for sins past, and hardness of heart makes the sinner continue in a course of sinning.

Deliver us and them from opposing a known truth, and from ever envying those who embrace it.

Deliver us, good LORD, from relapses and counterfeit repentances.

Deliver us from resisting any lawful authority whatsoever; for therein we resist thee, our GOD.

O keep all that have been once enlightened, and have been made partakers of the HOLY GHOST; that they may not fall away, and crucify to themselves afresh the LORD of life.

Come HOLY SPIRIT, and enflame our hearts with thy celestial fire; come, and burn up in us all the dross of sin.

Deliver us from all inconsiderateness and rashness, from all frowardness and censoriousness, and from the pride and lust of our own spirit; that so there may be a way prepared for thee.

Then our souls will be ready for thy impressions, and fitted for thy inspirations. Amen.

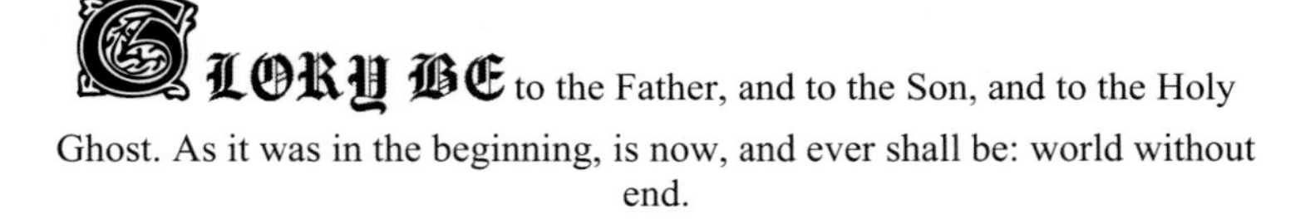

GLORY BE to the Father, and to the Son, and to the Holy Ghost. As it was in the beginning, is now, and ever shall be: world without end.

Amen.

PSALM 13.

THY impressions, O LORD, who art Goodness itself, will make us good; thy inspirations, who art Holiness itself, will make us holy.

It is thy SPIRIT, O LORD, that gives thy Priests eloquence, and thy Ministers utterance in preaching; that none may resist the power with which they speak.

It is thy SPIRIT that enkindles a burning zeal in them for thy glory, and makes it more and more ardent, so that nothing can stand before it.

It is thy SPIRIT that gives them a fiery tongue to publish thy Holy Gospel, and boldness cheerfully to profess the truth in the face of all the world.

He is the worker of our sanctification, and by him we are made new men in CHRIST JESUS.

He is the Discerner of the thoughts and intentions of our hearts, and the Purifier of all our uncleanness.

He is the Opener of the eyes of the blind, the Raiser of them that are bowed down, by the corruptible body pressing the soul.

He is the Unsealer of wisdom, and knowledge, and power, and is the Discoverer of hidden truth, and the Revealer of the depths of GOD:

He is the SPIRIT of truth, and his work in the soul is a work of truth, which causes all the shadows to flee away, and all works which are not wrought by him, do shake and tremble at it.

His voice is a voice of fire, quick and powerful, slaying and making alive; and blessed is every one that hears in his temple the voice of the fire, and can speak of his glory.

An heart of stone he melts with his breath into water, and from a flinty conscience he cuts out flames of fire.

He cleaves the fountain, and the flood, and turns our dry and barren earth into watersprings, making us to flourish as the garden of the LORD.

He puts a holy fire and lively zeal into the hearts of those who are cold and frozen; so that they can run, and faint not.

He gives strength to the weak, and enables the feeble to condemn the world, and despise all worldly things.

He illuminates the understanding; he rectifies the will; he sanctifies the memory.

He fills the whole soul with the treasures of his goodness, and all the faculties and powers thereof are blessed by him.

As a pure influence from the Almighty Word, he shines into our understanding, subduing every thought by the light of faith.

A Light he is to our mind, holy and undefiled; a Flame to our will, most quick and powerful; and a most precious Cabinet to our memory, stored with the riches of the divine word.

He not only enflames our affections with an holy ardor, but sweetly draws them from all other things unto himself.

GLORY BE to the Father, and to the Son, and to the Holy Ghost. As it was in the beginning, is now, and ever shall be: world without end.

Amen.

ALMIGHTY GOD, *and FATHER of all mercies, who alone can order the unruly wills and affections of sinful men, and who didst in the beginning powerfully instruct and graciously lead thy faithful servants, by sending them the light of thy HOLY SPIRIT; grant us by the same SPIRIT to have a right judgment in all things that are necessary to our salvation; and refusing the comforts and pleasures of this world, continually to rejoice in his holy consolation. Give us, we beseech thee, the SPIRIT of wisdom, and understanding, and counsel, that by the inspiration thereof we may think those things that be good; the SPIRIT of faith, and fortitude, and power, that by the guidance thereof we may perform the same in a manner most acceptable to thee; and give us the SPIRIT of prayer and supplication, that we may adore thee in spirit, with reverence, steadfastness, and perseverance. O confirm us by this Spirit, who are weak; reduce us, when we go astray from thee; let thy grace prevent our falling, by its power; and let thy mercy lift us up, when we are down; govern our senses, inspire our thoughts, guard our words, direct all our actions to thy glory; and now accept the offering of our whole spirit, soul and body, and all we are and have, as entirely devoted unto thee; and keep us always safe from both our visible and invisible enemies, for the merits of thy SON, JESUS CHRIST our LORD.* Amen.

The Office of the Saints

Morning Prayer.

Antiphon

Come, let us adore the King of saints.

PSALM 1.

GREAT is the Majesty of the King we serve, rich the splendor of his court; over all the world he sends his commands, and who dare resist, or dispute his power!

Come, let us adore the King of saints.

Great is the clemency of our gracious Sovereign, to pardon the offences of repentant sinners; great is the bounty of our glorious LORD, to crown with reward his faithful servants.

Come, let us adore the King of saints.

Thousands of saints attend at his presence, and millions of angels wait on his throne, all beauteously ranged in perfect order, all joyfully singing the praises of their Creator.

Come, let us adore the King of saints.

You art our King too, O blessed JESUS, and we, alas! thy unprofitable subjects; we cannot praise thee like those thine own bright choirs, yet humbly we offer our little tribute.

Come, let us adore the King of saints.

Let us bow down low our heads to him, before whom the Seraphim cover their faces: Let us bow down our faces to him, at whose feet the saints lay down their crowns.

Come, let us adore the King of saints.

GLORY BE to the Father, and to the Son, and to the Holy Ghost. As it was in the beginning, is now, and ever shall be: world without end.

Amen.

PSALM 2.

THEY who now are gladly arrived at the quiet harbor of eternal rest;

They behold us here below embarked in the same ship, and bound with all our interests for the same port.

They behold us struggling yet in this sea of storms, while they are safely landed on the coasts of everlasting light and joy.

O who is there that shall be able to help us, while the winds and the waves so beat upon us

Yea, who is there in heaven, that shall deliver us Is it not You, O LORD, even you alone

You art ready to guide us safely through all our dangers, even as you have guided them.

Let the heavens therefore hear thy voice, and let all the powers thereof give glory unto thee.

And You, O sovereign LORD of universal nature, on whom the celestial court continually waits!

Command now thy angels to watch about us, and carry us to the place of our desires.

Save us, O You, whom the sea and winds obey! Save us, O merciful LORD, or we perish.

Save us, who call on thee in all our distresses; save us, for whom there is intercession made in the heavenly temple, thy blood speaking better things for us than that of ABEL.

Save us, for whom thyself wert pleased to die, and graciously receive us into thy own blessed arms.

You art thyself, O LORD, the haven of repose; bring us to thyself, and our souls shall be safe.

GLORY BE to the Father, and to the Son, and to the Holy Ghost. As it was in the beginning, is now, and ever shall be: world without end.

Amen.

DELIVER *us, O LORD, from the deplorable end, which thy justice has prepared for the wicked, and deliver us from those vain deceitful ways that lead to so miserable an end. O make us always fear thy judgments, that we may never feel them; and always hope in thy mercies, that we never forfeit them. Bless us, O LORD, with a happy death, that our souls may depart in peace, and go up to dwell among the saints and angels: Bless us, O LORD, with a holy life, and then our death cannot but be happy.*

At Noon.

PSALM 3.

O PRAISE the LORD, all ye powers of my soul, praise the immortal King of saints and angels.

Praise him, the Author of all their graces; praise him, the Finisher of all their glories.

Praise him in the mighty hosts of angels, whom he sets about us, as the guard of our lives:

That they may safely keep us in all our ways, and carry us at last to their own home.

Praise him in the sacred college of Apostles, to whom he revealed the mysteries of his kingdom:

That they may teach us too those heavenly truths, and show us the same blessed way to felicity.

Praise him in the generous fortitude of Martyrs, whom he strengthened with courage to resist even to death:

That we might learn from them to hold fast our faith, and rather lose this life, than hazard the other.

Praise him in the eminent sanctity of Confessors, whose whole design was a course of virtue:

That we might raise our minds from earth, and with quick and active wing mount up towards heaven.

Praise him in the angelical purity of virgins, whose hearts he enflamed with his divine charity

That they might kindle our breasts with the same chaste fire, the same fervent love to the Bridegroom of our souls.

Praise him in the perfect holiness of all his saints, whose lives he beautifully has moulded into so various shapes:

That every size of ours might readily be furnished with a pattern fitted for itself.

O praise the LORD, all ye powers of my soul, praise the immortal King of saints and angels.

PSALM 4.

PRAISE every person of the sacred Deity, and give a shout of joy to the whole court of heaven.

Blessed for ever be the eternal FATHER, who has fixed his angels in so high a happiness.

Triumph, bright angels, on your radiant thrones, and shine continually in the presence of GOD.

Blessed for ever be the eternal Son, who has so honored human nature, as to exalt it above the very angels.

Blessed for ever be the eternal SPIRIT, whose grace brings all the saints to glory.

Rejoice, every happy saint, in your own felicity; rejoice every one in the felicity of all.

Blessed for ever be the holy and undivided Trinity, whose sight alone is the heaven of heaven.

Sing, all you holy citizens of heaven, sing ye all together everlasting hymns.

Sing aloud the triumphs of our dear Redeemer, and praise him for his mercies to us pilgrims here below.

Praise him, all ye angels, and magnify him with us, all ye stars of the morning.

Praise him, all his glorious hosts following him in white;

O praise him for his wondrous mercies, which endure for ever.

Praise him in his holiness, O praise him with us, for the mighty acts of his love; and let us together adore the GOD that has redeemed us.

Let the renowned society of Prophets, and the glorious college of Apostles, bless together the GOD that has redeemed us.

Let the goodly train of' Confessors, and the bright army of Martyrs, glorify him, who is the only strength of our salvation, even as he was of theirs.

Glory be to our LORD from the heavens, and praises to our GOD from the heights, for our LORD is glorious in his saints, but will not give his honor to another.

GLORY BE to the Father, and to the Son, and to the Holy Ghost. As it was in the beginning, is now, and ever shall be: world without end.

Amen.

PSALM 5.

LIFT up, my soul, and see the innumerable multitude of triumphing spirits.

See how they stand all clothed in white robes, with palms in their hands, and crowns on their heads.

Behold the glorious angels fall down before the throne, and prostrate adore him who liveth for ever.

Behold the blessed saints lay their crowns at his feet, and on their faces adore him who liveth forever.

Hark how they fill that spacious temple with their hymns, while night and day they continually sing:

Holy, holy, holy, LORD GOD Almighty; who was, and is, and is to come, **Hallelujah**.

Holy, holy, holy, LORD GOD of hosts! Heaven and earth are full of thy glory. **Hallelujah**.

Glorious art you in creating all things, glorious in preserving them every moment.

Glorious in governing them their several ways, glorious in appointing them their proper ends.

Glorious in rewarding thy servants above their hopes, glorious in punishing sinners below their demerits. Glorious, O LORD, art you in all thy works, but infinitely more in thine own self blessed essence.

Hallelujah. Thus they rejoice above, thus they triumph; and may their joy and triumph last for ever!

But O! were we not made, as well as they, to serve and glorify our great CREATOR

We owe him all we have, and they can owe no more; they can but do their best, and we should do no less.

Nor is envy in them, if we worms aspire to sing the same bright name which they adore;

Since there is but one family of us both in heaven and earth, under one Head, and all are knit together by one SPIRIT.

They stand as at the golden altar, compassing it about with songs of praise; but we, as without the porch, wait at a distance, till we also be admitted to be with them in the heavenly sanctuary.

Does not the smoke of this their incense, the sweet perfume of their praises, which comes with our prayers, ascend up before GOD, even our GOD and their God

O how sweet is the perfume of these their praises before the throne of GOD! O that our praises also and prayers could be but as the incense which they offer!

O that this our low service were now set forth in his sight as that heavenly incense! And that the lifting up of our hands were as the precious odours ascending out of the angel's hand!

But how, alas! can we sing those glorious songs which they now sing, while we are yet as in a strange land.

Yet fain would we join with you, O ye blessed spirits, and, as in one communion, together celebrate the glories of our triumphant LORD.

Praise this thy LORD, O Jerusalem that art above; praise thy GOD, O glorious Sion; and let all thy children shout aloud his triumphs.

Though we are now, alas! in this land of banishment, and indisposed for those songs of Sion;

Yet it is our hope one day to dwell above, and hear your holy harps, and learn to sing of you.

We hope to walk with you those ways of light, and follow the LAMB with you wherever he goes.

Meanwhile, we every day will join our vows to yours, and say a glad Amen to all ye sing.

We will every day repeat those short ends of your seraphic hymns:

> "Salvation to our GOD, who sits on the throne, and to the LAMB, that redeemed us with his blood. **Hallelujah**."
>
> "Blessing and honor, wisdom and power, be to him that sits on the throne, and to the LAMB for all eternity. **Hallelujah, Hallelujah**."

GLORY BE to the Father, and to the Son, and to the Holy Ghost. As it was in the beginning, is now, and ever shall be: world without end. Amen.

In the Afternoon.

PSALM 5.

TAKE courage, my soul, and chase away thy doubts; for more are with us than against us.

GOD and his holy angels are on our side, JESUS takes our part, and his blessed saints rejoice over us.

Our Almighty Creator looks on to excite us, our gracious Redeemer came down to instruct us.

The blessed SPIRIT is within us, to confirm our hearts, and the whole Trinity present, to crown our victories.

Whom then shall we fear, being thus safely guarded Who can resist so invincible a strength

None but our own corrupted nature dare contend, and the evil spirits that conspire with it against us.

Not that they can compel our wills, unless we yield, or make the least wound without our consent:

Much less prevail against the power of Heaven, and frustrate the purpose of almighty Wisdom:

Whose mercy has more arts to save us, than the craft of Satan can invent to destroy us.

O infinite Goodness, how generous is thy love! how liberally extended over all the world

You invitest little children to come unto thee, and the lame and the blind to sit down at thy feast.

None are shut out of heaven, but such as will not go in; none made unhappy, but those who care not to be otherwise.

Cheer then thyself, my heart, and let no fears molest thee, nor even death itself abate thy courage.

Lose not thy hope in so glorious an enterprise; eternity is at stake, and heaven the reward.

That heaven for which so many wandered about in old time in sheepskins and goatskins, being outwardly destitute, afflicted, tormented.

That heaven. for which so many have been content to lay out all they had, and have trampled under their feet all the flattering pomps of an earthly court.

That heaven for which the holy Confessors spent all their time, and innumerable Martyrs laid down their lives.

That heaven where millions of Angels continually sing, and all the blessed make one glorious choir.

That heaven, where the adored JESUS eternally reigns, and the immortal Deity shines bright for ever.

That very heaven is promised to thee, my soul, that blessed eternity you art commanded to hope for.

Raise now thy head, and see those beauteous prospects, that ravish the hearts of all their beholders.

Yonder is thy Savior's kingdom, yonder we must dwell when we leave this earth.

Yonder must our souls remove to rest, when the stroke of death shall divide them from their bodies.

And, when the Almighty Power shall join them again, yonder we must live with our GOD for ever.

O bounteous LORD, the only author of all we have, the only object of all we hope!

As you have prepared a heaven for us, O may thy grace prepare us for it!

O make us live the life of the righteous, and let our last end be like theirs!

O let us die the death of the righteous, and live for ever in their blessed society!

GLORY BE to the Father, and to the Son, and to the Holy Ghost. As it was in the beginning, is now, and ever shall be: world without end.

Amen.

O GOD, *whose merciful providence has still from the beginning sown the seeds of grace in the hearts of thy chosen servants, which, at the resurrection of thy SON, (the first fruits of them that sleep,) sprang up into glory, who, by his holy doctrine, and life, and precious death, have infinitely increased the means of salvation, and number of thy saints! Grant, we beseech thee, that we, whom you have favored with so many advantages, by calling us into communion with them, may obtain thy grace to imitate them here, and to rejoice with them in thy kingdom hereafter, through the same our LORD JESUS CHRIST, their and our merciful Redeemer: To whom, with thee and the HOLY GHOST, be all glory for ever.* Amen.

In the Evening.

PSALM 6.

THUS we have passed another day, another step towards our long home.

We have seen the sun a few hours more, and our day is lost in its own night.

But is it lost and all the holy words we have heard and read

Leave they no mark in our memories behind them but make a little sound and vanish into air

Have we not been at a solemn feast and do we so soon forget our entertainment

Was there no fit provision for some virtue we want no proper remedy for some weakness we have

Are we devout already, as the saints of GOD, and chaste, " and temperate, and resigned as they

Do we despise the world with a zeal like theirs, and value heaven at the same rate with them

Would we give all we have just now to be there; and part with life itself to go thither

Alas! how short are we of these perfections! how slowly do we follow those excellent guides!

O that we lived, like you, whose aim was high, and a generous heat glowed in your breasts!

At least let us learn to humble ourselves, and check the vanity of our proud conceits.

Let us mourn and blush at our many infirmities, and so much the louder call to Heaven for relief.

Let us worship and' fall down, and kneel, like you, before our LORD and Maker.

We hope assuredly to be with you, and enter into his Test, where you already are arrived.

GLORY BE to the Father, and to the Son, and to the Holy Ghost. As it was in the beginning, is now, and ever shall be: world without end.

Amen.

PSALM 7.

LET US humble ourselves, but not grow faint, at the sight of others so far before us.

Rather let us quicken ourselves by their swift pace, and encourage our fears with their happy success.

We, who profess the religion of all those saints, who lived and died in the same Church with us:

We, who partake of the same holy Sacraments, and eat the same celestial food;

Why should we fear one day to shine above, and rejoice together with you, O glorious saints

Are we not all redeemed with the same rich price and is not the same eternal crown proposed to us all

You lived in a dangerous world, like this, and were tied to bodies frail as ours.

But, by a constant vigilance, you overcame the world, and subdued those bodies to the service of your mind.

You overcame with a joyful heart, and we thus congratulate the triumphs of your victories.

You overcame, but not with your own strong hand; you now triumph, but it is by the bounty of your GOD.

Cheer up then thyself, my soul, and raise thy head, and open thy bosom to the hopes of heaven.

If we perform, with them, the part of faithful servants, we shall surely, with them, have the portion of children.

GLORY BE to the Father, and to the Son, and to the Holy Ghost. As it was in the beginning, is now, and ever shall be: world without end.

Amen.

PSALM 8.

PRECIOUS, O LORD, in thy sight is the death of thy saints, which finishes thy greatest work, the perfecting of souls:

Whom you esteemest as the jewels of heaven, and choicely gatherest them into thine own treasury.

Precious to themselves, O LORD, is the death of thy saints, which takes off the dusty cover that hides their brightness:

Which shapes and polishes them to a beautiful lustre, and sets them as stars round about thy throne.

Precious to us, O LORD, is the death of thy saints, which makes us heirs of so great a wealth:

Which leaves us furnished with so rich variety of examples, that every want is abundantly supplied.

O gracious LORD, whose love still looks about, and searches every way to save us sinners!

Who tamest thyself, bright Sun of Glory, to enlighten our darkness, and warm our frozen hearts!

Who, with thy fruitful beams, still kindlest others, to burn as tapers in thy Church's hands:

O make us bless thy name for all these mercies, and let not one be lost by our ingratitude.

Let us not see in vain the crowns at the race's end, and sit down in the shades of ease.

Let us not keep in vain these sacred memorials, to be only a reproach to our unprofitable lives.

But let us stretch out ourselves, and pursue to the mark, for the glorious prize that is set before us.

Still with our utmost speed let us follow them, whose travels ended in so sweet a rest. And when our life's last day begins to fail, and bids us hasten to prepare for night:

Then, O you dear Redeemer of the world, and sovereign King of life and death,

You that despisest not the tears of the penitent, nor turnest away from the sighs of the afflicted!

You that preserve all that rely on thee, and fulfillest their desires that long to be with thee!

Call us to thyself with thine own blessed voice, call us, O JESUS! in thine own sweet words:

> "Come, ye blessed of my FATHER, inherit the kingdom prepared for you from the beginning of the world."

Then, O my happy soul, immediately obey, and go forth with gladness to meet thy LORD:

To live with him, and behold his glory; to rejoice with him, and sing his praise.

GLORY BE to the Father, and to the Son, and to the Holy Ghost. As it was in the beginning, is now, and ever shall be: world without end.

Amen.

The Preparatory Office for Death

Morning Prayer.

Antiphon

Come, let us adore our GOD, to whom all things live.

PSALM 1.

HE is the great Creator of the world, and sovereign Judge of all mankind; he sits above on his glorious throne, and in his hands are the keys of life and death.

Whatever he pleases he brings to pass, and none can resist his almighty power; whatever he does is still the best, and none can accuse his, all knowing goodness.

All things live to thee, O LORD, you sole Preserver of universal nature; the blessed saints rejoice in thy glory, and with pleasure expect from thee the accomplishment of their bliss.

Even the unhappy spirits declare thy justice; and the rest of thy creatures look up for mercy, expecting at last to be removed from corruption, into the glorious liberty of the sons of GOD.

LORD! whilst we breathe, let us live to thee; and when we expire, depart in thy peace; that whether we live or die, we may be always thine, and after death still live with thee.

GLORY BE to the Father, and to the Son, and to the Holy Ghost. As it was in the beginning, is now, and ever shall be: world without end.

Amen.

PSALM 2.

WHAT, O glorious God, is our business here, but to trim our lamps, and wait for thy coming

But to sow the immortal seed of hope, and expect hereafter to reap the increase

No matter how late the fruit be gathered, if still it go on in growing better.

No matter how soon it fall from the tree, if not blown down before it be ripe.

O you most just, but secret Providence, who governest all things by the counsel of thy will;

Whose powerful hand can wound, and heal, lead down to the grave, and bring back again:

Behold, to thee we bow our heads, and freely submit our dearest concerns.

Strike, as you pleasest, our health, our lives; we cannot be safer than at thy disposal.

Only these few requests we humbly make; which, O may thy clemency vouchsafe to hear!

Cut us not off in the midst of our folly, nor suffer us to expire with our sins unpardoned;

But make us, Loon, first ready for thyself; then take us to thyself in thine own fit time.

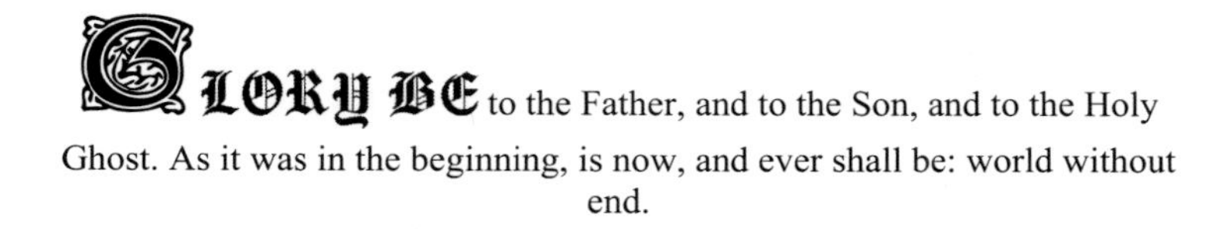

GLORY BE to the Father, and to the Son, and to the Holy Ghost. As it was in the beginning, is now, and ever shall be: world without end.

Amen.

PSALM 3.

O THAT we may rightly use the day of grace; and repent, while repentance is available to salvation!

O Sun of Righteousness, arise upon us with healing in thy wings!

O enlighten, and water our hard frozen souls with the radiant beams of thy HOLY SPIRIT!

You who earnest humble once to redeem us, come graciously now to deliver us, whom you have redeemed with thy precious blood.

Come, LORD, come quickly, and rescue with thy power thine own inheritance.

O may that happy day make haste to come, and cheer our darkness with its radiant beams!

O may that Light of lights speedily arise, and disperse the mist that intercepts our sight!

Come, LORD, come quickly! and lead thy servants forth out of the house of bondage.

Come, and deliver us out of the snare of the enemy; O deliver all the captives of Satan out of the hands of that wicked one;

That they may pass from death to life, and dwell with thee in thy blessed peace.

GLORY BE to the Father, and to the Son, and to the Holy Ghost. As it was in the beginning, is now, and ever shall be: world without end. Amen.

At Noon.

PSALM 4.

WHEN we have shed our solemn tears, and paid our due sighs to the memory of our friend,

Let us wipe our eyes with the comfort of hope, and change our grief into a charitable joy.

The friends we mourn for are delivered from this world, and all the miseries we deplore.

They quietly rest in the silent grave, till they rise again to immortal glory; which whilst they there expect in peace, their souls are enlarged to a spacious liberty.

No longer confined to this prison of the body, but gone to dwell in the region of spirits:

No longer exposed to these stormy seas, but gladly arrived at their safe harbor.

O glorious LORD, the free original source and final end of universal nature!

Since by thy grace you have thus begun, and sown in our hearts the seeds of glory:

O may the same blessed hand go on to finish its own blessed work.

Ripen the fruit you reserve for thyself, and hasten the days of our joyful harvest.

Send forth thy angels to reap thy grain, and lay it up safe in thy heavenly magazine,

There to supply the place of those unhappy tares, which thy justice threw down into everlasting fire;

There to assist among those holy angelic choirs, which thy mercy established in everlasting bliss;

There to join with thy perfectly blessed, to sing eternal hallelujahs unto thee.

GLORY BE to the Father, and to the Son, and to the Holy Ghost. As it was in the beginning, is now, and ever shall be: world without end.

Amen.

PSALM 5.

CAME, let us praise the goodness of our GOD, who orders every thing to the best for his servants:

Whose providence governs us all our life, and takes so particular care of our death.

He casts us down on our bed of sickness, and draws the curtain between the world and us:

Shutting out all its vain designs, and contracting our business to a little chamber.

There, in that quiet solitude, he speaks to our hearts, and sets before us all our life.

Thither he sends even his only Son, to secure our passage and conduct us unto himself.

Blessed for ever be thy name, O LORD! whose mercy sanctifies even thy punishments into favors.

You commandest the grave to dispense with none, but indifferently seize on all alike;

That all may alike provide for that hour, and none be undone with mistaken hopes.

You tellest us plainly that all must die, but kindly concealest the time and place,

That every where we may stand on our guard, and every moment expect thy coming.

You teachest the use of decent funerals, and the duty we owe to our deceased friends,

That we may often renew the memory of our own grave and the wholesome thoughts of our future state.

Let not, O LORD, these gracious arts be lost, which thy merciful wisdom contrives for our sakes.

But whilst we thus remember the death of others, make us still seriously reflect upon our own.

And let every time we reflect upon our own, the more diligent in preparing for it.

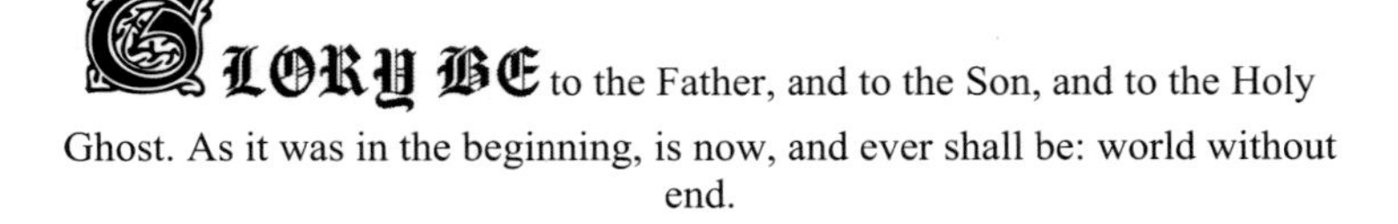

GLORY BE to the Father, and to the Son, and to the Holy Ghost. As it was in the beginning, is now, and ever shall be: world without end.

Amen.

PSALM 6.

O PRAISE the LORD, all ye nations of the earth, whom his providence yet sustains alive;

Whom he so long forbears to strike, though our sins have so oft provoked his wrath.

O praise the LORD, all ye faithful souls, for his mercy shall preserve the just.

Though, we lie below in this valley of tears, and sit lamenting in the shades of sorrow,

Yet he will bring us up to his eternal mountains, and fill our eyes with glorious light.

Though our bones stare us in the face, and our hearts faint with age or sickness,

Yet we shall be clothed with strength and beauty, and placed to sing among the blessed saints.

O praise the LORD, all you blessed above, whom his bounty has already crowned with glory.

You who were weaned from the allurements of the world, and fit to die at the hour of death.

O praise the LORD, all you glorious angels, whose bright felicity began so early:

Stars that arose in the morning of the world, and still maintain your unchangeable lustre.

O praise the LORD, all ye his works; praise and magnify him for ever.

Praise his almighty power that gave you being, and still preserves you from relapsing into nothing.

Praise his all seeing wisdom, O ye saints, that here directs your steps, and leads you on to your eternal end.

Praise above all his boundless goodness, that pours into every thing as much as it can hold.

And though our short sight now reaches not so far, but often mistakes and repines at his government:

Yet at the last day we shall easily discern a perfect concord in the harshest note.

When our adored REDEEMER shall come in the clouds, and summon all nature to appear before him,

There to receive each one their proper part, exactly fitted to their best capacity;

There to behold the whole creation strive, to express in itself the perfections of its Maker,

Whose admirable wisdom shall guide that last universal scene, and finish all into a beauteous close.

GLORY BE to the Father, and to the Son, and to the Holy Ghost. As it was in the beginning, is now, and ever shall be: world without end.

Amen.

ALMIGHTY GOD, *with whom do live the spirits of them that depart in the LORD, and with whom the souls of the faithful, after they are delivered from the burden of the flesh, do rest from their labors; we give thee hearty " thanks for that it has pleased thee to deliver our dear friends, who have gone before us, out of the miseries of this sinful world, [Here any of our dear, virtuous friends or relations, natural, civil, or spiritual, whom we believe to have died in the peace of GOD, may be commemorated by saying, " Particularly thy servant, our late father, mother, brother, " &c.,] beseeching thee, that it may please thee to accomplish the number of thine elect, and to hasten thy kingdom; that we, with all those that have departed in the true faith of thy holy Church, may have our perfect consummation and bliss, both in body and soul, in thy eternal kingdom, through JESUS CHRIST our LORD.* Amen.

In the Afternoon.

PSALM 7.

HEAR our prayers, O LORD, for thy sick servants, that are visited with thy rod at this time.

Hear their own prayers, O LORD, and tenderly regard their complaints.

Look upon them with the eyes of thy mercy, and give them, we beseech thee, comfort and sure confidence in thee, their strong salvation.

Quench not, O GOD of, mercy, the smoking flax, nor break the bruised reed.

But sanctify thy fatherly correction to them that fear thee, and pardon the sins of the days of their folly.

O let thy saving word leap down from heaven, and heal all their infirmities.

Let thy grace at this time mercifully assist them; that the sense of their weakness may add strength to their faith, and seriousness to their repentance:

That they, being sincerely contrite for their sins, may by thee mercifully be delivered:

And being themselves forgiven may from their hearts both forgive all that have offended them, and make satisfaction to' all whom they may have injured:

That being reconciled to thee, and all the world, they may, with a constant faith and firm hope, cast themselves upon thy mercy, and continue to the end in thy grace and favor:

That howsoever it shall please thee to dispose of them, either for life or death, they may cheerfully submit to thy most holy will.

O LORD, according to the multitude of the sorrows in their souls or bodies, let thy comforts refresh their hearts.

And as the sufferings of CHRIST abound in any; so may their consolation much more abound by CHRIST, to thy glory.

Favorably accept our petitions for all those who are any ways afflicted in mind or distressed in body.

O show thy mercy unto them, and let thy kingdom come both unto them and us!

Make haste, O LORD, you GOD of our salvation, and suffer not thy servants to faint when they are proved by thee!

But may their diseases, and all their bodily infirmities, work together for good to them.

And may these momentary and light afflictions work for us all an eternal weight of glory.

Make haste, O GOD of Truth, to accomplish thy word, and give all thy faithful perfect rest in thee.

Let the days of misery and sin be brought to an end, and may thy light gloriously shine upon them for ever.

O how long delayeth our LORD to come! Why are the wheels of his chariot so slow

Have you not said, O LORD of Glory, " Behold, I come quickly, and my reward is with me"

Come, glorious JESUS with all thy holy angels, and the bright attendance of rejoicing saints.

The Spirit says, "Come," and the Bride says, "Come:" Even so "come" to all that are athirst for thee, most gracious JESU!

Come, and redeem the captivity of thy children: And lead them away as trophies of thy victory.

Come, and redeem us from this body of sin: Yea, come, and redeem all thy Israel from their iniquities.

In the Evening.

PSALM 8.

THE Wisdom of GOD cries in the streets, in the temples, and in the chief places of concourse, she cries daily, saying,

"Today if ye will hear his voice, harden not your hearts."

O LORD, we hear thy voice: O melt you down our hearts, we pray thee!

O merciful LORD! thy voice do we hear with gladness: Though we have erred and strayed from thy ways, yet are we the sheep of thy pasture, and know thy voice.

The voice of our LORD is mighty in operation; the voice of our LORD is a glorious voice.

At this thy voice, O GOD, death and hell are made to flee, and in thy temple shall every one speak of thy honor.

You have by thy powerful voice graciously called us out of darkness, into thy marvelous light.

Whence we trust that that day shall never surprise us; but that when it comes we shall be found already in the light of it.

O lift you up the light of thy countenance upon us, so that we may walk all the day long in thy light, and continually behold light in this thy light.

And when thy day shall be revealed, with the night of this world; then let a garment of light be ready for us:

In which we may be led into the bride chamber of the Lamb; and there, by his grace, take possession of the saints' inheritance in light.

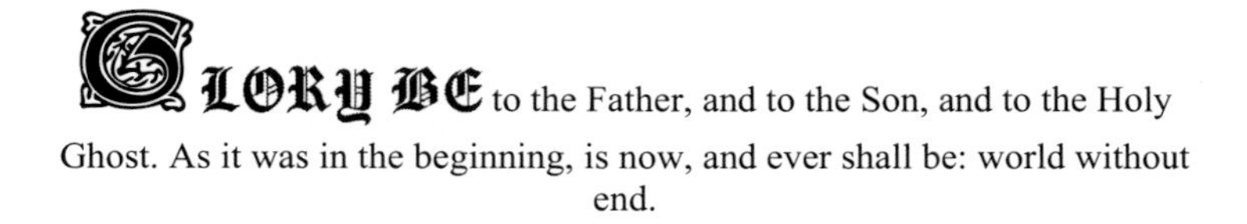

GLORY BE to the Father, and to the Son, and to the Holy Ghost. As it was in the beginning, is now, and ever shall be: world without end.

Amen.

PSALM 9.

WE confess Him that is the resurrection and the light; we acknowledge Him that is the light of angels and saints.

Our LORD CHRIST is the very light of life; whosoever truly seeks him shall live and not die.

He is the life everlasting; and to know him is also life everlasting, as to serve him an unfading crown.

O come, let us worship, then, and fall down before our LORD, the LORD of life, to whom all things live.

Come, let us adore the LORD our Redeemer, by whom all things live, and kneel before him who visits the chambers of the dead, and opens the graves:

Who causes his dew to fall upon the mown grass, and remembering the prayers of his dead Israelites calls them forth by name.

For faithful is he in all his promises; and his covenant. is confirmed to all the generations of his saints.

They live in him, and he in them; and as he liveth, so also must they live, and death can have no power over them.

They have sought him, and they have found him; and they know that with him is life, and that his mercy endured), for ever.

Lo! How is the shadow of death by him turned into the glorious morning of the resurrection!

The shadows are passed, and the LAMB is risen as a glorious Sun, shining upon them with healing in his wings.

Healing all their former maladies, and wiping away all tears from their eyes.

GLORY BE to the Father, and to the Son, and to the Holy Ghost. As it was in the beginning, is now, and ever shall be: world without end.

Amen.

ALMIGHTY GOD, *with whom do live the spirits of the just made perfect, we bless thee for all thy faithful, whom you have delivered out of the snares and miseries of this sinful world; more especially those of thy blessed saints, whom you madest burning and shining lamps in their generation, filling them with thy righteousness and true holiness; and we likewise pray thee to hasten thy kingdom, that all those that are departed in thy faith and fear, may have their perfect consummation and bliss; and that we who here wait and sigh after the day of our deliverance, may together with them see thee, and in the light of thy glory rejoice everlastingly; through JESUS CHRIST our LORD.* Amen.

GRANT, *O blessed LORD, the Father of mercies, to whom alone belong the issues of life and death, that whether we live, we may live unto thee, or whether we die, we may die unto thee; that CHRIST thy Son may be glorified in our bodies and in our souls, whether we live or die, that neither life nor death, nor any other creature, may be able to separate us from the love of thee in CHRIST JESUS our LORD: That so as the earthly house of this our tabernacle shall be dissolved, we may possess an eternal habitation, not made with hands, in the heavens; through the same thy Son, and our only Redeemer and Mediator, JESUS CHRIST.* Amen.

THE *Divine assistance abide with us henceforth and evermore; that even walking in the midst of the shadow of death, and by the gates of hell, we may fear no evil, because GOD is with us, even IMMANUEL, who is LORD and CHRIST blessed for ever.* Amen.

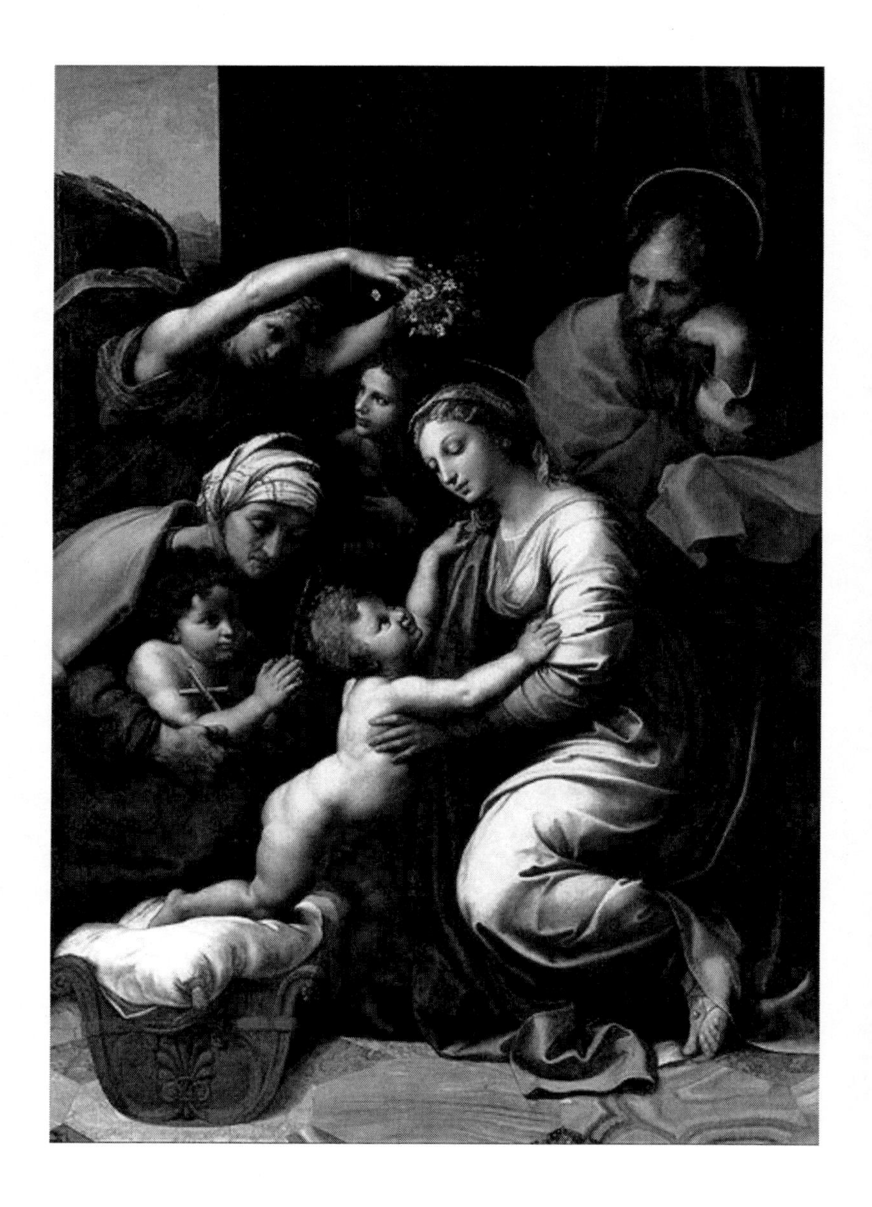

The Office for a Family.

Morning Prayer.

IN the name of the FATHER, and of the ✠ SON, and of the HOLY GHOST. Amen.

PREVENT US, O LORD, in all our actions with thy holy inspiration, and carry on the same by thy gracious assistance, that both every prayer and every work of ours may from thee always begin, and by thee always be happily ended; through JESUS CHRIST our LORD. Amen.

LORD, have mercy upon us.

CHRIST, have mercy upon us.

LORD, have mercy upon us.

OUR FATHER, which art in heaven, hallowed be thy name. Thy kingdom come. Thy will be done in earth, as it is in heaven. Give us this day our daily bread. And forgive us our trespasses, as we forgive them that trespass against us. And lead us not into temptation: But deliver us from evil. For thine is the kingdom, the power, and the glory, for ever and ever. Amen.

O eternal, infinite and omnipotent GOD! whose gracious wisdom vouchsafes to command such things as are necessary to fit us for everlasting bliss, and forbids such as are apt to render us eternally unhappy; we, miserable sinners, humbly prostrate our souls and bodies before thy most adorable Majesty; and with a true and hearty sorrow, each of us particularly accuse and condemn ourselves.

Here pause a while to examine and repent, and make holy purposes.

We confess, O LORD GOD, that we have grievously sinned against thee in thought, [ ] word, [ ] and deed: [ ] But have you mercy upon us, O most merciful FATHER, for thy SON's sake, JESUS CHRIST, our only LORD and Advocate. Amen.

The great and glorious LORD of heaven and earth, have mercy upon us, forgive us our sins, and bring us to everlasting life. Amen.

O GOD the FATHER, Creator of the world, have mercy upon us.

O GOD the SON, Redeemer of mankind, have mercy upon us.

O GOD the HOLY GHOST, Perfecter of the faithful, have mercy upon us.

Holy, holy, holy, LORD GOD of hosts!

Have mercy on this family we beseech thee:

And spare every soul therein for thy name's sake.

PSALM 1.

THE night is far spent, the day is at hand; yea, the night is past, and the day is now risen: Let us therefore cast off the works of darkness, and let us put on the armor of light.

Come, let us adore the Dayspring from on high.

They that walk in darkness have seen a great light; and upon them that dwell in the land of the shadow of death has this glorious light shined.

Come, let us. adore the Dayspring from on high.

CHRIST is that Dayspring from on high, whence only there is joy to GOD in the highest.

Come, let us adore the Dayspring from on high.

He is the Light that shines in our darkness; but the darkness of our understanding comprehends him not.

Come, let us adore the Dayspring from on high.

The LORD is our Light; for with him, and with none else, is indeed the light of life; and in this light shall we, by faith, behold light.

Come, let us adore the Dayspring from on high.

GLORY BE to the Father, and to the Son, and to the Holy Ghost. As it was in the beginning, is now, and ever shall be: world without end.

Amen.

O glorious JESUS! without whom we are dead, quicken us with thy SPIRIT, that we may live by thy life; and so putting thee on, may make no more provision for the flesh, to fulfill its desires; but for the spirit only, thereby to fulfill all righteousness in thee, and bring forth the fruits of the HOLY GHOST: While, by thy power, we cast away the works of darkness, and put on the impregnable armor of light.

Almighty GOD, and most merciful FATHER, give us, we beseech thee, that grace, that we may duly examine the inmost of our hearts, and our most secret thoughts, how we stand before thee; and that we may henceforth never be drawn to do any thing that may dishonor thy name, but may persevere in all good purposes, and in thy holy service unto our lives' end: And grant that we may this day begin to walk before thee, as becometh those that are called to an inheritance of light in CHRIST.

LORD, you knows what is best for us to do, according to thy will; give us, we beseech thee, to at you wilt, as much as you wilt, and when you wilt. Do with us in all things, as you knows best to be done; and. as it shall please thee, and as may be most for thy honor, put us where you wilt, and freely do with us in all things after thy will and pleasure. We are thy creatures, and in thy hands; lead us, O GOD, and turn us wheresoever you wilt. Lo! we are thy servants, ready to do all things that you cornmandest us; for we desire not to live to ourselves, but to thee, through JESUS CHRIST our LORD. Amen.

O LORD, we give thee humble and hearty thanks for all the benefits and blessings, both spiritual and temporal, which in the riches of thy great mercy you have bountifully poured down upon us; but especially for the spiritual. Let us not live, but to praise and magnify thee and thy glorious name. Particularly we give thee most unfeigned thanks for our preservation from the time of our birth to this present; [and yet more particularly for thy late mercies vouchsafed us, for bringing us safe to the beginning of this day; in which, and all the days of our life, we beseech thee, preserve us from sin, and from danger; so governing and leading us, that all our thoughts, words, and works may tend to the honor and glory of thy name, the good of thy Church, the discharge of our duties, and the salvation of our souls in the day of our appearance and account to be made before thee, through JESUS CHRIST our only Savior and Redeemer. Amen.

O eternal GOD and merciful FATH ac, we humbly beseech thee, bless thy holy Catholic Church, wheresoever spread upon the whole earth. Good LORD, purge it from all heresy, schism, superstition, and factious maintenance of groundless opinions; that one faith, one LORD, one baptism, may in all places be uniformly professed, as thy Church is and can be but one. And grant that we here present may be, and continue, faithful, living, and working members under CHRIST the Head, in that Church the Body, all the days of our lives, and through the hour of our death; for the merits, and by the grace, of the same JESUS CHRIST our LORD and only Savior. Amen.

O merciful GOD, bless this particular Church in which we live; make it, and all the members of it, sound in faith, and holy in life; but especially so illuminate all its Bishops, Priests and Deacons, [Particularly N. or N., under whose care we are by thee placed,] with the true knowledge of CHRIST, and understanding of thy word, according as thy SPIRIT meant it; that both by their preaching and living, they may set it forth to thy glory, and that all thy people committed to their charge may from their mouths meekly hear thy word, receive it with pure affection, and through thy gracious assistance bring forth the fruits of the SPIRIT, for the honor of JESUS CHRIST, our Mediator and Advocate. Amen.

O LORD, bless all the afflicted members of the body of thy Son, wheresoever or howsoever distressed; [More especially those/or whom our prayers are desired;] send them constant patience, or speedy deliverance, as seems best to thee, and is best for them, according to their several wants and necessities whatsoever, known unto thee: And do unto them according to all those mercies, which we would desire you should show unto our own souls, if at any time you shall be pleased to make our estate as theirs is at this present. And this we beg of thee, O merciful FATHER, in the name, and for the' merits of thy dear SON CHRIST JESUS, our LORD and only Advocate. Amen.

The LORD bless this family, and keep us; the LORD lift up the light of his countenance upon us all, and give us peace now and for evermore.

Evening Prayer.

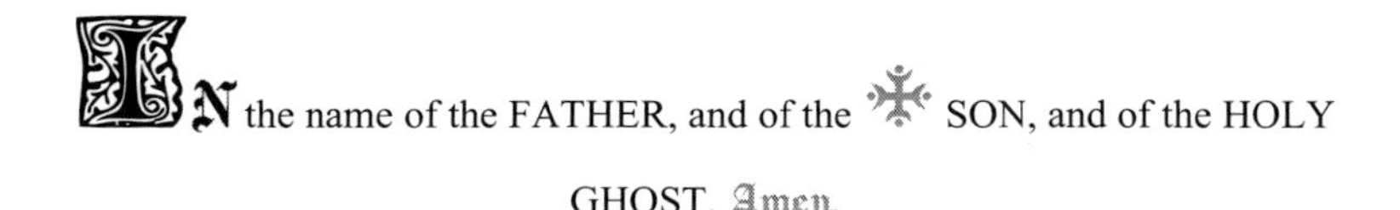

IN the name of the FATHER, and of the ✠ SON, and of the HOLY GHOST. Amen.

Blessed be the holy and undivided Trinity. Amen.

PSALM 2.

THIS day is past, and the night is come; but the day has taught us, and the night shall teach us also.

One day, O GOD, shall tell another of thy wondrous works; and one night shall certify another of thy marvelous goodness.

How deep are thy thoughts towards the children of men; and how unsearchable the ways of thy Providence!

As thy judgments, so thy mercies, are past finding out; and there is none in heaven or in earth that can utter the mighty acts of thy love.

GOD is exalted above all the earth; and as high as the heaven is in comparison of the earth, so high and so great is his mercy towards us.

Praise then the LORD, O ye nations of the earth; praise him, and his mighty deeds.

Praise the LORD in the heights; praise him also in the depths, O ye children of men.

Praise our LORD, all ye nations of the earth; O praise him for the mercies he has vouchsafed us.

Praise our LORD, ye happy nations of heaven; O praise him, ye saints, whom praise becomes.

But praise, alas! becomes not us; impure lips pollute the holy sacrifice.

Our lips should be first touched with a coal from the altar; we should first learn to praise him with our lives.

My GOD, when shall I thoroughly shake off this drowsiness; and rise, and run in the ways of thy commandments

What sweetness is it to think of thee What happiness to love thee

What an hell is it to be without thee What an heaven to possess thee

Overcome our perverse laziness, Almighty Goodness! and mercifully compel us to come to thee.

Add this one more, we beseech thee, to the vast heap of thy mercies; but one, without which all the rest are useless:

Give us effectually both to will and to do; and suffer not, LORD, thy grace in us to be void, and to return to thee empty.

Do you open our lips, and open our hearts; that so, loving thee perfectly, we may worthily praise thy holy name;

With angels and archangels, and with all the heavenly host of the blessed saints, that are now following the Lamb upon his holy hill.

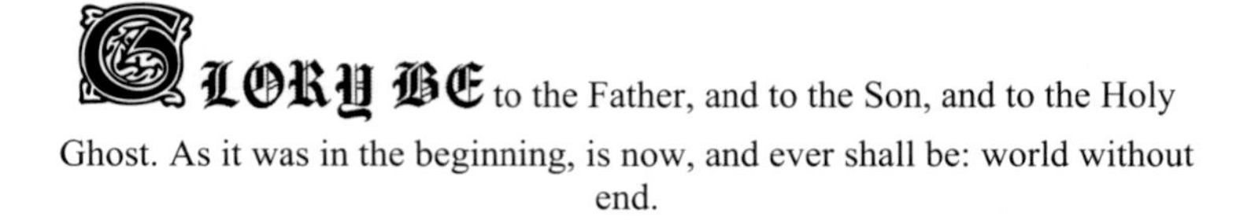

GLORY BE to the Father, and to the Son, and to the Holy Ghost. As it was in the beginning, is now, and ever shall be: world without end.

Amen.

PSALM 3.

PRAISE the LORD, ye heavens; praise him, O you Jerusalem which art above.

Let all the heavenly congregation praise him; let the whole church of the firstborn, written in heaven, praise him.

Let the spirits of the Prophets, and just men made perfect, praise him; let the souls of the Apostles, and all holy Martyrs, praise him.

O praise the LORD in his noble acts; and let all his saints rejoice before him with glory.

Let us praise him for his excellent greatness; let us praise him for the way by which he has appointed us to be happy.

By forsaking all things, we come to possess all things; and by our desire of nothing; we attain to want nothing.

By our being careful for nothing, but how to serve and please him, we come to be provided of all things.

As the heavens are above the earth, so is his wisdom above our reason.

How are the most cunning devices of human reason brought to nought by him! Yea, how has the LORD scattered the proud reasoner in the imaginations of his heart!

For the foolishness of GOD is wiser than the wisdom of men, and the weakness of GOD stronger than the strength of men.

So the race is not to the swift, nor the battle to the strong;

Neither is bread to the wise, nor favor to the skillful, nor riches to the understanding, nor honor to the learned.

But as our LORD distributes these, even so they are; in wisdom he disposes of them all, yet is there none that can find out his ways.

O'LORD, our GOD, how glorious art you in all thy works! and how excellent is thy name throughout the heavens and the earth!

You have showed strength, O LORD, with thy arm; and with the Son of thy righthand have you loosed the prisoners, and led captivity captive.

You feedest by him the hungry with the bread of life; by him you givest sight to the blind;

By him you have helped them that were fallen, and raised up those that were bowed down.

Therefore shall thy praises be in our hearts, and our mouths shall also speak the glorious honor of thy Majesty.

Day by day we will speak of the glory of thy empire; and night after night will we utter the memory of thy great goodness, and of thy tender mercies that are over all thy works.

All thy works shall praise thee, and we will bless thy name for ever.

Thy mercies shall be our songs of the night; and concerning thy righteousness, O GOD, will we sing and rejoice upon our beds.

Praise the LORD, O ye heavens; praise him, O you Jerusalem which art above. **Hallelujah**.

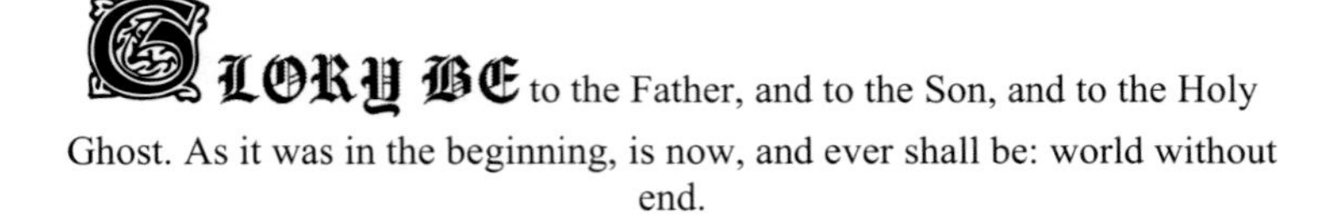

GLORY BE to the Father, and to the Son, and to the Holy Ghost. As it was in the beginning, is now, and ever shall be: world without end.

Amen.

Hallelujah.

ALMIGHTY and everlasting GOD, we render thee most humble and hearty thanks, for that you have vouchsafed of thy great goodness to preserve us this day; we beseech thee also to preserve and keep us this night from all danger, as well of body as of soul, but especially so enlighten the eyes of our souls, that we may never sleep in sin; that, being by thee graciously preserved, we may (if it be thy good pleasure) rise again in health to praise thy Majesty, and joyfully serve thee in thanksgiving, with chaste bodies and clean hearts; nor may fail finally of attaining thy everlasting light, through JESUS CHRIST Our LORD. Amen.

Save us, good LORD, waking, and keep us sleeping; that we may watch with CHRIST, and rest in peace. Amen.

Pause a while, to reflect on what you have now performed, and renew your attention.

 **GOD**, the comfortable Repose of thy servants in hope, and their blissful Rest in thy everlasting possession! Obedient to thy call by the voice of our nature, we retire, to lay down our weary heads; and, instructed by thy grace, confidently resign all we are and have, while we sleep, into the hands of thy ever waking Providence; most humbly beseeching thee, that if it please thee to take us hence this night, the eyes of our souls (as those of our bodies) may be found closed to all this world's goods, and at the same time wide open to receive thy ardently expected vision; or if you vouchsafest to protract our lives, we may rise from our beds cheerfully disposed, by works of faith and true righteousness, in our several vocations, to make our calling and election sure, and advance to our glorious mansion for ever with thee; through our LORD JESUS CHRIST, thy SON, who, with thee and the HOLY GHOST, lives and reigns, one GOD, world without end. Amen

O eternal, infinite, and Almighty God! whose goodness has vouchsafed to command us such things as are necessary to fit us for everlasting bliss, and forbid us such things as will make us eternally miserable; we, wretched sinners, the sinful offspring of our disobedient first parents, humbly prostrate our souls and bodies before the throne of thy adorable Majesty, to accuse and condemn ourselves with true and hearty sorrow for all the sins of our lives, and particularly for those we have committed this day by thought, word, or deed, against thy holy laws, provoking most justly thy wrath and indignation against us. We confess them with shame and confusion of face before thee, humbly beseeching thee to have pity upon us, according to thy great goodness, and according to the multitude of thy tender mercies, blot out our transgressions. But as is thy Majesty so is thy Mercy, O gracious FATHER, and therefore we beseech thee to hear our humble supplication, for the forgiveness of our sins: Forgive them all, O LORD, of what kind or degree soever they be; our sins of omission, and our sins of commission; the sins of our youth, and the sins of our riper years; the sins of our souls, and the sins of our bodies; our secret, and our more open sins; our sins of ignorance and surprise, and our more deliberate and presumptuous sins; the sins we have done to please ourselves, and the sins we have done to please others; the sins we know and remember, and the sins we have forgotten; the sins we have strove to hide from others, and the sins by which we have made others offend forgive them, O LORD, forgive them all for his sake, who died, for our sins, and rose again for our justification, and now stands at thy right hand to make intercession for us, JESUS CHRIST our LORD. Amen.

The Litany for Family Worship

Here followeth the LITANY, to be used after morning or evening prayer for a family, especially upon days of fasting and abstinence, or at other times, according to the discretion of the head of the family.

 GOD, the FATHER, Creator of the world,

Have mercy upon us.

O GOD the Son, Redeemer of mankind;

Have mercy upon us.

O GOD the HOLY GHOST, Sanctifier, Comforter, and Perfecter of the faithful;

Have mercy upon us.

Holy, holy, holy LORD GOD of all the hosts of heaven and earth;

Have mercy upon us.

O GOD, the eternalfulness of all perfection; the overflowing Source of all beings; the bountiful Author of all our good; O GOD, in whom we live, move, and have our being;

Have mercy upon us.

O GOD, who has made us out of nothing after thine own image, who preserve us every moment from returning into nothing; O GOD, who has made the world for our use, and us for thyself;

Have mercy upon us.

O GOD, who has prepared a glorious inheritance for those who love thee, and keep thy commandments; who art thyself that glorious inheritance and the end of all our labors;

Have mercy upon us.

O GOD, the only rest of our wearied souls, the only joy of our time and of our eternity; O GOD, our GOD, and all things that we can desire;

Have mercy upon us.

From all manner of evil, but especially from sin; from all occasions of offending thy divine Majesty, and from the particular temptations to which, by time, place, or temper, we are most exposed;

Deliver us, O LORD.

From the treachery of our own hearts, and the violence of our passions; from unprovided death here, and from everlasting death hereafter;

Deliver us, O LORD.

By thy almighty power and unsearchable wisdom; by thy adorable goodness, and all thy other glorious attributes;

Deliver us, O LORD.

By the mystery of thy holy incarnation, and humble birth; by the sanctity of thy heavenly doctrine, the perfect example of thy heavenly life; and by all the miracles you didst work for us;

Deliver us, O LORD.

By the merits of thy bitter passion and death; by thy victorious resurrection; by thy triumphant ascension, and by the glory of thy kingdom, who art King of Kings and LORD of LORDs, in the hour of death, and in the day of judgment;

Deliver us, O LORD.

WE sinners beseech thee to hear us, O LORD GOD; and that it may please thee to give us true repentance for all our past offences, and to work in us a firm and effectual resolution to amend our lives for the time to come;

We beseech thee to hear us, O LORD.

That it may please thee to pardon the sins of our life, and so to prevent and assist us with thy grace while we live here, that we may not fail to be eternally happy hereafter;

We beseech, &c.

That it may please thee to have pity on the infirmities of our frail nature, and in all our dangers, trials, and temptations, to strengthen and relieve us;

We beseech, &c.

That seeing our daily imperfections, we may quicken our diligence, depend on thee, and love to pray unto thee;

We beseech, &c.

That acknowledging all we have is derived from thy free bounty, we may delight to praise and glorify thee, and, above all thy benefits, love thee our Benefactor;

We beseech, &c.

That knowing all we hope for proceeds from thy free gracious promises, we may faithfully endeavor to serveand please thee, and secure to ourselves thy everlasting rewards;

We beseech, &c.

That believing you governest the world by thy providence, we may humbly and thankfully accept of any condition of life you assignest us, and not murmur at the part you givest us to act, but strive to act it well;

We beseech, &c.

That we may religiously observe the rules and duties of our several places, and contentedly submit to the meanest works of our condition;

We beseech, &c.

That we may live in peace and charity with all the world, especially among ourselves, united into one family, patiently forbearing, freely forgiving, and readily assisting one another;

We beseech, &c.

That in the midst of our daily business we may lift up our hearts to heaven, and thereby comfort and refresh our spirits, and increase our desires of a glorious eternity;

We beseech, &c.

That whether we sleep or wake, we may be safe under thy protection, who never slumberest or sleep; and whether we live or die, we may always be thine;

We beseech, &c.

SON of GOD, we beseech thee to hear us.

SON of GOD, we beseech thee to hear us.

 LAMB of GOD, that takest away the sins of the world; Grant us thy peace.

O LAMB of GOD, that takest away the sins of the world; Have mercy upon us.

ORD have mercy upon us.

CHRIST have mercy upon us.

LORD have mercy upon us.

OUR FATHER, which art in heaven, hallowed be thy name. Thy kingdom come. Thy will be done in earth, as it is in heaven. Give us this day our daily bread. And forgive us our trespasses, as we forgive them that trespass against us. And lead us not into temptation: But deliver us from evil. For thine is the kingdom, the power, and the glory, for ever and ever. Amen.

BLESS, O LORD, thy spouse, the holy Catholic Church; And evermore mightily defend her.

Deliver her from all strange doctrines, heresies, and schisms;

And bless her with truth, unity, and concord.

Clothe her Priests with righteousness and holiness;

And give her people grace to hold fast their holy profession, and adorn it with good works.

Comfort her where she is distressed;

And strengthen her where she is languishing and weak.

Deliver her where she is in danger;

And restore her where she is laid waste.

Bless her friends;

Convert her enemies.

Reduce those who have wandered from her fold;

And may all the kingdoms of the world be the kingdoms of our LORD and of his CHRIST. Bless all our kindred and acquaintance;

And abundantly reward our friends and benefactors.

Bless our enemies and slanderers, and all that persecute us, and despitefully use us.

Turn their hearts, O LORD, and make them become our f Mends.

Have mercy, O LORD, on the nations who do not know thee;

And those who knew thee once, but since have fallen from the truth.

Have mercy on the poor, helpless, and afflicted

And hear their prayers, when they cry unto thee.

Have mercy on us thy servants here assembled in thy presence;

And guard and defend us from all evil this day [night]. At night, add here as follows:

Keep us from the terror and danger of fire;

And from all assaults of wicked men and wicked spirits.

Into thy hands, O LORD, we commend our souls;

O LORD, our refuge, our strength, and our Redeemer.

Into thy hands, O LORD, we commend our spirits;

O bless us, and keep us this night without sin.

ACCEPT, O gracious FATHER, this our evening sacrifice of most humble and hearty thanks for all the mercies and blessings of this day, and not only of this day, but of all the days of our past lives. Thy daily care has been of us, and our daily praises are due unto thee, to whom we owe our being and well. being, even all that we are, and all that we have. You have ordained the day for labor and business, and the night for moderate and refreshing sleep; and now, in obedience to thy order and the voice of our nature, we desire to lay down our wearied heads upon our beds, humbly beseeching thee, that as you have dwelt with us this day, it may please thee to watch over us this night; and to grant each of us such convenient refreshment, as the necessities of our common nature make us stand in need of. Keep us, therefore, gracious LORD, in safety under the shadow of thy wings; for unto thy almighty protection we4 commit ourselves this night; humbly beseeching thee, that, after due rest, we may rise from our beds with thankful hearts, and return with cheerful dispositions to the duties of our several vocations, to glorify thee by our good works, through JESUS CHRIST our LORD; to whom, with thee, and the HOLY GHOST, be all honor and glory, world without end. Amen.

GOD the FATHER of our LORD JESUS CHRIST, the GOD of the Patriarchs and Prophets, the GOD of the Apostles, Martyrs and Confessors, and of all true believers, increase our faith, confirm our hope, and enlarge our charity; and grant that we may faithfully serve him, by doing and suffering his will all the days of our short pilgrimage here, and after death be made partakers of immortal glory. Amen.

THE grace of our LORD JESUS CHRIST, and the love of GOD, and the fellowship of the HOLY GHOST, be with us all. Amen.

Prayers of Intercession

For the Church.

O GOD, who gatherest thy flock out of all nations into the saving fold of one holy Catholic Church, purchased by the precious blood of thy Son, wherein you hast, in thy providence, graciously ordained Bishops. and Pastors to feed thy sheep and lambs; let thy continual pity cleanse and defend the same, and because without thee it cannot continue in safety, preserve it evermore by thy help and goodness; and so govern the minds of thy servants the Bishops, that they may never lay hands suddenly on any man, but may always make a wise and faithful choice of fit and worthy persons to serve in the ministry of thy church. Bless them all, we beseech thee, and their Clergy with courage and skill and fatherly care, to edify and guard their several charges by thee committed to them. Bless also the faithful with an humble filial love, and due obedience for thy sake, to their superiors whom you have set over them; that so the clearness of truth, and beauty of holiness, daily increasing in this thy church, through every one's devout pursuance of his duties, all may come at last into the way of truth, and hold the faith in unity of spirit, in the bond of peace, and in righteousness of life; all heresies and schisms may vanish away, and all Jews, Turks, and Infidels, may be brought home, and saved among the remnants of thy true Israelites, and be made with us, and with all who profess themselves Christians, one fold under one Shepherd, JESUS CHRIST our LORD, who liveth and reigneth with thee and the HOLY GHOST, one GOD, world without end. Amen.

For the State.

O GOD, by whom alone Kings reign, and all kinds and degrees of lawful magistracy are substituted, to provide for the public peace, among such infinite varieties of humors and interests; and by restraining private injuries, to remove the impediments of true charity, that so the whole state and each member be built up together, to their greatest fitness for thy heavenly kingdom. Preserve, we beseech thee, and govern with thy grace those whom you have adorned with thy power: Rule their hearts in thy faith, fear, and love, that they may not seek their own, but thy honor and glory only, O LORD of LORDs,' and King of Kings; and may at all times, and in all cases, truly and indifferently minister justice, to the punishment of all wickedness and vice, and to the furtherance of thy true religion and virtue. Make both them and their subjects to know that you reignest, that so they may seek in all things truly to obey and please thee, and Kings may be, indeed, the nursing fathers and Queens, the nursing mothers of the church. Grant this, O LORD, we humbly pray thee; and for this end save and defend all Christian Kings, Princes, and Governors; inspire them with a true zeal for thee, and so give by their means to all nations unity, peace, and concord, that they may become the kingdoms of thee and of thy Son; who, with thee and the HOLY GHOST, liveth and reigneth in the one only eternal Majesty, GOD and King for ever, world without end. Amen.

For All Conditions of Men

 LORD, who has commanded us to make prayers and supplications for all others as well as for ourselves, we beseech thee, O you Creator and Preserver of all mankind, for all sorts and conditions of men, that you wouldest be pleased to extend thy mercy to them all, to open and enlighten the eyes of them that sit in darkness, and to guide their feet into the way of peace; that thy ways may be made known upon earth, and thy saving health among all nations. More especially we pray for the good estate of all orders and degrees in thy church, that both Priests and people may, by their faith and holy conversation, shine as lights, set in candlesticks of gold: Distribute, therefore, thy graces and blessings to every one, as you shall judge most meet, and as may best fit, and enable, and encourage them in their several callings, in performance of their duties of worship and obedience to thee, and of justice, and truth, and charity to their brethren. Particularly bless and keep all those to whom we are bound by any special relation, whether of nature or otherwise. [And in special N. N. or N. N.] You knows our several desires and wants: Now, therefore, mercifully proportion thy blessings to every one accordingly, that we may be mutual helps and comforts in our passage through this vale of misery. Finally, we commend to thy fatherly goodness all those who are under any calamity in mind or body, or outward condition; more especially those that suffer for righteousness sake. Give them, we beseech thee, patience to bear, and prudence to make a right use of their afflictions, and, in thine own good time, relieve and restore them here, or take them to thine eternal rest, through thy mercies in JESUS CHRIST our LORD and mighty REDEEMER. Amen.

For Enemies.

O GOD, our heavenly FATHER, who makest thy sun to rise on the evil and on the good, and sendest rain on the just and unjust; and who of thy tender love towards us, while we were enemies, didst send thy beloved SON JESUS CHRIST to take upon him our flesh, and to suffer death for us upon the cross, that we might all follow the example of his great love and deep humility; mercifully grant that we may follow his most blessed example, and being filled with his SPIRIT, may learn to love and bless all those that trespass against us, and in any wise despitefully use us. Wherefore, we beseech thee, O merciful FATHER, in obedience to thy command, and in conformity to thy SON's practice, that it may please thee to forgive our enemies, persecutors, and slanderers; especially those that have either caused or increased the destructions in Church or State. Have mercy upon them, good LORD, have mercy upon them; remember not their offences, neither take you vengeance of their sins: Spare them, because they are the work of thy hands; spare them, because they are redeemed with thy SON's precious blood; and lay not to their charge whatever they have said or done against us thy servants, who stand bound unto thee in ten thousand talents. Deliver them both from the secret crafts and open assaults of their and our great enemy; open their eyes and hearts, that they may see and consider the errors of their own ways, and so turn into the straight path, walking therein in all meekness and brotherly love, in all charity, condescension, and humility; that we may live together in peace here, and reign together in thy glory hereafter; for the love of JESUS CHRIST our LORD, to whom, with thee and the HOLY GHOST, be all honor and glory, world without end. Amen.

For Friends and Natural Relations.

O GOD, our heavenly FATHER, who have commanded us to love one another, as thy children, and have ordained the highest friendship in the bond of thy SPIRIT; we beseech thee to preserve us always in the same bond, to thy glory, and our mutual comfort, with all those to whom we are bound by any special tie, either of nature or of choice; that we may be perfected together in that love which is from above, and which never faileth. Bless more particularly this family by thy grace; bless our kindred, our acquaintance, our friends, our benefactors, [especially N. or N. to whom, by the wisdom of thy providence, we are in a peculiar manner obliged,] and all thy servants whom you wiliest to be more nearly knit unto us in any relation whatever. Distribute thy blessings among them according as may, on all accounts, be fittest for them, O you that knows their several desires and necessities; give them such temporal blessings as it shall seem best unto thee, and may be most for the advancement of their eternal interest; but, above all, send down the dew of thy heavenly grace upon them, and pour the light of thy SPIRIT into their hearts, which may lead them steadfastly in thy way, and enable them to walk in the same all the days of their life; that we may have joy in each other that passes not away; and having lived together in love here, may live for ever together with them, in the glory of thy kingdom, through JESUS CHRIST our LORD. Amen.

For the Saints.

 ETERNAL FATHER, whose holy SPIRIT, by thy blessed Apostles, has planted in the world the saving doctrine of thy Son, and watered it with so much blood that it has overspread the earth, and borne much fruit to heaven! most thankfully we praise thee for the gracious lives and deaths of all thy saints here, and for the glorious crowns with which they are recompensed; beseeching thee to give us grace so to follow their good examples, applying home to our hearts their precious memories, that we, living and dying like them, may together with them be partakers also of thy heavenly kingdom, and numbered with these thy holy ones in glory everlasting. Grant this, O FATHER, for the merits of JESUS CHRIST, our only Mediator and Advocate. Amen.

For a Sick Family Member.

 SOVEREIGN LORD of life and death! by the order of whose providence thy servant now lies dangerously sick, and summons the utmost of our charity in his [or her] assistance; hear, we beseech thee, our humble supplications for him, that, if possible, this sickness may only be for thy greater glory, and he recover his health, better instructed by this thy discipline duly to value and use it; or, if it must be to death, that he may be strengthened by thy grace to b ear the approaches to his dissolution, however painful, and yield up his soul with that courage and constancy as becometh a Christian. Hear us also, good LORD, for ourselves, and grant that wisely improving this opportunity of exercising our right judgments, both in discourse and practice with him, we may sink them deeper into our own selves, and thereby be more strongly disposed to pass

fearless through the same rough way to immortality, through our LORD JESUS CHRIST. Amen.

Spare thy people o lord

The Litany

Here follows the LITANY or GENERAL SUPPLICATION, to be said after Morning Prayer, chiefly upon the days of fasting and humiliation, or according as discretion or devotion shall prompt.

 **GOD** the FATHER of Heaven, Maker of all things,

Have mercy upon us.

O GOD the SON, Redeemer of the world,

Have mercy upon us.

O GOD the HOLY GHOST, Sanctifier of the Church,

Have mercy upon us.

Holy, blessed, and glorious Trinity, that art but one GOD,

Have mercy upon us.

Holy, holy, holy, LORD GOD Omnipotent, who art, who wast, and who art to come,

Have mercy, &c.

O GOD of GODs, who didst unto Moses manifest thy name, " I Am that I Am," whom the heaven of heavens cannot contain,

Have mercy, &c.

Everlasting King, immortal, invisible; who inhabitest that light unto which no man can approach, great in council and mighty in work, and of whose wisdom there is no end,

Have mercy, &c.

Who only doest great things, and unsearchable marvelous things without number; who workest all things according to the purpose of thy will, and madest all things for thyself,

Have mercy, &c.

One GOD and Father of us all, who art above all, and through all, and in us all; from whom, by whom, and in whom are all things; in whom we live and have our being;

Have mercy, &c.

O GOD, who have disposed of all things in number, weight, and measure, who madest heaven and earth, and all things therein, who createdst the earth by thy power, and the universe by thy wisdom,

Have mercy, &c.

The LORD forming light and creating darkness, making peace and creating evil for punishment of transgressors; in whose hand is the life of every living thing, and the breath of all flesh,

Have mercy, &c.

O LORD, who searchest the heart and triest the reins, who quickenest the dead, and tallest those things that were not, as if they; were whose eyes are brighter than the sun, beholding all the ways of men,

Have mercy, &c.

O LORD GOD, who killest and makest alive, who sendest to the grave and bringest back again, who increasest the nations and destroyest them, who enlargest the nations and straitenest them,

Have mercy, &c.

O God, who takest no pleasure in iniquity, with whom is no acceptance of persons, terrible in thy counsels concerning the sons of men, the strong and jealous GOD, visiting the iniquities of the fathers upon the children,

Have mercy, &c.

O God, whose anger none can withstand, but whose mercy is above all thy works; O GOD most gracious, showing mercy even to a thousand generations,

Have mercy, &c.

The LORD, compassionate, longsuffering, of great mercy and truth, our Protector and exceeding great Reward,

Have mercy, &c.

O Father of mercies, and GOD of all consolation, who only can comfort us in all our tribulations,

Have mercy, &c.

O God, who by the death of thy Son has redeemed, and by the grace of thy SPIRIT dost sanctify us, and all thy faithful people,

Have mercy, &c.

Have mercy, O LORD, and spare us

Have mercy, &c.

Have mercy, O LORD, and hear us:

Have mercy, &c.

FROM all evil and from all sin, but particularly from all pride, obstinacy, and vainglory, and from all covetousness, Deliver us, O LORD.

From gluttony and surfeiting, from envy and hatred, from anger and illwill, from luxury and uncleanness, from does and inordinate heaviness, and anxiety,

Deliver us, &c.

From all hypocrisy, and all uncharitableness, from all baseness and cowardice, from all blindness and hardness of heart;

Deliver us, &c.

By the might of thy omnipotency, by the Majesty of thy glory, and by the multitude of thy mercies;

Deliver us, &c.

Now, and at all times, when we look unto thee; but especially in the hour of death, and in the clay of judgment;

Deliver us, &c.

WE sinners beseech thee to hear us, O LORD; that it would please thee to give us thy grace that we may worship thee our LORD GOD, in spirit and in truth;

We beseech thee to hear us, O LORD.

That we may love thee with all our hearts, with all our minds, with all our souls and with all our strength; that we may steadfastly believe in thee, give thee thanks always, and put our trust in thee;

We beseech, &c.

That we may honor thy holy name and thy word, that we may remember our covenant with thee in baptism, and all our renewed vows to adhere unto thee only, against all manner of opposition from the world, the flesh, or the Devil;

We beseech, &c.

That we may love our neigbour as ourselves; that we may do to all men as we would they should do unto us;

We beseech, &c.

That we may obey and reverence our parents and superiors, and may submit ourselves to every ordinance of man for thy sake;

We beseech, &c.

That we may be perfectly true and just in all our dealings, that we may injure no man's life, good name or honor, and may be ready to do them all the good we can;

We beseech, &c.

That we may forbear one another in love, being careful to keep the unity of the SPIRIT in the bond of peace; that we may bear one another's burdens, and so fulfil the law of GOD;

We beseech, &c.

That you wouldest cleanse our hearts from all inordinate desires and impure affections, by pouring into us thy holy love; that we may obtain the true love of thee and our neighbors, with the contempt of ourselves and the things of this world;

We beseech, &c.

That we may present our bodies a living and holy sacrifice, wellpleasing to thee, and at length attain to that kingdom which you have prepared for us from the beginning of the world;

We beseech, &c.

That it may please thee to rule thy Church universal, as in the beginning; and to deliver the same, in every branch thereof, from all false doctrine, heresy and schism;

We beseech, &c.

That you wouldest give to all Christian Princes and states, unity, peace, and firm concord, with zeal for thy glory;the same, thy name may be great among all the Gentiles, and that all the kingdoms of the earth may become the kingdoms of thy SON;

We beseech, &c.

That thy kingdom may come into us, and all that truly call upon thee, with peace, righteousness, and joy in the HOLY SPIRIT; and that both thy name may be sanctified, and thy will done in us and by us on earth, as it is done in heaven by thy holy angels;

We beseech, &c.

That you wouldest be pleased to give us, with all thy faithful people, this day our daily bread, spiritual and bodily;

We beseech, &c.

That you wouldest graciously forgive us our trespasses as we forgive them that trespass against us; and lead us not into temptation, or suffer us not to be tempted above what weare able, but deliver us from the evil one, and all evil;

We beseech, &c.

That you wouldest have mercy upon all Jews, Turks, Infidels, and Heretics, and take from them all ignorance, stubbornness, pride, and contempt of thy word;

We beseech, &c.

That you wouldest open and enlighten the eyes of all them that sit in darkness, and in the shadow of death; and guide their feet into the way of peace;

We beseech, &c.

That you wouldest bring into the way of truth all such as have erred or are deceived by themselves and others, and fetch all wandering souls home to thy flock;

We beseech, &c.

That you wouldest vouchsafe to strengthen all such as stand, to comfort and assist all that are weak and broken, and to raise up again them that fall;

We beseech, &c.

That you wouldest vouchsafe to defend the cause of the orphans and widows, to succor all that are desolate and

We beseech, &c.

That from the rising of the sun even unto the setting of oppressed, and to have pity upon all that are under any calamity in body or mind, or outward estate;

We beseech, &c.

That you wouldest give them perfect patience in all their afflictions, and wisdom to receive spiritual profit by all that thine hand has laid upon them;

We beseech, &c.

That neither by frailty, enticements, or any tortures, you wouldest permit any of us to fall from thee, but wouldest perfect thy praise in us by the steadfastness of our faith, and by the invincibleness of our charity;

We beseech, &c.

That you wouldest hear always the prayers of thy Church; and that whatever we faithfully ask, either for ourselves or for others, may through thy grace be effectually obtained;

We beseech, &c.

O FATHER, in the name of thy SON,

We beseech, &c.

O LORD, our Protector, behold us; And look upon the face of thy CHRIST. Remember thy people, O LORD, with thy good pleasure; And visit them with thy salvation.

Convert us, O LORD GOD of hosts;

And show us the light of thy countenance. Let thy Priests be clothed with righteousness; And make thy faithful people joyful. Turn the scourge of thine anger from the earth; And give peace in our time, O LORD.

 Lamb of GOD, that takest away the sins of the world;

Grant us thy peace.

O LAMB of GOD, &c.

Have mercy upon us.

O Lamb of GOD, &c.

Send thy HOLY SPIRIT into us.

OUR FATHER, which art in heaven, hallowed be thy name. Thy kingdom come. Thy will be done in earth, as it is in heaven. Give us this day our daily bread. And forgive us our trespasses, as we forgive them that trespass against us. And lead us not into temptation: But deliver us from evil. For thine is the kingdom, the power, and the glory, for ever and ever. Amen.

Save thy servants, O LORD;

And send us help, from thy holy place

O Almighty everlasting GOD, by whose SPIRIT the whole body of thy Church is sanctified and governed, mercifully hear us for all estates of the same; that by all degrees you mayst be faithfully served and glorified, from the gift of thy grace, through JESUS CHRIST, our LORD. Amen.

The Collects

After which may be added one or more of the following COLLECTS, according to discretion.

I.

O GOD, the Author of peace, and the Lover of charity, give, we beseech' thee, unto all our enemies that peace and charity which are thy gift, and are without all hypocrisy; and mercifully grant unto them forgiveness of all their sins, and unto us protection from all their snares and assaults; that we, securely trusting in thy almighty defense, may not fear either the policy or the power of our adversaries, but may evermore give thanks unto thee for thy great deliverances and mercies to us; through CHRIST our LORR. Amen.

II.

BLESSED GOD, from whom all holy desires, all good designs, and all just enterprises do proceed, inspire, we humbly pray thee, all Christians Princes and states with principles of righteousness and peace; pour into their hearts reasonable and religious desires, instruct them secretly with good counsels and wise resolutions, for the honor and peace of the Church, and for the true interest of them and their subjects: And so bring down the pride of man, disarm the power, baffle the designs, and confound the devices, of all that put their confidence not in thee, but in their own strength, and sacrifice to their own nets; that so thy servants being armed with thy defense, and secure from the fear of their enemies, may in thy holy Church pass their time in rest and quietness; through the merits of JESUS CHRIST our SAVIOR Amen.

III.

 **GOD** of peace, and Author of concord, whom to know is to live, and whom to serve is to reign, mercifully defend us thy humble servants in all assaults of our enemies; that we, putting our whole trust and confidence in thee our mighty Deliverer, and only Refuge, may not be afraid of any weapons of the enemy, but may continually triumph in thy salvation; through the might of JESUS CHRIST our LORD. Amen.

IV.

 **GOD**, who rulest in the kingdoms of men, and in whose hand are the hearts of the Kings and mighty ones of the earth which you turnest as the course of waters is turned; so dispose all hearts, and remove all obstacles, that none may longer have the will, much less the power, to hinder the establishment of thy peaceful kingdom throughout all the Churches: And give hereby to all nations unity, peace, and concord; that the course of the world may be so peaceably ordered, according to thy holy will, that thy Church universal may joyfully serve thee in all Godly quietness; through JESUS CHRIST our LORD. Amen.

 **PROVIDENT LORD**, who permittest the power of darkness in this world to persecute the children of light; that their sufferings may exercise themselves, and attest to those without, the utter contempt of all temporal goods, in comparison of their eternal hope: Sustain us, we humbly beseech thee, against being shaken by the dread of men, or rage of Devils; support us under the present burden you have seen fit to lay upon us for our trial; maintain us by thy grace under all difficulties, in the strictest obedience to all thy commandments; and never suffer us basely to start from the cross, which we have been so powerfully commanded to take up, and therewith to follow Him who was made perfect by sufferings; neither suffer us to be discouraged at all by the outward prosperity of our persecutors: But grant that, in due compassion both to them and to ourselves, no temptation maybe able to sway us from our duty, or prevail on us to violate any obligation, public or private, that we may stand in, and may we be ready continually to render them all good offices, and to pray unto thee forthem, that you wouldest not lay this sin to their charge, but have mercy upon them, and bring them back into the path of peace and true righteousness, through our LORD JESUS CHRIST. Amen.

Here may be added also one or other of the following COLLECTS, as discretion shall direct.

I.

MOST powerful and righteous LORD GOD, mercifully assist our prayers when we cry unto thee, powerfully defend the cause of thy truth against the face of the wicked, and put forth now thy right arm, and let those evils which the craft and subtlety of the Devil or man worketh against us be brought to nought, and by thy good Providence dispersed; that we thy servants, being hurt by no persecutions, may evermore glorify thee, and give thee thanks, through CHRIST our LORD. Amen.

II.

RANT, we beseech thee, O GOD, the Strength of all that put their trust in thee, that in all our sufferings here upon earth, for the testimony of thy truth, and for righteousness sake, we may steadfastly look up to heaven, and by faith behold the glory that shall be revealed, and being filled with the HOLY GHOST, may learn to love and bless our persecutors, by the examples that you have set before us: And that we may not be afraid through many tribulations and persecutions to enter into the kingdom of heaven; but may count all things dross and dung so we may but gain CHRIST. To whom with thee, O FATHER, and the HOLY GHOST, be all glory, now and for ever. Amen.

III.

KEEP, we beseech thee, O LORD, thy household the Church; and because it cannot continue in safety without thv succor, preserve it evermore by thy help and goodness; and let the course of this world be so peaceably ordered by thy government, that we and all the members of thy Church may henceforth joyfully serve thee in all Godly quietness, through JESUS CHRIST our LORD. Amen.

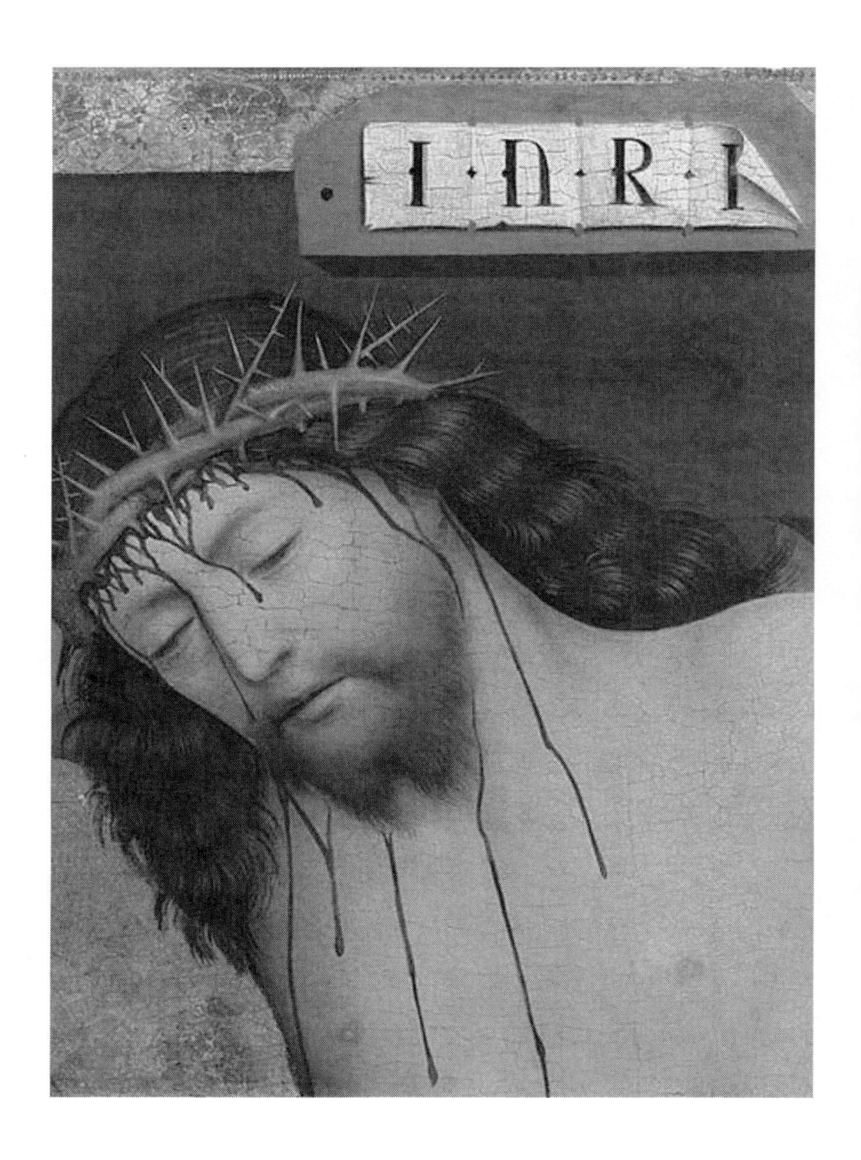
I·N·R·I

Private Prayers for Persons in Deep Affliction.

O MOST blessed, and gracious GOD, who only can heal a wounded spirit, and quiet a troubled mind, look with pity on the misery of thy most unworthy creature, that load of misery which I feel within me, but am not able to express. Unto thee do I cry for help, O you great Physician of body and soul: Uphold and comfort my weak and dejected spirit. As you alone can relieve me, so unto thee do I call for relief; O hear my most earnest supplication, and make me to possess an easy, quiet, and cheerful spirit, as my trust is in thee. I ask this, O LORD, as the greatest of blessings you can bestow upon me; I ask it, because I cannot enjoy any other of thy blessings without it; I ask it, because you alone can give it; and if you art pleased to glorify thy goodness in granting this my earnest request, then shall I serve thee faithfully, with a cheerful and thankful heart, and glorify thy goodness, all the remainder of my life, through JESUS CHRIST My LORD. Amen.

O blessed JESUS, who has made man, and who in our nature tookest our infirmities, and wast once exceeding sorrowful unto death, and who in anguish of spirit upon the cross, cried out to thy FATHER, and our FATHER, " My GOD, my GOD, why have you forsaken me!" O you most merciful, faithful, and unchangeable High Priest, who wast made like unto thy brethren, and can not but be touched with the sense of our infirmities, I beseech thee by thy infinite compassion to look down from heaven upon me, who am a miserable object of thy pity, being sore afflicted, and sore let and hindered in the course of my Christian duties by sadness and dejection of spirit. You knows, O LORD, how exceedingly my soul is troubled: You seest how much it is disquieted within me; I take no delight in any thing I do, no not in my spiritual exercises. I am wholly indisposed for my own business, and loathe to do any thing, even to pray unto thee, though I will not forbear to pray unto thee, O LORD, my Strength and my Redeemer. I beseech thee, blessed SAVIOR, hear my complaint, and take away this plague from me. It is with this most earnest petition that I now he prostrate at the throne of mercy: Remove it, I beseech thee, be it fixed in the body, or In the soul, of thy afflicted servant, or in both; speak but the word, and I shall be whole. I ask this in submission to thy good will and pleasure: If it is sent to me to punish me for my sins past, or restrain me from sins to come, or to correct my pride, or exercise my patience and trust in thee, not my will but thine be done. I am content to bear it to my life's end: If you shall think fit to continue it, and support me under it with the assistances of thy HOLY SPIRIT. But if it please thee, O let this torment of soul depart from me, that, being restored to an easy, free, cheerful, and active spirit, I may serve thee with delight, and vigor, in all the duties of my heavenly calling, and enjoy all other blessings and comforts of life, which you art pleased to continue unto me, and better bear any other sufferings which you shall fit, for the exercise of my patience, to lay upon me. O LORD, hear this prayer, which in anguish of spirit I make unto thee. I come to thee at this time in hopes to obtain this great mercy of thee, who art all mercy. O grant it for thy own merits' sake, who wast a man of sorrows, and acquainted with grief, and now live, and reignest with the FATHER, and the HOLY GHOST, one GOD, world without end. Amen.

Soliloquy of a Troubled Soul.

WHY art you so vexed, O my soul; and why art you so disquieted within me

The LORD has covered me with a cloud in his anger; and with darkness am I compassed about.

My soul is sore troubled; but, LORD, how long wilt you punish me

I am bowed down greatly; for mine iniquities are gone over my head, and as an heavy burden too heavy for me.

There is no peace in my spirit, for it is grievously wounded; neither is there quiet found in my soul, because the hand of the LORD presseth me hard.

And I said, Surely my strength and my hope are pershed from the LORD.

O my GOD, why have you caused the arrows of thy quiver to enter thus into my reins And why have you so filled me with bitterness, and made me drunk with wormwood

Why have you led me, and brought me into darkness; and turned thy hand against me all the day

You have removed my soul far off from peace, whence I go mourning all the day long.

But why art you so cast down, O my soul; and why art you so full of heaviness

Put thy trust yet in the LORD, of whose mercies it is that you art not utterly consumed.

It is good that you both hope and quietly wait for the salvation of the LORD, who will not cast off for ever.

But though he cause grief, yet will he have compassion according to the multitude of his mercies.

Hope you therefore in GOD, O my soul, for thy hope is not yet perished from the LORD; yea, hope you in GOD, for I shall yet praise him for the help of his countenance.

He will make me to hear of joy and gladness, that the bones which have been broken may rejoice.

Return therefore unto thy rest, O my soul; and be no longer disquieted within me.

Return unto thy rest, O my soul, in GOD: For he is thy resting place and thy salvation.

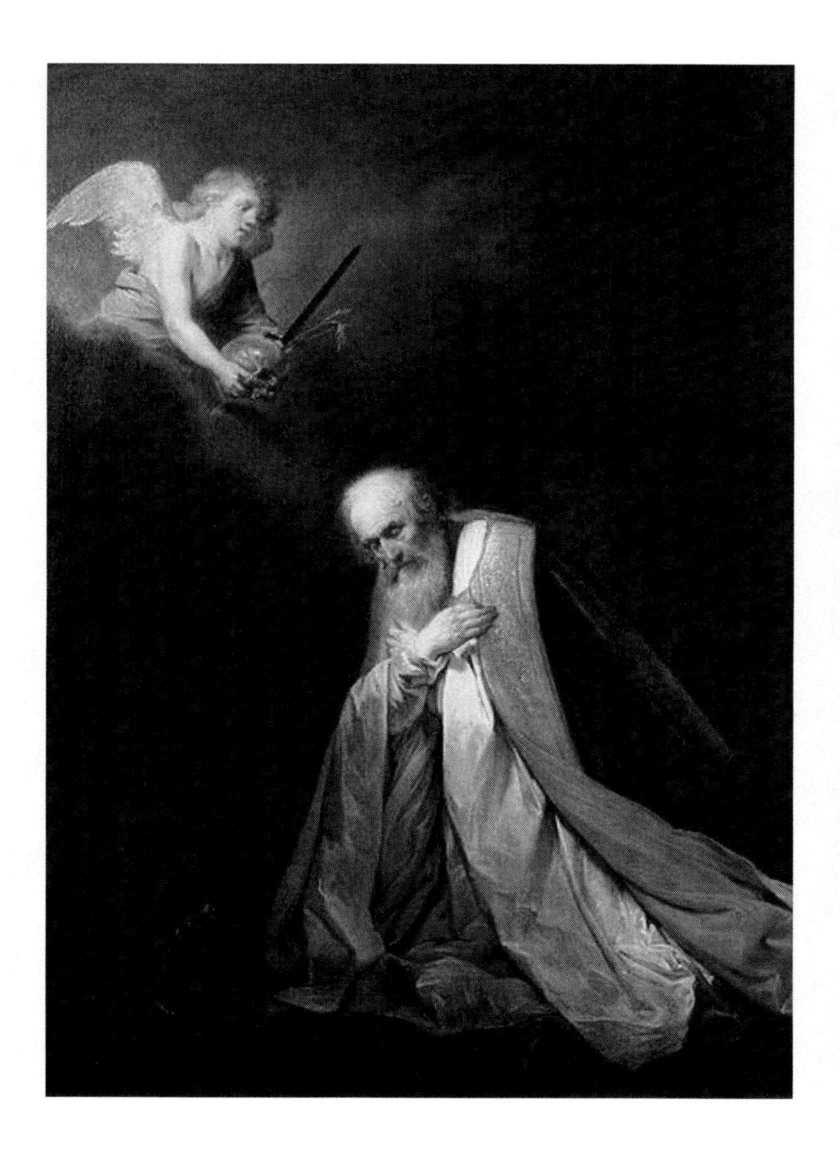

The Psalter

Adapted from John Wesley's, Sunday Service of the People called Methodists in North America.

PSALM 1

BLESSED is the man that hath not walked in the counsel of the ungodly, nor stood in the way of sinners: and hath not sat in the seat of the scornful.
2 But his delight is in the law of the Lord: and in his law will he exercise himself day and night.
3 He shall be like a tree planted by the water-side; that will bring forth his fruit in due season.
4 His leaf also shall not wither: and look, whatsoever he doeth, it shall prosper.
5 As for the ungodly, it is not so with them: but they are like the chaff which the wind scattereth away from the face of the earth.
6 Therefore the ungodly shall not be able to stand in the judgment: neither the sinners in the congregation of the righteous.
7 But the Lord knoweth the way of the righteous: and the way of the ungodly shall perish.

PSALM 2

WHY do the heathen so furiously rage together: and why do the people imagine a vain thing?

2 The kings of the earth stand up, and the rulers take counsel together: against the Lord, and against his Anointed.
3 Let us break their bonds asunder: and cast away their cords from us.
4 He that dwelleth in heaven shall laugh them to scorn: the Lord shall have them in derision.
5 Then shall he speak unto them in his wrath: and vex them in his sore displeasure.
6 Yet have I set my King: upon my holy hill of Sion.
7 I will declare the decree; the Lord hath said unto me: Thou art my Son, this day have I begotten thee.
8 Desire of me, and I shall give thee the heathen for thine inheritance: and the uttermost parts of the earth for thy possession.
9 Thou shalt bruise them with a rod of iron: and break them to pieces like a potter's vessel.
10 Be wise now, therefore, O ye kings: be learned, ye that are judges of the earth.
11 Serve the Lord in fear: and rejoice unto him with reverence.
12 Kiss the Son, lest he be angry, and so ye perish from the right way: when his wrath is kindled but a little. Blessed are all they that put their trust in him.

PSALM 3

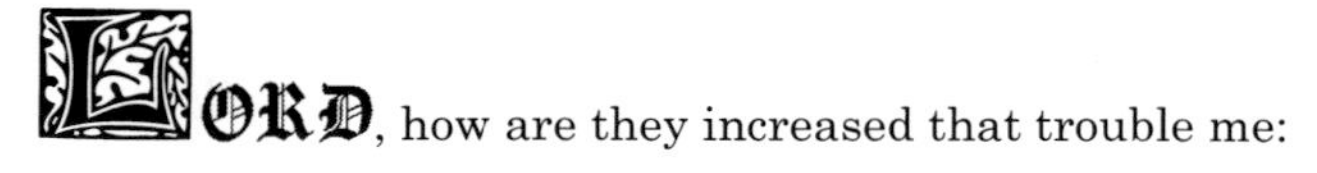
LORD, how are they increased that trouble me:
many are they that rise against me.
2 Many are they that say of my soul: There is no help for him in his God.
3 But thou, O Lord, art my defender: thou art my glory, and the lifter up of my head.
4 I did call upon the Lord with my voice: and he heard me out of his holy hill.

5 I laid me down and slept, and rose up again: for the Lord sustained me.
6 I will not be afraid for ten thousands of the people: that have set themselves against me round about.
7 Up, Lord, and help me, O my God: for thou smitest all mine enemies upon the cheek-bone; thou hast broken the teeth of the ungodly.
8 Salvation belongeth unto the Lord: and thy blessing is upon thy people.

PSALM 4

EAR me when I call, O God of my righteousness: thou hast set me at liberty when I was in trouble; have mercy upon me, and hearken unto my prayer.
2 O ye sons of men, how long will ye blaspheme mine honor: and have such pleasure in vanity, and seek after lying?
3 Know this also, that the Lord hath chosen to himself the man that is godly: when I call upon the Lord, he will hear me.
4 Stand in awe, and sin not: commune with your own heart, and in your chamber, and be still.
5 Offer the sacrifice of righteousness: and put your trust in the Lord.
6 There are many that say: Who will show us any good?
7 Lord, lift thou up: the light of thy countenance upon us.
8 Thou hast put gladness in my heart: more than in the time that their corn and their wine increased.
9 I will lay me down in peace, and take my rest: for it is thou, Lord, only that makest me dwell in safety.

PSALM 5

PONDER my words, O Lord: consider ray meditation.

2 O hearken thou unto the voice of my calling, my King and my God: for unto thee will I make my prayer.
3 My voice shalt thou hear betimes, O Lord: early in the morning will I direct my prayer unto thee, and will look up.
4 For thou art the God that hast no pleasure in wickedness: neither shall any evil dwell with thee.
5 Such as be foolish shall not stand in thy sight: for thou hatest all them that work vanity.
6 Thou shalt destroy them that speak lies: the Lord will abhor both the blood-thirsty and deceitful man.
7 But as for me, I will come into thine house, even upon the multitude of thy mercy: and in thy fear will I worship toward thy holy temple.
8 Lead me, O Lord, in thy righteousness, because of mine enemies: make thy way plain before my face.
9 And let all them that put their trust in thee rejoice: they shall ever be giving of thanks, because thou defendest them; they that love thy name shall be joyful in thee.
10 For thou, Lord, wilt give thy blessing unto the righteous: and with thy favorable kindness wilt thou defend him, as with a shield.

PSALM 6

LORD, rebuke me not in thine indignation: neither chasten me in thy displeasure.
2 Have mercy upon me, O Lord, for I am weak: O Lord, heal me; for my bones are vexed.

3 My soul also is sore troubled: but, Lord, how long wilt thou punish me?
4 Turn thee, O Lord, and deliver my soul: save me, for thy mercy's sake.
5 For in death no man remembereth thee: and who will give thee thanks in the pit?
6 I am weary of my groaning: every night wash I my bed, and water my couch with my tears.
7 My beauty is gone for very trouble: and worn away because of all mine enemies.
8 Away from me, all ye that work vanity: for the Lord hath heard the voice of my weeping.
9 The Lord hath heard my petition: the Lord will receive my prayer.
10 All mine enemies shall be confounded, and sore vexed: they shall be turned back, and put to shame suddenly.

PSALM 7

 **LORD**, my God, in thee have I put my trust: save me from all them that persecute me, and deliver me;
2 Lest he devour my soul like a lion: and tear it in pieces while there is none to help.
3 O Lord, my God, if I have done any such thing: or if there be any wickedness in my hands;
4 If I have rewarded evil unto him that dealt friendly with me: (yea, I have delivered him that without any cause is mine enemy ;)
5 Then let mine enemy persecute my soul, and take me: yea, let him tread my life down upon the earth, and lay mine honor in the dust.
6 Stand up, O Lord, and lift up thyself because of the indignation of mine enemies: arise up for me to the judgment that thou hast commanded.

7 And so shall the congregation of the people come about thee: for their sakes therefore lift up thyself again.
8 The Lord shall judge the people; give sentence with me, O Lord: according to my righteousness, and according to the innocency that is in me.
9 O let the wickedness of the ungodly come to an end: but guide thou the just.
10 For the righteous God: trieth the very hearts and reins.
11 My help cometh of God: who preserveth them that are true of heart.
12 God is a righteous Judge, strong and patient: and God is provoked every day.
13 If a man will not turn, he will whet his sword: he hath bent his bow, and made it ready.
14 He hath prepared for him the instruments of death: he ordaineth his arrows against the persecutors.
15 Behold, he travaileth with mischief: he hath conceived sorrow, and brought forth ungodliness.
16 He hath graven and digged up a pit: and is fallen himself into the destruction that he made for others.
17 I will give thanks unto the Lord, according to his righteousness: and I will praise the name of the Lord most high.

PSALM 8

 **LORD** our Governor, how excellent is thy name in all the world: thou that hast set thy glory above the heavens!
2 Out of the mouths of very babes and sucklings hast thou ordained strength, because of thine enemies: that thou mightest still the enemy and the avenger.
3 I will consider thy heavens, even the works of thy fingers: the moon and the stars which thou hast ordained.

4 What is man, that thou art mindful of him: and the son of man, that thou visitest him?
5 Thou madest him a little lower than the angels: to crown him with glory and honor.
6 Thou makest him to have dominion over the works of thy hands: and thou hast put all things in subjection under his feet;
7 All sheep and oxen: yea, and the beasts of the field;
8 The fowls of the air, and the fishes of the sea: and whatsoever passeth through the paths of the seas.
9 O Lord our Governor: how excellent is thy name in all the world!

PSALM 9

 **WILL** give thanks unto thee, O Lord, with my whole heart: I will speak of all thy marvelous works.
2 I will be glad and rejoice in thee: yea, my songs will I make of thy name, O thou most Highest.
3 When mine enemies are driven back: they shall fall and perish at thy presence.
4 For thou hast maintained my right and my cause: thou art set in the throne judging right.
5 Thou hast rebuked the heathen, and destroyed the ungodly: thou hast put out their name forever and ever.
6 O thou enemy, destructions are come to a perpetual end: even as the cities which thou hast destroyed; their memorial is perished with them.
7 But the Lord shall endure forever: he hath also prepared his seat for judgment.
8 For he shall judge the world in righteousness: and minister true judgment unto the people.

9 The Lord will also be a defense for the oppressed: even a refuge in times of trouble.

10 And they that know thy name will put their trust in thee: for thou, Lord, hast never failed them that seek thee.

11 O praise the Lord, who dwelleth in Sion: show the people his doings.

12 For when he maketh inquisition for blood, he remembereth them: and forgetteth not the complaint of the humble.

13 Have mercy upon me, O Lord; consider the trouble which I suffer of them that hate me: thou that liftest me up from the gates of death.

14 That I may show all thy praises within the gates of the daughter of Sion: I will rejoice in thy salvation.

15 The heathen are sunk down in the pit that they made: in the same net which they hid privily is their foot taken.

16 The Lord is known to execute judgment: the ungodly is trapped in the work of his own hands.

17 The wicked shall be turned into hell: and all the people that forget God.

1 8 For the poor shall not always be forgotten: the patient abiding of the meek shall not perish forever.

19 Up, Lord, and let not man have the upper hand: let the heathen be judged in thy sight.

20 Put them in fear, O Lord: that the heathen may know themselves to be but men.

PSALM 10

WHY standest thou so far off, O Lord: and hidest thy face in the needful time of trouble?

2 The ungodly, for his own lust, doth persecute the

poor: they shall be taken in the crafty wiliness that they have imagined.

3 For the ungodly hath made boast of his own heart's desire: and speaketh good of the covetous, whom God abhorreth.

4 The ungodly is so proud, that he careth not for God: neither is God in all his thoughts.

5 His ways are always grievous: thy judgments are far above out of his sight, and therefore defieth he all his enemies.

6 Arise, O Lord God, and lift up thine hand: forget not the poor.

7 Wherefore should the wicked blaspheme God: while he doth say in his heart, Thou God carest not for it?

8 Surely thou hast seen it: for thou beholdest ungodliness and wrong.

9 That thou mayest take the matter into thy hand: the poor committeth himself unto thee; for thou art the helper of the friendless.

10 Break thou the power of the ungodly and malicious: seek out his wickedness till thou find none.

11 The Lord is King forever and ever: and the heathen are perished out of the land.

12 Lord, thou hast heard the desire of the poor: thou preparest their heart, and thine ear hearkeneth thereto;

13 To help the fatherless and poor unto their right: that the man of the earth be no more exalted against them.

PSALM 11

IN the Lord I put my trust: how say ye then to my soul, that she should flee as a bird unto the hill?

2 For, lo, the ungodly bend their bow, and make

ready their arrows within the quiver: that they may privily shoot at them who are true of heart.

3 If the foundations be destroyed: what can the righteous do?

4 The Lord is in his holy temple: the Lord's seat is in heaven.

5 His eyes consider the poor: and his eyelids try the children of men.

6 The Lord trieth the righteous: but the ungodly, and him that delighteth in wickedness, doth his soul abhor.

7 Upon the ungodly he shall rain snares, fire and brimstone, storm and tempest: this shall be their portion to drink.

8 For the righteous Lord loveth righteousness: his countenance will behold the thing that is just.

PSALM 12

ELP me, Lord: for the faithful are minished from among the children of men.

2 They talk of vanity every one with his neighbor: they do but flatter with their lips, and dissemble in their double heart.

3 The Lord shall root out all deceitful lips: and the tongue that speaketh proud things;

4 Which have said, With our tongue will we prevail: we are they that ought to speak; who is Lord over us?

5 Now, for the comfortless troubles' sake of the needy: and because of the deep sighing of the poor;

6 I will up, saith the Lord: and will help every one from him that swelleth against him, and will set him at rest.

7 The words of the Lord are pure words: even as the silver, which from the earth is tried, and purified seven times in the fire.

8 Thou shalt keep them, O Lord: thou shalt preserve

them from this generation forever.
9 The ungodly walk on every side: when they arc exalted, the children of men are put to rebuke.

PSALM 13

OW long wilt thou forget me, O Lord? Forever?

How long wilt thou hide thy face from me?
2 How long shall I seek counsel in my soul, and be vexed in my heart? How long shall mine enemies triumph over me?
3 Consider, and hear me, O Lord, my God: lighten mine eyes, that I sleep not in death:
4 Lest mine enemy say, I have prevailed against him: for if I be cast down, they that trouble me will rejoice at it.
5 But my trust is in thy mercy: and my heart is joyful in thy salvation.
6 I will sing of the Lord, because he hath dealt so lovingly with me: yea, I will praise the Name of the Lord most Highest.

PSALM 15

ORD, who shall dwell in thy tabernacle: or who

shall rest upon thy holy hill?
2 Even he that leadeth an uncorrupt life: and doeth the thing which is right, and speaketh the truth from his heart;
3 He that hath used no deceit with his tongue, nor done evil to his neighbor: and hath not slandered his neighbor.
4 He that setteth not by himself, but is lowly in his own eyes: and maketh much of them that fear the Lord.

5 He that sweareth unto his neighbor, and disappointeth him not: though it were to his own hinderance.
6 He that hath not given up his money upon usury: nor taken reward against the innocent.
7 Whoso doeth these things: shall never fall.

PSALM 16

RESERVE me, O God: for in thee have I put my trust.
2 O my soul, thou hast said unto the Lord, Thou art my God: my goodness extendeth not to thee.
3 All my delight is upon the saints that are in the earth: and upon such as excel in virtue.
4 But they that run after another god: shall have great trouble.
5 Their drink-offerings of blood will I not offer: neither make mention of their names within my lips.
6 The Lord himself is the portion of mine inheritance, and of my cup: thou shalt maintain my lot.
7 The lot is fallen unto me in a fair ground: yea, I have a goodly heritage.
8 I will thank the Lord for giving me warning: my reins also chasten me in the night season.
9 I have set God always before me: for he is on my right hand, therefore I shall not fall.
10 Wherefore my heart is glad, and my glory rejoiceth: my flesh also shall rest in hope.
11 For why? thou shalt not leave my soul in hell: neither shalt thou suffer thy Holy One to see corruption.
12 Thou shalt show me the path of life; in thy presence is the fulness of joy: and at thy right hand there is pleasure forevermore.

PSALM 17

EAR the right, O Lord, consider my complaint:

and hearken unto my prayer, that goeth not out of feigned lips.

2 Let my sentence come forth from thy presence: and let thine eyes look upon the thing that is equal.

3 Thou hast proved, and visited mine heart in the night season; thou hast tried me, and shalt find no wickedness in me: for I am utterly purposed that my mouth shall not offend.

4 Because of men's works that are done against the words of thy lips: I have kept me from the ways of the destroyer.

5 O hold thou up my goings in thy paths: that my footsteps slip not.

6 I have called upon thee, O God, for thou shalt hear me: incline thine ear to me, and hearken unto my words.

7 Show thy marvelous lovingkindness, O thou that savest by thy right hand them who put their trust in thee: from those that rise up against them.

8 Keep me as the apple of an eye: hide me under the shadow of thy wings.

9 Arise, O Lord, and deliver my soul from the wicked: who are thy sword:

10 From men who are thy hand, O Lord; from men of the world: who have their portion in this life, and whose belly thou fillest with thy hid treasure.

11 They have children at their desire: and leave the rest of their substance for their babes.

12 But as for me, I will behold thy presence in righteousness: and when I awake up after thy likeness, I shall be satisfied with it.

PSALM 18. PART 1.

 **WILL** love thee, O Lord, my strength: the Lord is my stony rock and my defense; my Savior, my God, and my might, in whom I will trust; my buckler, the horn also of my salvation, and my refuge.

2 I will call upon the Lord, who is worthy to be praised: so shall I be safe from mine enemies.

3 The sorrows of death compassed me: and the overflowings of ungodliness made me afraid.

4 The pains of hell came about me: the snares of death overtook me.

5 In my trouble I will call upon the Lord: and complain unto my God.

6 So shall he hear my voice out of his holy temple: and my complaint shall come before him; it shall enter even into his ears.

7 The earth trembled and quaked: the very foundations also of the hills shook, and were removed, because he was wroth.

8 There went a smoke out in his presence, and a consuming fire out of his mouth: so that coals were kindled at it.

9 He bowed the heavens also, and came down: and it was dark under his feet.

10 He rode upon the cherubim, and did fly: he came flying upon the wings of the wind.

11 He made darkness his secret place: his pavilion round about him with dark water, and thick clouds to cover him.

12 At the brightness of his presence his clouds removed: hail-stones, and coals of fire.

13 The Lord also thundered out of heaven, and the Highest gave his voice: hail-stones, and coals of fire.

14 He sent out his arrows, and scattered them: he cast forth lightnings, and destroyed them.

15 The springs of water were seen, and the foundations of the round world were discovered at thy chiding,

O Lord: at the blasting of the breath of thy displeasure.
16 He shall send down from on high to fetch me: and shall take me out of many waters.
17 He shall deliver me from my strongest enemy, and from them who hate me: for they are too mighty for me.
18 They prevented me in the day of my trouble: but the Lord was my upholder.
19 He brought me forth also into a place of liberty: he brought me forth, even because he had a favor unto me.
20 The Lord shall reward me after my righteous dealing: according to the cleanness of my hands shall he recompense me.
21 Because I have kept the ways of the Lord: and have not forsaken my God, as the wicked doth.
22 For I have an eye unto all his laws: and will not cast his commandments from me.
23 I was also uncorrupt before him: and kept myself from mine own iniquity.
24 Therefore shall the Lord reward me after my righteous dealing: and according unto the cleanness of mine hands in his eye-sight.

PSALM 18. PART 2.

HOU shalt light my candle: the Lord my God shall make my darkness to be light.
2 The way of God is an undefined way: the word of the Lord is also tried in the fire; he is the defender of all them that put their trust in him.
3 For who is God but the Lord: or who hath any strength except our God?
4 It is God that girdeth me with strength of war: and maketh my way perfect.
5 He maketh my feet like harts' feet: and setteth me up on high.

6 He teacheth mine hands to fight: and mine arms shall break even a bow of steel.
7 Thou hast given me the defense of thy salvation: thy right hand also shall hold me up, and thy loving correction shall make me great.
8 Thou shall make room enough under me to go: that my footsteps shall not slide.
9 The Lord liveth; and blessed be my strong Helper: and praised be the God of my salvation.
10 It is he that delivereth me from my cruel enemies, and setteth me up above mine adversaries: thou shalt deliver me from the wicked man.
11 For this cause will I give thanks unto thee, O Lord, among the Gentiles: and sing praises unto thy Name.

PSALM 19

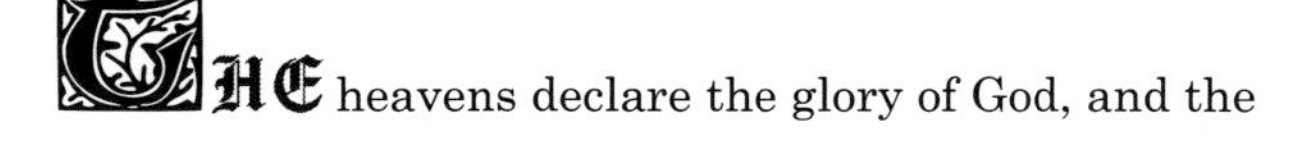
THE heavens declare the glory of God, and the firmament showeth his handy work.
2 One day telleth another: and one night certifieth another.
3 There is neither speech nor language: but their voices are heard among them.
4 Their sound is gone out into all lands: and their words unto the ends of the world.
5 In them hath he set a tabernacle for the sun: which cometh forth as a bridegroom out of his chamber, and rejoiceth as a giant to run his course.
6 It goeth forth from the uttermost part of the heaven, and runneth about unto the end of it again: and there is nothing hid from the heat thereof.
7 The law of the Lord is an undefiled law, converting the soul: the testimony of the Lord is sure, and giveth wisdom unto the simple.
8 The statutes of the Lord are right, and rejoice the

heart: the commandment of the Lord is pure, and giveth light unto the eyes.
9 The fear of the Lord is clean, and endureth for ever: the judgments of the Lord are true and righteous altogether.
10 More to be desired are they than gold, yea, than much fine gold: sweeter also than honey and the honey-comb.
11 Moreover by them is thy servant taught: and in keeping of them there is great reward.
12 Who can tell how oft he offendeth? O cleanse thou me from my secret faults.
13 Keep thy servant from all presumptuous sins, lest they get the dominion over me: so shall I be undefiled, and innocent from the great offence.
14 Let the words of my mouth, and the meditation of my heart, be always acceptable in thy sight,
15 O Lord, my Strength and my Redeemer.

PSALM 20

THE Lord hear thee in the day of trouble: the

I Name of the God of Jacob defend thee:
2 Send thee help from the sanctuary: and strengthen thee out of Sion.
3 We will rejoice in thy salvation, and triumph in the Name of the Lord our God: the Lord perform all thy petitions.
4 Now know I that the Lord helpeth his Anointed, and will hear him from his holy heaven: even with the wholesome strength of his right hand.
5 Some put their trust in chariots, and some in horses: but we will remember the Name of the Lord our God.
6 They are brought down, and fallen: but we are risen, and stand upright.

7 Save, Lord, and hear us, King of heaven: when we call upon thee.

PSALM 22. PART 1.

y God, my God, look upon me: why hast thou forsaken me; and art so far from helping me and from the words of my complaint?
2 O my God, I cry in the daytime, but thou hearest not: and in the night season also I take no rest.
3 But thou continuest holy: O thou Worship of Israel.
4 Our fathers hoped in thee: they trusted in thee, and thou didst deliver them.
5 They called upon thee, and were holpen: they put their trust in thee, and were not confounded.
6 But as for me, I am a worm, and no man: a very scorn of men, and the outcast of the people.
7 All they that see me, laugh me to scorn: they shoot out their lips, and shake their heads, saying,
8 He trusted in God, that he would deliver him: let him deliver him, if he will have him.
9 But thou art he that took me out of my mother's womb: thou wast my hope when I hanged yet upon my mother's breasts.
10 I have been left unto thee ever since I was born: thou art my God, even from my mother's womb.
11 O go not from me, for trouble is hard at hand: and there is none to help me.
12 I am poured out like water, and all my bones are out of joint: my heart also in the midst of my body is like melting wax.
13 My strength is dried up like a potsherd, and my tongue cleaveth to my gums: and thou hast brought me into the dust of death.
14 They pierced my hands and my feet; I may tell

all my bones: they stand staring and looking upon me.
15 They part my garments among them: and cast lots upon my vesture.
16 But be not thou far from me, O Lord: thou art my succour; haste thee to help me.
17 Deliver my soul from the sword: my darling from the power of the dog.
18 Save me from the lion's mouth: thou hast heard me also from among the horns of the unicorns.

PSALM 22. PART 2.

 WILL declare thy name unto my brethren: in the midst of the congregation will I praise thee.
2 O praise the Lord, ye that fear him: magnify him, all ye of the seed of Jacob; and fear him, all ye seed of Israel.
3 For he hath not despised, nor abhorred the low estate of the poor: he hath not hid his face from him; but when he called unto him, he heard him.
4 My praise is of thee in the great congregation: my vows will I perform in the sight of them that fear him.
5 The poor shall eat and be satisfied: they that seek the Lord shall praise him; your heart shall live forever.
6 All the ends of the world shall remember themselves, and be turned unto the Lord: and all the kindreds of the nations shall worship before him.
7 For the kingdom is the Lord's: and he is the Governor among the people.
8 All they that go down into the dust shall bow before him: and none can keep alive his own soul.
9 A seed shall serve him: they shall be accounted to the Lord for a generation.
10 They shall come, and the heavens shall declare nis righteousness: unto a people that shall be born,

whom the Lord hath made.

PSALM 23

THE Lord is my shepherd: therefore can I lack
I nothing.
2 He shall feed me in a green pasture: and lead me
forth beside the waters of comfort.
3 He shall convert my soul: and bring me forth in
the paths of righteousness, for his Name's sake.
4 Yea, though I walk through the valley of the
shadow of death, I will fear no evil: for thou art with
me; thy rod and thy staff comfort me.
5 Thou shalt prepare a table before me in the presence of them that trouble me: thou hast anointed my
head with oil, and my cup shall be full.
6 Surely thy lovingkindness and mercy shall follow
me all the days of my life: and I will dwell in the
house of the Lord forever.

PSALM 24

THE earth is the Lord's, and all that therein is: the
compass of the world, and they that dwell therein.
2 For he hath founded it upon the seas: and prepared it upon the floods.
3 Who shall ascend into the hill of the Lord: or who
shall rise up in his holy place?
4 Even he that hath clean hands and a pure heart:
and that hath not lifted up his mind unto vanity, nor
sworn to deceive his neighbor.
5 He shall receive the blessing from the Lord: and
righteousness from the God of his salvation.
6 This is the generation of them that seek him: even
of them that seek thy face, O Jacob.
7 Lift up your heads, O ye gates, and be ye lifted

up, ye everlasting doors: and the King of glory shall come in.
8 Who is the King of glory? It is the Lord, strong and mighty, even the Lord mighty in battle.
9 Lift up your heads, O ye gates, and be ye lifted up, ye everlasting doors: and the King of glory shall come in.
10 Who is the King of glory? Even the Lord of hosts, he is the King of glory.

PSALM 25

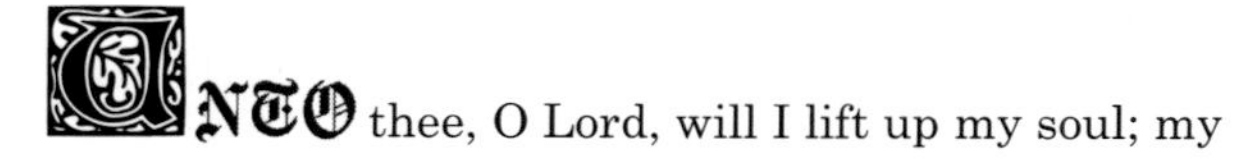
UNTO thee, O Lord, will I lift up my soul; my God, I have put my trust in thee: O let me not be confounded, neither let mine enemies triumph over me.
2 For all they that hope in thee shall not be ashamed: but such as transgress without a cause shall be put to confusion.
3 Show me thy ways, O Lord: and teach me thy paths.
4 Lead me forth in thy truth, and teach me: for thou art the God of my salvation; in thee hath been my hope all the day long.
5 Call to remembrance, O Lord, thy tender mercies: and thy lovingkindnesses, which have been ever of old.
6 O remember not the sins and offences of my youth: but according to thy mercy, think thou upon me, O Lord, for thy goodness.
7 Gracious and righteous is the Lord: therefore will he teach sinners in the way.
8 Them that are meek shall he guide in judgment: and such as are gentle, them shall he teach his way.
9 All the paths of the Lord are mercy and truth: unto such as keep his covenant and his testimonies.
10 For thy Name's sake, O Lord: be merciful unto

my sin; for it is great.
11 What man is he that feareth the Lord? him shall he teach in the way that he shall choose.
12 His soul shall dwell at ease: and his seed shall inherit the land.
13 The secret of the Lord is among them that fear him: and he will show them his covenant.
14 Mine eyes are ever looking unto the Lord: for he shall pluck my feet out of the net.
15 Turn thee unto me, and have mercy upon me: for I am desolate and in misery.
16 The sorrows of my heart are enlarged: O bring thou me out of my troubles.
17 Look upon my adversity and misery: and forgive me all my sin.
18 O keep my soul, and deliver me: let me not be confounded, for I have put my trust in thee.
19 Let perfectness and righteous dealing wait upon me: for my hope hath been in thee.
20 Deliver Israel, O God: out of all his troubles.

PSALM 26

E thou my Judge, O Lord, for I have walked innocently: my trust hath been also in the Lord, therefore shall I not fall.
2 Examine me, O Lord, and prove me: try my reins, and my heart.
3 For thy lovingkindness is ever before mine eyes: and I will walk in thy truth.
4 I have not dealt with vain persons: neither will I have fellowship with the deceitful.
5 I have hated the congregation of the wicked: and will not sit among the ungodly.
6 I will wash my hands in innocency, O Lord: and so will I go to thine altar.

7 That I may show the voice of thanksgiving: and tell of all thy wondrous works.
8 Lord, I have loved the habitation of thy house: and the place where thine honor dwelleth.
9 O shut not up my soul with the sinners: nor my life with the blood-thirsty.
10 As for me, I will walk innocently: O deliver me, and be merciful unto me.
11 My foot standeth right: I will praise the Lord in the congregation.

PSALM 27

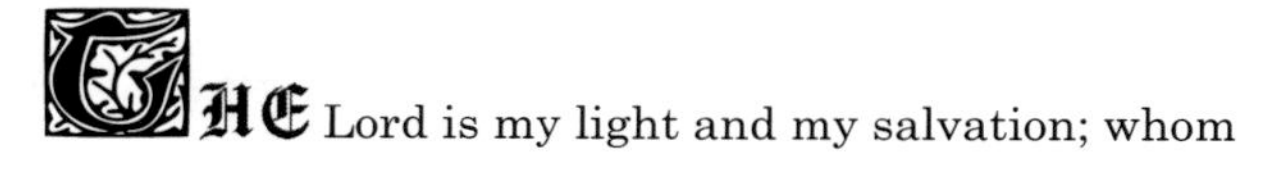

THE Lord is my light and my salvation; whom then shall I fear? the Lord is the strength of my life; of whom then shall I be afraid?
2 When the wicked, even mine enemies and my foes, came upon me to eat up my flesh: they stumbled and fell.
3 Though an host of men were encamped against me, yet shall not my heart be afraid: and though there rose up war against me, yet will I put my trust in him.
4 One thing have I desired of the Lord, which I will require: even that I may dwell in the house of the Lord all the days of my life, to behold the fair beauty of the Lord, and visit his temple.
5 For in the time of trouble he shall hide me in his tabernacle: yea, in the secret place of his dwelling shall he hide me, and set me upon a rock of stone.
6 And now shall he lift up mine head: above mine enemies round about me.
7 Therefore will I offer in his dwelling an oblation with great gladness: I will sing, and speak praises unto the Lord.
8 Hearken unto my voice, O Lord, when I cry unto thee: have mercy upon me, and hear me.

9 When them saidst, Seek ye my face: my heart said unto thee, Thy face, Lord, will I seek.
10 O hide not thou thy face from me: nor cast thy servant away in displeasure.
11 Thou hast been my succor: leave me not, neither forsake me, O God of my salvation.
12 When my father and my mother forsake me: the Lord taketh me up.
13 Teach me thy way, O Lord: and lead me in the right way, because of mine enemies.
14 Deliver me not over unto the will of mine adversaries: for there are false witnesses risen up against me, and such as speak wrong.
15 I should utterly have fainted: but that I believe verily to see the goodness of the Lord in the land of the living.
16 O tarry thou the Lord's leisure: be strong, and he shall comfort thine heart, and put thou thy trust in the Lord.

PSALM 28

NTO thee will I cry, O Lord, my strength: think no scorn of me; lest if thou make as though thou nearest not, I become like them that go down into the pit.
2 Hear the voice of my humble petitions, when I cry unto thee: when I hold up my hands towards the mercy-seat of thy holy temple.
3 O pluck me not away, neither destroy me with the ungodly and wicked doers: who speak friendly to their neighbors, but imagine mischief in their hearts.
4 Praised be the Lord: for he hath heard the voice of my humble petitions.
5 The Lord is my strength and my shield; my heart hath trusted in him, and I am helped: therefore my

heart danceth for joy, and in my song will I praise him
6 The Lord is my strength: and he is the wholesome defense of his Anointed.
7 O save thy people, and give thy blessing unto thine inheritance: feed them, and set them up forever.

PSALM 29

ASCRIBE unto the Lord, O ye mighty: ascribe unto the Lord glory and strength.
2 Give the Lord the honor due unto his name: worship the Lord with holy worship.
3 It is the Lord that commandeth the waters: it is the glorious God that maketh the thunder.
4 It is the Lord that ruleth the sea: the voice of the Lord is mighty in operation; the voice of the Lord is a glorious voice.
5 The voice of the Lord breaketh the cedar-trees: yea, the Lord breaketh the cedars of Libanus.
6 He maketh them also to skip like a calf: Libanus also, and Sirion, like a young unicorn.
7 The voice of the Lord divideth the flames of fire: the voice of the Lord shaketh the wilderness; yea, the Lord shaketh the wilderness of Kadesh.
8 The voice of the Lord maketh the hinds to^-bring forth young, and discovereth the thick bushes: in his temple doth every man speak of his honor.
9 The Lord sitteth above the water-flood: and the Lord remaineth a King forever.
10 The Lord shall give strength unto his people: the Lord shall give his people the blessing of peace.

PSALM 30

 WILL magnify thee, O Lord; for thou hast set me up: and not made my foes to triumph over me.

2 O Lord my God, I cried unto thee: and thou hast healed me.

3 Thou, Lord, hast brought my soul out of hell: thou hast kept me alive, that I should not go down to the pit.

4 Sing praises unto the Lord, O ye saints of his: and give thanks unto him for a remembrance of his holiness.

5 For his wrath endureth but the twinkling of an eye, and in his pleasure is life: heaviness may endure for a night, but joy cometh in the morning.

6 And in my prosperity I said, I shall never be removed: thou, Lord, of thy goodness hadst made my hill so strong.

7 Thou didst turn thy face from me: and I was troubled.

8 Then cried I unto thee, O Lord: and gat me to my Lord right humbly.

9 What profit is there in my blood: when I go down to the pit?

10 Shall the dust give thanks unto thee: or shall it declare thy truth?

11 Hear, O Lord, and have mercy upon me: Lord, be thou my helper.

12 Thou hast turned my heaviness into joy: thou hast put off my sackcloth, and girded me with gladness.

13 Therefore shall every good man sing of thy praise without ceasing: O my God, I will give thanks unto thee forever.

PSALM 31

IN thee, O Lord, have I put my trust: let me never be put to confusion; deliver me in thy righteousness.
2 Bow down thine ear to me: make haste to deliver me.
3 And be thou my strong rock and house of defence: that thou mayest save me.
4 For thou art my strong rock and my castle: be thou also my guide, and lead me for thy Name's sake.
5 Draw me out of the net that they have laid privily for me: for thou art my strength.
6 Into thy hands I commend my spirit: for thou hast redeemed me, O Lord, thou God of truth.
7 I will be glad and rejoice in thy mercy: for thou hast considered my trouble, and hast known my soul in adversities.
8 Thou hast not shut me up into the hand of the enemy: but hast set my feet in a large room.
9 My hope hath been in thee, O Lord: I have said, Thou art my God.
10 My time is in thy hand: deliver me from the hand of mine enemies, and from them that persecute me.
11 Show thy servant the light of thy countenance: and save me for thy mercies' sake.
12 O how plentiful is thy goodness, which thou hast laid up for them that fear thee: and which thou hast prepared for them that put their trust in thee, even before the sons of men!
13 Thou shalt hide them privily by thine own presence from the provoking of all men: thou shalt keep them secret in thy tabernacle from the strife of tongues.
14 O love the Lord, all ye his saints: for the Lord preserveth them that are faithful; and plenteously rewardeth the proud doer.
15 Be strong, and he shall establish your heart: all ye that put your trust in the Lord.

PSALM 32

LESSED is he whose unrighteousness is forgiven:
and whose sin is covered.
2 Blessed is the man unto whom the Lord imputeth no sin: and in whose spirit there is no guile.
3 While I held my tongue, my bones consumed away through my daily complaining.
4 For thy hand was heavy upon me, day and night: and my moisture is like the drought in summer.
5 I acknowledge my sin unto thee: and mine unrighteousness have I not hid.
6 I said, I will confess my sins unto the Lord and so thou forgavest the wickedness of my sin.
7 For this shall every one that is godly make his prayer unto thee, in a time when thou mayest be found: but in the great waterfloods they shall not come nigh him.
8 Thou art a place to hide me in, thou shalt preserve me from trouble: thou shalt compass me about with songs of deliverance.
9 I will inform thee, and teach thee in the way wherein thou shalt go: and I will guide thee with mine eye.
10 Be ye not like to horse and mule, which have no understanding: whose mouths must be held with bit and bridle, lest they fall upon thee.
11 Great plagues remain for the ungodly: but whoso putteth his trust in the Lord, mercy embraceth him on every side.
12 Be glad, O ye righteous, and rejoice in the Lord: and be joyful, all ye that are true of heart.

PSALM 33

REJOICE in the Lord, O ye righteous: for it becometh well the just to be thankful.
2 Sing unto the Lord a new song: sing praises lustily unto him with a good courage.
3 For the word of the Lord is true: and all his works are faithful.
4 He loveth righteousness and judgment: the earth is full of the goodness of the Lord.
5 By the word of the Lord were the heavens made: and all the hosts of them by the breath of his mouth.
6 He gathereth the waters of the sea together, as it were upon a heap: and layeth up the deep as in a treasure-house.
7 Let all the earth fear the Lord: stand in awe of him, all ye that dwell in the world.
8 For he spake, and it was done: he commanded, and it stood fast.
9 The Lord bringeth the counsel of the heathen to nought: and maketh the devices of the people to be of none effect, and casteth out the counsels of princes.
10 The counsel of the Lord shall endure for eyer: and the thoughts of his heart from generation to generation.
11 Blessed are the people whose God is the Lord Jehovah: and blessed are the folk that he hath chosen to him to be his inheritance.
12 The Lord looketh down from heaven, and beholdeth all the children of men: from the habitation of his dwelling he considereth all them that dwell on the earth.
13 He fashioneth all the hearts of them: and understandeth all their works.
14 There is no king that can be saved by the multitude of a host: neither is any mighty man delivered by much strength.
15 A horse is counted but a vain thing to save a man: neither shall he deliver any man by his great

strength.
16 Behold, the eye of the Lord is upon them that fear him: and upon them that put their trust in his mercy;
17 To deliver their soul from death: and to feed them in the time of dearth.
18 Our soul hath patiently tarried for the Lord: for he is our help and our shield.
19 For our heart shall rejoice in him: because we have hoped in his holy Name.
20 Let thy merciful kindness, O Lord, be upon us: like as we do put our trust in thee.

PSALM 34

 WILL always give thanks unto the Lord: his praise shall ever be in my mouth.
2 My soul shall make her boast in the Lord: the humble shall hear thereof, and be glad.
3 O praise the Lord with me: and let us magnify his Name together.
4 I sought the Lord, and he heard me: yea, he delivered me out of all my fear.
5 They had an eye unto him, and were lightened: and their faces were not ashamed.
6 Lo, the poor crieth, and the Lord heareth him: yea, and saveth him out of all his troubles.
7 The angel of the Lord tarrieth round about them that fear him: and delivereth them.
8 O taste and see how gracious the Lord is: blessed is the man that trusteth in him.
9 O fear the Lord, ye that are his saints: for they that fear him lack nothing.
10 The lions do lack and suffer hunger: but they who seek the Lord shall want no manner of thing that is good.
11 Come, ye children, and hearken unto me: I will

teach you the fear of the Lord,
12 What man is he that desireth to live: and would fain see good days?
13 Keep thy tongue from evil: and thy lips that they speak no guile.
14 Eschew evil, and do good: seek peace, and ensue it.
15 The eyes of the Lord are over the righteous: and his ears are open unto their prayers.
16 The countenance of the Lord is against them that do evil: to root out the remembrance of them from the earth.
17 The righteous cry, and the Lord heareth them: and delivereth them out of all their troubles.
18 The Lord is nigh unto them that are of a contrite heart: and will save such as are of a humble spirit.
19 Great are the troubles of the righteous: but the Lord delivereth him out of all.
20 He keepeth all his bones: so that not one of them is broken.
21 But misfortune shall slay the ungodly: and they that hate the righteous shall be desolate.
22 The Lord delivereth the souls of his servants: and all they that put their trust in him shall not be destitute.

PSALM 35

PLEAD thou my cause, O Lord, with them that strive with me: and fight thou against them that fight against me.
2 Lay hand upon the shield and buckler: and stand up to help me.
3 Bring forth the spear, and stop the way against them that persecute me: say unto my soul, I am thy salvation.

4 My soul, be joyful in the Lord: it shall rejoice in his salvation.
5 All my bones shall say, Lord, who is like unto thee, who deliverest the poor from him that is too strong for him: yea, the poor, and him that is in misery, from him that spoileth him?
6 I will give thee thanks in the great congregation: I will praise thee among much people.
7 Let them be glad and rejoice that favor my righteous dealing: yea, let them say always, Blessed be the Lord, who hath pleasure in the prosperity of his servant,
8 And as for my tongue, it shall be talking of thy righteousness: and of thy praise, all the day long.

PSALM 36

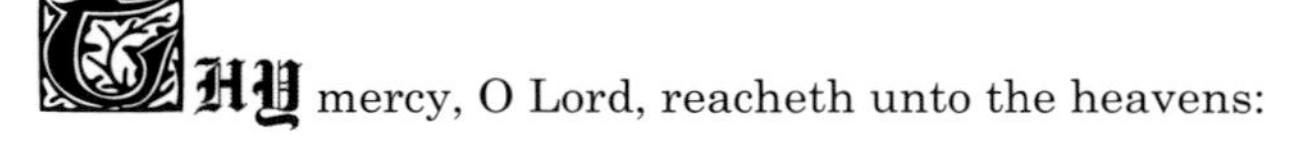

THY mercy, O Lord, reacheth unto the heavens: and thy faithfulness unto the clouds.
2 Thy righteousness standeth like the strong mountains: thy judgments are like the great deep.
3 Thou, Lord, preservest both man and beast. How excellent is thy mercy, O God: and the children of men shall put their trust under the shadow of thy wings.
4 They shall be satisfied with the plenteousness of thy house: and thou shalt give them drink of thy pleasures, as out of the river.
5 For with thee is the well of life: and in thy light shall we see light.
6 O continue thy lovingkindness unto them that know thee: and thy righteousness unto them that are true of heart.
7 O let not the foot of pride come against me: and let not the hand of the ungodly cast me down.
8 There are they fallen, all that work wickedness:

they are cast down, and shall not be able to stand.

PSALM 37. PART 1.

FRET not thyself because of the ungodly: neither be thou envious against the evil doers.

2 For they shall be soon cut down like the grass: and be withered even as the green herb.

3 Put thou thy trust in the Lord, and be doing good: dwell in the land, and verily thou shalt be fed.

4 Delight thou in the Lord: and he shall give thee thy heart's desire.

5 Commit thy way unto the Lord, and put thy trust in him: and he shall bring it to pass.

6 He shall make thy righteousness as clear as the light: and thy just dealing as the noon-day.

7 Hold thee still in the Lord, and abide patiently upon him: but grieve not thyself at him whose way doth prosper, at the man that doeth after evil counsels.

8 Cease from wrath, and let go displeasure: fret not thyself, else thou shalt be moved to do evil.

9 Wicked doers shall be rooted out: but they that patiently wait upon the Lord, those shall inherit the land.

10 Yet a little while, and the ungodly shall be clean gone thou shalt look after his place, and he shall be away.

11 But the meek-spirited shall possess the earth: and shall be refreshed in the multitude of peace.

12 The ungodly seeketh counsel against the just: and gnasheth upon him with his teeth.

13 The Lord shall laugh him to scorn: for he seeth that his day is coming.

14 A small thing that the righteous hath: is better than great riches of the ungodly.

15 For the arms of the ungodly shall be broken:

and the Lord upholdeth the righteous.
16 The Lord knoweth the days of the godly: and their inheritance shall endure forever.
17 They shall not be confounded in the perilous time: and in the days of dearth they shall have enough.
18 As for the ungodly, they shall perish; and the enemies of the Lord shall consume as the fat of lambs: yea, even as the smoke shall they consume away.
19 The ungodly borroweth, and payeth not again: but the righteous is merciful and liberal.
20 Such as are blessed of God shall possess the land: and they that are cursed of him shall be rooted out.

PSALM 37. PART 2.

THE Lord ordereth a good man's going: and maketh his way acceptable to himself.
2 Though he fall, he shall not be cast away: for the Lord upholdeth him with his hand.
3 I have been young, and now am old: and yet saw I never the righteous forsaken, nor his seed begging their bread.
4 The righteous is ever merciful, and lendeth: and his seed is blessed.
5 Flee from evil, and do the thing that is good: and dwell forevermore.
6 For the Lord loveth the thing that is right: he forsaketh not his saints; but they are preserved for ever.
7 The righteous shall be punished: as for the seed of the ungodly, it shall be rooted out.
8 The righteous shall inherit the land: and dwell therein forever.
9 The mouth of the righteous is exercised in wisdom: and his tongue will be talking of judgment.
10 The law of his God is in his heart: and his going

shall not slide.
11 The ungodly seeth the righteous: and seeketh occasion to slay him.
12 The Lord will not leave him in his hand: nor condemn him when he is judged.
13 Hope thou in the Lord, and keep his way, and he shall promote thee, that thou shalt possess the land: when the ungodly shall perish, thou shalt see it.
14 I myself have seen the ungodly in great power: and flourishing like a green bay-tree.
15 I went by, and, lo, he was gone: I sought him, but his place could nowhere be found.
16 Keep innocency, and take heed unto the thing that is right: for that shall bring a man peace at the last.
17 As for the transgressors, they shall perish together: and the end of the ungodly is, they shall be rooted out at last.
18 But the salvation of the righteous cometh of the Lord: who is also their strength in the time of trouble.
19 And the Lord shall stand by them, and save them: he shall deliver them from the ungodly, and shall save them, because they put their trust in him.

PSALM 38

UT me not to rebuke, O Lord, in thine anger: neither chasten me in thy heavy displeasure.
2 For thine arrows stick fast in me: and thy hand presseth me sore.
3 There is no health in my flesh, because of thy dis pleasure: neither is there any rest in my bones, by reason of my sin.
4 For my wickednesses are gone over my head: and are like a sore burden, too heavy for me to bear.
5 My wounds stink, and are corrupt: through my foolishness.

6 I am brought into so great trouble and misery: that I go mourning all the day long.
7 I am feeble and sore smitten: I have roared for the very disquietness of my heart.
8 Lord, thou knowest all my desire: and my groaning is not hid from thee.
9 My heart panteth, my strength hath failed me: and the sight of mine eyes is gone from me.
10 My lovers and my neighbors did stand looking upon my trouble: and my kinsmen stood afar off.
11 In thee, O Lord, have I put my trust: thou shalt answer for me, O Lord my God.
12 I will confess my wickedness: and be sorry for my sin.
13 Forsake me not, O Lord, my God: be not thou far from me.
14 Haste thee to help me: O Lord God of my salvation.

PSALM 39

SAID, I will take heed to my ways: that I offend not with my tongue.
2 I will keep my mouth as it were with a bridle i while the ungodly is in my sight.
3 I held my tongue, and spake nothing: I kept silence, yea, even from good words; but it was pain and grief to me.
4 My heart was hot within me, and while I was thus musing, the fire kindled: and at the last I spake with my tongue.
5 Lord, let me know my end, and the number of my days: that I may be certified how long I have to live.
6 Behold, thou hast made my days as it were a span long, and mine age is even as nothing in respect of thee: and verily every man living is altogether vanity.
7 For man walketh in a vain shadow, and disquieteth

himself in vain: he heapeth up riches, and cannot tell who shall gather them.

8 And now, Lord, what is my hope? truly my hope is even in thee.

9 Deliver me from all mine offences: and make me not a rebuke unto the foolish.

10 I became dumb, and opened not my mouth: for it was thy doing.

11 Take thy plague away from me: I am even consumed by the means of thy heavy hand.

12 When thou with rebukes dost chasten man for sin, thou makest his beauty to consume away, like as it were a moth fretting a garment: every man therefore is but vanity.

13 Hear my prayer, O Lord, and with thine ears consider my calling: hold not thy peace at my tears;

14 For I am a stranger with thee: and a sojourner, as all my fathers were.

15 O spare me a little, that I may recover my strength: before I go hence, and be no more seen.

PSALM 40

WAITED patiently for the Lord: and he inclined unto me, and heard my calling.

2 He brought me also out of the horrible pit, out of the mire and clay: and set my feet upon the rock, and ordered my goings.

3 And he hath put a new song in my mouth: even a thanksgiving unto our God.

4 Many shall see it, and fear: and shall put their trust in the Lord.

5 Blessed is the man that hath set his hope in the Lord: and turned not unto the proud, and to such as go about with lies.

6 O Lord, my God, great are the wondrous works

which thou hast done, like as are also thy thoughts, which are to us-ward: and yet there is no man that ordereth them unto thee.

7 If I should declare them, and speak of them: they would be more than I am able to express.

8 Sacrifice and meat-offering thou wouldest not: but mine ears hast thou opened.

9 Burnt-offerings and sacrifice for sin hast thou not required: then said I, Lo, I come,

10 In the volume of the book it is written of me, that I should fulfil thy will, O my God: I am content to do it; yea, thy law is within my heart.

11 I have declared thy righteousness in the great congregation: lo, I will not refrain my lips, O Lord, and that thou knowest.

12 I have not hid thy righteousness within my heart: my talk hath been of thy truth, and of thy salvation.

131 have not kept back thy loving mercy and truth: from the great congregation.

14 Withdraw not thou thy mercy from me, O Lord: let thy loving-kindness and thy truth always preserve me.

15 For innumerable troubles are come about me; my sins have taken such hold upon me, that I am not able to look up: yea, they are more in number than the hairs of my head, and my heart hath failed me.

16 O Lord, let it be thy pleasure to deliver me: make haste, O Lord, to help me.

17 Let all those that seek thee, be joyful and glad in thee: and let such as love thy salvation say always, The Lord be praised.

18 As for me, I am poor and needy: but the Lord careth for me.

19 Thou art my helper and redeemer: make no long tarrying, O my God.

PSALM 41

LESSED is he that considereth the poor and needy: the Lord shall deliver him in the time of trouble.

2 The Lord will preserve him, and keep him alive, and he shall be blessed upon the earth: and thou wilt not deliver him unto the will of his enemies.

3 The Lord will comfort him, when he lieth sick upon his bed: thou wilt make all his bed in his sickness.

4 I said, Lord, be merciful unto me: heal my soul; for I have sinned against thee.

5 By this I know thou favorest me: that mine enemy doth not triumph against me.

6 And when I am in my health, thou upholdest me: and shalt set me before thy face forever.

7 Blessed be the Lord God of Israel: world without end. Amen.

PSALM 42

S the hart panteth after the water-brooks: so panteth my soul after thee, O God.

2 My soul is athirst for God, yea, even for the living God: when shall I come to appear before the presence of God?

3 My tears have been my meat day and night: while daily they say unto me, Where is now thy God?

4 Now when I think thereupon, I pour out my heart by myself: for I went with the multitude, and brought them forth into the house of God;

5 In the voice of praise and thanksgiving: among such as keep holy-day.

6 Why art thou so full of heaviness, O my soul: and

why art thou so disquieted within me?
7 Put thy trust in God: for I shall yet give him thanks for the help of his countenance.
8 The Lord hath granted his lovingkindness in the day-time: and in the night season did I sing of him, and made my prayer unto the God of my life.
9 I will say unto the God of my strength, Why hast thou forgotten me: why go I thus heavily, while the enemy oppresseth me?
10 Why art thou so vexed, O my soul: and why art thou so disquieted within me?
11 O put thy trust in God: for I shall yet thank him, who is the help of my countenance, and my God.

PSALM 43

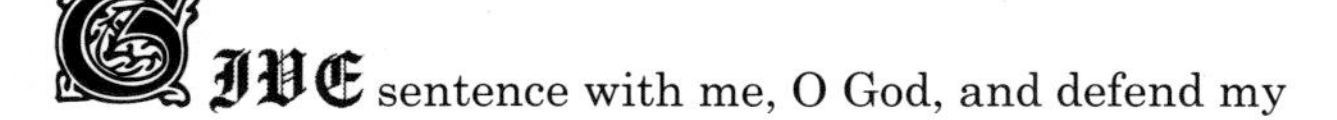

GIVE sentence with me, O God, and defend my cause against the ungodly people: O deliver me from the deceitful and wicked man.
2 For thou art the God of my strength, why hast thou put me from thee: and why go I so heavily, while the enemy oppresseth me?
3 O send out thy light and thy truth, that they may lead me: and bring me unto thy holy hill, and to thy dwelling.
4 Then will I go unto the altar of God: even unto God, my exceeding joy.
5 Why art thou so heavy, O my soul: and why art thou so disquieted within me?
6 O put thy trust in God: for I shall yet give him thanks, who is the help of my countenance, and my God.

PSALM 44

WE have heard with our ears, O God: our fathers have told us what thou hast done in their time of old.

2 How thou hast driven out the heathen with thy hand, and planted them in: how thou hast destroyed the nations, and cast them out.

3 For they gat not the land in possession through their own sword: neither was it their own arm that helped them;

4 But thy right hand, and thine arm, and the light of thy countenance: because thou hadst a favor unto them.

5 Thou art my King, O God: send help unto Jacob.

6 Through thee will we overthrow our enemies: and in thy name will we tread them under that rise up against us.

7 For I will not trust in my bow: it is not my sword that shall help me.

8 But it is thou that savest us from our enemies: and puttest them to confusion that hate us.

9 We make our boast of God all day long: and will praise thy Name forever.

PSALM 45

My heart is indicting of a good matter: I speak of the things which I have made touching the King.

2 My tongue is the pen of a ready writer.

3 Thou art fairer than the children of men: full of grace are thy lips, because God hath blessed thee for ever.

4 Gird thee with thy sword upon thy thigh, O thou most Mighty: according to thy glory and renown.

5 Good luck have thou with thine honor: ride on, because of the word of truth, of meekness, and righteousness; and thy right hand shall teach thee terrible

things.

6 Thy arrows are very sharp in the heart of the King's enemies: whereby the people shall be subdued unto thee.

7 Thy seat, O God, endureth forever: the sceptre of thy kingdom is a right sceptre.

8 Thou hast loved righteousness, and hated iniquity: wherefore God, even thy God, hath anointed thee with the oil of gladness above thy fellows.

9 I will remember thy Name from one generation to another: therefore shall the people give thanks unto thee world without end.

PSALM 46

OD is our hope and strength: a very present help in trouble.

2 Therefore will we not fear, though the earth be moved: and though the hills be carried into the midst of the sea.

3 Though the waters thereof rage and swell: and though the mountains shake at the tempest of the same.

4 There is a river, the streams whereof shall make glad the city of God: the holy place of the tabernacle of the Most High.

5 God is in the midst of her, therefore shall she not be removed: God shall help her, and that right early.

6 The heathen make much ado, and the kingdoms are moved: but God hath showed his voice, and the earth shall melt away.

7 The Lord of hosts is with us: the God of Jacob is our refuge.

8 O come hither, and behold the works of the Lord: what destruction he hath brought upon the earth.

9 He maketh wars to cease in all the world: he

breaketh the bow, and knappeth the spear in sunder, and burneth the chariots in the fire.

10 Be still, then, and know that I am God: I will be exalted among the heathen, and I will be exalted in the earth.

11 The Lord of hosts is with us: the God of Jacob is our refuge.

PSALM 47

 CLAP your hands together, all ye people: O sing unto God with the voice of melody.

2 For the Lord is high, and to be feared: he is the great King upon all the earth.

3 He shall subdue the people under us: and the nations under our feet.

4 He shall choose out a heritage for us: even the excellency of Jacob, whom he loved.

5 God is gone up with a merry noise: and the Lord with the sound of the trump.

6 O sing praises, sing praises unto our God: O sing praises unto our King.

7 For God is the King of all the earth: sing ye praises with understanding.

8 God reigneth over the heathen: God sitteth upon his holy seat.

9 God, who is very high exalted, doth defend the earth as it were with a shield.

PSALM 48

 REAT is the Lord, and greatly to be praised: in the city of our God, even upon his holy hill.

2 Like as we have heard, so we have seen in the

city of the Lord of hosts, in the city of our God: God upholdeth the same forever.

3 We wait for thy lovingkindness, O God: in the midst of thy temple.

4 O God, according to thy Name, so is thy praise unto the world's end: thy right hand is full of righteousness.

5 Let the mount Sion rejoice, and the daughter of Judah be glad: because of thy judgments.

6 Walk about Sion, and go round about her: and tell the towers thereof.

7 Mark well her bulwarks, set up her palaces: that ye may tell them that come after.

8 For this God is our God forever and ever: he shall be our guide unto death.

PSALM 49

 HEAR ye this, all ye people: ponder it with your ears, all ye that dwell in the world.

2 High and low, rich and poor: one with another.

3 My mouth shall speak of wisdom: and my heart shall muse of understanding.

4 There are some that put their trust in their goods: and boast themselves in the multitude of their riches.

5 But no man may deliver his brother: or make an agreement unto God for him;

6 For it cost more to redeem their souls: so that he must let that alone forever;

7 That he should still live forever, and not see corruption.

8 For he seeth that wise men also die and perish together: as well as the ignorant and foolish, and leave their riches for other.

9 And yet they think that their houses shall continue forever, and that their dwelling-places shall endure from one generation to another: and call the

lands after their own names.
10 Nevertheless, man being in honor abideth not: he is like the beasts that perish.
11 This their way is their folly: yet their posterity approve their sayings.
12 Like sheep they are laid in the grave, death shall feed on them, and the upright shall have dominion over them in the morning: their beauty shall consume in the grave from their dwelling.
13 But God will redeem my soul from the power of the grave: for he shall receive me.
14 Be not thou afraid, when one is made rich: when the glory of his house is increased.
15 For when he dieth, he shall carry nothing away: his glory shall not descend after him.
16 Though while he lived, he blessed his soul: and men will praise thee when thou doest well to thyself.
17 He shall go to the generation of his fathers: they shall never see fight.
18 Man that is in honor, and understandeth not, is like the beasts that perish.

PSALM 50

HE Lord, even the most mighty God, hath spoken: and called the world, from the rising up of the sun unto the going down thereof.
2 Out of Sion hath God appeared: in perfect beauty.
3 Our God shall come, and shall not keep silence: there shah 1 go before him a consuming fire, and a mighty tempest shall be stirred up round about him.
4 He shall call the heaven from above: and the earth, that he may judge his people.
5 Gather my saints together unto me: those that have made a covenant with me with sacrifice.
6 And the heavens shall declare his righteousness:

for God is judge himself.
7 Hear, O my people, and I will speak: I myself will testify against thee, O Israel; for I am God, even thy God.
8 I will not reprove thee, because of thy sacrifices, or for thy burnt-offerings: because they were not always before me.
9 I will take no bullock out of thine house: nor he-goat out of thy folds.
10 For all the beasts of the forest are mine: and so are the cattle upon a thousand hills.
11 I know all the fowls upon the mountains: and the wild beasts of the field are in my sight.
12 If I were hungry, I would not tell thee: for the whole world is mine, and all that is therein.
13 Thinkest thou that I will eat bulls' flesh: and drink the blood of goats?
14 Offer unto God thanksgiving: and pay thy vows unto the Most High;
15 And call upon me in the time of trouble: so will I hear thee, and thou shalt praise me.
16 But unto the ungodly said God: Why dost thou preach my laws, and takest my covenant in thy mouth;
17 Whereas thou hatest to be reformed: and hast cast my words behind thee?
18 Consider this, ye that forget God: lest I pluck you away, and there be none to deliver you.
19 Whoso offereth me thanks and praise, he honoreth me: and to him that ordereth his conversation aright, will I show the salvation of God.

PSALM 51.

HAVE mercy upon me, O God, after thy great goodness: according to the multitude of thy mercies do away mine offences.

2 Wash me thoroughly from my wickedness: and cleanse me from my sin.
3 For I acknowledge my faults: and my sin is ever before me.
4 Against thee only have I sinned, and done this evil in thy sight: that thou mightest be justified in thy saying, and clear when thou art judged.
5 Behold, I was shapen in wickedness: and in sin hath my mother conceived me.
6 But, lo, thou requirest truth in the inward parts: and shalt make me to understand wisdom secretly.
7 Thou shalt purge me with hyssop, and I shall be clean: thou shalt wash me, and I shall be whiter than snow.
8 Thou shalt make me hear of joy and gladness: that the bones which thou hast broken may rejoice.
9 Turn thy face from my sins: and put out all my misdeeds.
10 Make me a clean heart, O God: and renew a right spirit within me.
11 Cast me not away from thy presence: and take not thy Holy Spirit from me.
12 O give me the comfort of thy help again: and establish me with thy free Spirit.
13 Then shall I teach thy ways unto the wicked: and sinners shall be converted unto thee.
14 Deliver me from blood-guiltiness, O God, thou that art the God of my health: and my tongue shall sing of thy righteousness.
15 Thou shall open my lips, O Lord: and my mouth shall show thy praise.
16 For thou desirest no sacrifice, else would I give it thee: but thou delightest not in burnt-offerings.
17 The sacrifice of God is a troubled spirit: a broken and a contrite heart, O God, shall thou not despise.

PSALM 52

EAR my prayer, O God: and hide not thyself from my petition.

2 Attend unto me, and hear me: how I mourn in my prayer, and am vexed.

3 My heart is disquieted within me: and the fear of death is fallen upon me:

4 Fearfulness and trembling are come upon me: and an horrible dread hath overwhelmed me.

5 And I said, O that I had wings like a dove: for then I would flee away, and be at rest.

6 Lo, then would I get me away far off: and remain in the wilderness.

7 I would make haste to escape: because of the stormy wind and tempest.

8 For it is not an open enemy that hath done me this dishonor: for then I could have borne it.

9 Neither was it mine adversary that did magnify himself against me: for then, peradventure, I would have hid myself from him.

10 But it was even thou, my companion: my guide, and mine own familiar friend.

11 We took sweet counsel together: and walked in the house of God as friends.

12 As for me, I will call upon God: and the Lord shall save me.

13 In the evening and morning, and at noon-day, will I pray, and that instantly: and he shall hear my voice.

14 It is he that hath delivered my soul in peace, from the battle that was against me: for there were many with me.

15 Yea, even God, that endureth forever, shall hear me, and bring them down: for they will not turn, nor fear God.

16 O cast thy burden upon the Lord, and he shall nourish thee: and shall not suffer the righteous to fall

forever.
1 7 And as for them: thou, O God, shalt bring them into the pit of destruction.
18 The blood-thirsty and deceitful men shall not live out half their days: but my trust shall be in thee, O Lord.

PSALM 56

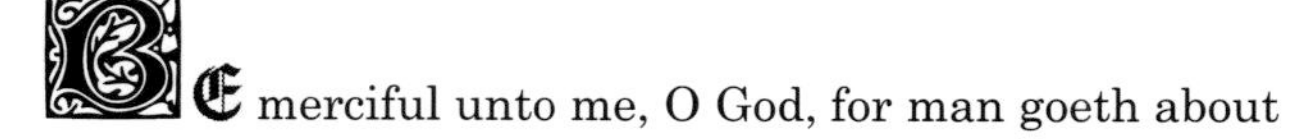
E merciful unto me, O God, for man goeth about to devour me: he is daily fighting and troubling me.
2 Nevertheless, though I am sometimes afraid: yet put I my trust in thee.
3 I will praise God because of his word: I have put my trust in God, and will not fear what flesh can do unto me.
4 Whensoever I call upon thee, then shall mine enemies be put to flight: this I know, for God is on my side.
5 In God's word will I rejoice: in the Lord's word will 1 comfort me.
6 Yea, in my God have I put my trust: I will not be afraid what man can do unto me.
7 Unto thee, O God, will I pay my vows: unto thee will I give thanks.
8 For thou hast delivered my soul from death, and my feet from falling: that I may walk before God in the light of the living.

PSALM 57

BE merciful unto me, O God, be merciful unto me, for my soul trusteth in thee: and under the shadow

of thy wings shall be my refuge, until this tyranny be overpast.
2 I will call unto the most high God: even unto the God that shall perform the cause which I have in hand.
3 Set up thyself, O God, above the heavens: and thy glory above all the earth.
4 My heart is fixed, O God, my heart is fixed: I will sing and give praise.
5 I will give thanks unto thee, O Lord, among the people: and I will sing unto thee among the nations.
6 For the greatness of thy mercy reacheth unto the heavens: and thy truth unto the clouds.
7 Set up thyself, O God, above the heavens: and thy glory above all the earth.

PSALM 59

DELIVER me from mine enemies, O God: defend me from them that rise up against me.
2 O deliver me from the wicked doers: and save me from the blood-thirsty men.
3 My strength will I ascribe unto thee: for thou art the God of my refuge.
4 God showeth me his goodness plenteously: and God shall let me see my desire upon mine enemies.
5 As for me, I will sing of thy power, and will praise thy mercy betimes in the morning: for thou hast been my defense and refuge in the day of my trouble.
6 Unto thee, O my strength, will I sing: for thou, O God, art my refuge, and my merciful God.

PSALM 61

EAR my cry, O God: give ear unto my

prayer.
2 From the ends of the earth will I call upon thee: when my heart is in heaviness.
3 O set me upon the rock that is higher than I: for thou hast been my hope, and a strong tower for me against the enemy.
4 I will dwell in thy tabernacle forever: and my trust shall be under the covering of thy wings.
5 For thou, O Lord, hast heard my desires: and hast given an heritage unto those that fear thy Name.
6 I will always sing praise unto thy Name: that I may daily perform my vows.

PSALM 62

Y soul truly waiteth still upon God: for of him cometh my salvation.
2 He verily is my strength and my salvation: he is my defense, so that I shall not greatly fall.
3 My soul, wait thou still upon God: for my hope is in him.
4 He truly is my strength and my salvation: he is iny defense, so that I may not fall.
5 In God is my health, and my glory, the rock of my might: and in God is my trust.
6 O put your trust in him always, ye people, pour out your hearts before him: for God is our hope.
7 As for the children of men, they are but vanity: the children of men are deceitful in the balance, they are altogether lighter than vanity itself.
8 Give not yourselves unto vanity: if riches increase, set not your heart upon them.
9 God spake once, and twice I have also heard the same: That power belongeth unto God;
10 And that thou, Lord, art merciful: for thou rewardest every man according to his work.

PSALM 63

 GOD, thou art my God: early will I seek thee.

2 My soul thirsteth for thee, my flesh also longeth after thee: in a barren and dry land, where no water is.

3 Thus have I looked for thee in holiness: that I might behold thy power and glory.

4 For thy lovingkindness is better than the life itself: my lips shall praise thee.

5 As long as I live I will magnify thee on this manner: and lift up my hands in thy Name.

6 My soul shall be satisfied even as it were with marrow and fatness: when my mouth praiseth thee with joyful lips.

Have I not remembered thee in my bed: and thought upon thee when I was waking?

8 Because thou hast been my helper: therefore under the shadow of thy wings will I rejoice.

9 My soul hangeth upon thee: thy right hand hath upholden me.

PSALM 65

HOU, O God, art praised in Sion: and unto thee shall the vow be performed in Jerusalem.

2 Thou that hearest the prayer: unto thee shall all flesh come.

3 My misdeeds prevail against me: O be thou merciful unto our sins.

4 Blessed is the man whom thou choosest, and receivest unto thee: he shall dwell in thy court, and shall be satisfied with the pleasures of thy house, even

of thy holy temple.
5 Thou shalt show us wonderful things in thy righteousness, O God of our salvation: thou that art the hope of all the ends of the earth, and of them that remain in the broad sea.
6 Who in his strength setteth fast the mountains: and is girded about with power.
7 Who stilleth the raging of the sea: and the noise of his waves, and the madness of the people.
8 They also that dwell in the uttermost parts of the earth shall be afraid at thy tokens: thou that makest the outgoings of the morning and evening to praise thee.
9 Thou visitest the earth, and blessest it: thou makest it very plenteous.
10 The river of God is full of water: thou preparest their corn, for so thou providest for the earth.
11 Thou waterest her furrows, thou sendest rain into the little valleys thereof: thou makest it soft with the drops of rain, and blessest the increase of it.
12 Thou crownest the year with thy goodness: and thy clouds drop fatness.
13 They shall drop upon the dwellings of the wilderness: and the little hills shall rejoice on every side.
14 The folds shall be full of sheep: the valleys also shall stand so thick with corn, that they shall laugh and sing.

PSALM 66

BE joyful in God, all ye lands: sing praises unto the honor of his Name, make his praise to be glorious.
2 Say unto God, O how wonderful art thou in thy works: through the greatness of thy power shall thine enemies submit themselves unto thee.

3 For all the world shall worship thee: sing of thee, and praise thy Name.
4 O come hither, and behold the works of God: how wonderful he is in his doing toward the children of men.
5 He turned the sea into dry land: so that they went through the water on foot; there did we rejoice in him.
6 He ruleth with his power forever; his eyes behold the people: and such as will not believe shall not be able to exalt themselves.
7 O praise our God, ye people: and make the voice of his praise to be heard.
8 Who holdeth our soul in life: and suffereth not our feet to slip.
9 For thou, O God, hast proved us: thou also hast tried us like as silver is tried.
10 Thou broughtest us into the snare: and laidest trouble upon our loins.
11 We went through fire and water: and thou broughtest us out into a wealthy place.
12 I will pay thee my vows, which I promised with my lips, and spake with my mouth, when I was in trouble.
13 O come hither, and hearken, all ye that fear God: and I will tell you what he hath done for my soul.
14 I called unto him with my mouth: and gave him praises with my tongue.
15 If I incline unto wickedness with mine heart: the Lord will not hear me.
16 But God hath heard me: and considered the voice of my prayer.
17 Praised be God, who hath not cast out my prayer: nor turned his mercy from me.

PSALM 67

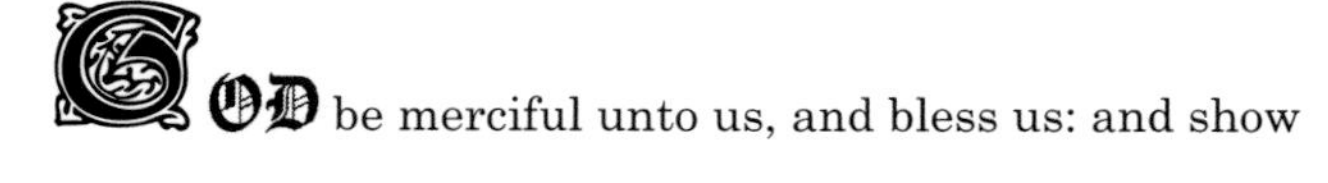

GOD be merciful unto us, and bless us: and show us the light of his countenance, and be merciful unto us;
2 That thy way may be known upon earth: thy saving health among all nations.
3 Let the people praise thee, O God: yea, let ail the people praise thee.
4 O let the nations rejoice and be glad: for thou shalt judge the people righteously, and govern the nations upon earth.
5 Let the people praise thee, O God: yea, let all the people praise thee.
6 Then shall the earth bring forth her increase: and God, even our own God, shall give us his blessing.
7 God shall bless us: and all the ends of the world shall fear him.

PSALM 68

LET God arise, and let his enemies be scattered: let them also that hate him, flee before him.
2 Like as the smoke vanisheth, so shalt thou drive them away: and like as wax melteth at the fire, so let the ungodly perish at the presence of God.
3 But let the righteous be glad, and rejoice before God: let them also be merry and joyful.
4 O sing unto God, and sing praises unto his Name: magnify him that rideth upon the heavens, as it were upon a horse; praise him in his Name JAH, and rejoice before him.
5 He is a Father of the fatherless, and defendeth the cause of the widows: even God in his holy habitation.

6 He is the God that maketh men to be of one mind in an house, and bringeth the prisoners out of captivity: but letteth the rebellious continue in scarceness.
7 O God, when thou wentest forth before the people: when thou wentest through the wilderness;
8 The earth shook, and the heavens dropped at the presence of God: even as Sinai also was moved at the presence of God, who is the God of Israel.
9 Thou, O God, sentest a gracious rain upon thine inheritance: and refreshedst it when it was weary.
10 Thy congregation shall dwell therein: for thou, O God, hast of thy goodness prepared for the poor.
11 Thou art gone up on high, thou hast led captivity captive, and received gifts for men: yea, even for thine enemies, that the Lord God might dwell among them.
12 Praised be the Lord daily: even the God who helpeth us, and poureth his benefits upon us.
13 He is our God, even the God of whom cometh salvation: God is the Lord, by whom we escape death.
14 Thy God hath sent forth strength for thee: stablish the thing, O God, that thou hast wrought in us.
15 Sing unto God, O ye kingdoms of the earth: O sing praises unto the Lord.
16 Who sitteth in the heavens over all, from the beginning: lo, he doth send out his voice, yea, and that a mighty voice.
17 Ascribe ye the power to God over Israel: his excellency and strength is in the clouds.
18 O God, wonderful art thou in thy holy places, even the God of Israel: he will give strength and power unto his people; blessed be God.

PSALM 69

AVE me, O God: for the waters have come in even unto my soul.

2 I sink in deep mire, where there is no standing:
I am come into deep waters, so that the floods run
over me.
3 I am weary of crying, my throat is dry: my sight
faileth me for waiting so long upon my God.
4 Let not them that trust in thee, O Lord God of
hosts, be ashamed for my sake: let not those that
seek thee be confounded through me, O Lord God of
Israel.
5 And why? for thy sake have I suffered reproof:
shame hath covered my face.
6 I am become a stranger unto my brethren: even
an alien unto my mother's children.
7 For the zeal of thine house hath even eaten me:
and the rebukes of them that rebuked thee are fallen
upon me.
8 I wept and chastened myself with fasting: and
that was turned to my reproof.
9 But, Lord, I make my prayer unto thee: in an
acceptable time.
10 Hear me, O God, in the multitude of thy mercy:
even in the truth of thy salvation.
11 Take me out of the mire, that I sink not: O let
me be delivered from them that hate me, and out of
the deep waters.
12 Let not the water-flood drown me, neither let
the deep swallow me up: and let not the pit shut her
mouth upon me.
13 Hear me, O Lord, for thy lovingkindness is
comfortable: turn thee unto me, according to the multitude of thy
mercies;
14 And hide not thy face from thy servant, for I am
in trouble: O haste thee, and hear me.
15 Draw nigh unto my soul, and save it: O deliver
me, because of mine enemies.
16 Thou hast known my reproof, my shame, and my
dishonor: mine adversaries are all in thy sight.
17 Reproach hath broken my heart, I am full of

heaviness: I looked for some to have pity on me, but there was no man, neither found I any to comfort me.
18 They gave me gall to eat: and when I was thirsty, they gave me vinegar to drink.
19 But as for me, when I am poor and in heaviness, thy help, O God, shall lift me up.
20 I will praise the name of God with a song: and magnify it with thanksgiving.
21 The humble shall consider this, and be glad: seek ye after God, and your soul shall live.
22 For the Lord heareth the poor: and despiseth not his prisoners.
23 Let heaven and earth praise him: the sea, and all that moveth therein.

PSALM 70

ASTE thee, O God, to deliver me: make haste to help me, O Lord.
2 Let all those that seek thee be joyful and glad in thee: and let all such as delight in thy salvation, say always, The Lord be praised.
3 As for me, I am poor and in misery: haste thou unto me, O God.
4 Thou art my Helper and my Redeemer: O make no long tarrying.

PSALM 71

IN thee, O Lord, have I put my trust, let me never be put to confusion: but rid me and deliver me in thy righteousness; incline thine ear unto me, and save me.

Be thou my strong hold, whereunto I may always resort: thou hast promised to help me, for thou art my house of defense, and my castle.
3 Deliver me, O my God, out of the hand of the ungodly: out of the hand of the unrighteous and cruel man.
4 For thou, O Lord God, art the thing that I long for: thou art my hope, even from my youth.
5 Through thee have I been holden up ever since I was born: thou art he that took me out of my mother's womb; my praise shall be always of thee.
6 I am become as it were a monster unto many: but my sure trust is in thee.
7 O let my mouth be filled with thy praise: that I may sing of thy glory and honor all the day long.
8 Cast me not away in the time of age: forsake me not when my strength faileth me.
9 Go not far from me, O God: my God, haste thee to help me.
10 As for me, I will patiently abide always: and will praise thee more and more.
11 My mouth shall daily speak of thy righteousness and salvation: for I know no end thereof.
12 I will go forth in the strength of the Lord God: and will make mention of thy righteousness only.
13 Thou, O God, hast taught me from my youth up until now: therefore will I tell of thy wondrous works.
14 Forsake me not, O God, in mine old age, when I am grey headed: until I have showed thy strength unto this generation, and thy power to all them that are yet for to come.
15 Thy righteousness, O God, is very high: and great things are they that thou hast done; O God, who is like unto thee?
16 O what great troubles and adversities hast thou showed me! and yet didst thou turn and refresh me: yea, and broughtest me from the deep of the earth again.

17 Thou hast brought me to great honor: and comforted me on every side.
18 My lips will be glad, when I sing unto thee: and so will my soul which thou hast delivered.
19 My tongue also shall talk of thy righteousness all the day long.

PSALM 73

RULY God is loving unto Israel: even unto such as are of a clean heart.
2 Nevertheless, my feet were almost gone: my leadings had well nigh slipped.
3 And why? I was grieved at the wicked: I do also see the ungodly in such prosperity.
4 Then thought I to understand this: but it was too hard for me,
5 Until I went into the sanctuary of God: then understood I the end of these men;
6 Namely, how thou dost set them in slippery places: and castest them down, and destroyest them.
7 O how suddenly do they consume: perish, and come to a fearful end!
8 Yea, even like as a dream when one awaketh: so shalt thou make their image to vanish out of the city.
9 Thus my heart was grieved: and it went even through my reins.
10 So foolish was I and ignorant: even as it were a beast before thee.
11 Nevertheless, I am always by thee: for thou hast holden me by my right hand.
12 Thou shalt guide me with thy counsel: and after that receive me to glory.
13 Whom have I in heaven but thee? and there is none upon earth that I desire in comparison of thee.
14 My flesh and my heart faileth: but God is the

strength of my heart, and my portion forever.

PSALM 75

NTO thee, O God, do we give thanks: yea, unto thee do we give thanks.

2 Thy name also is so near: and that do thy wondrous works declare.

3 When I receive the congregation: I shall judge according unto right.

4 I said unto the fools, Deal not so madly: and to the ungodly, Set not up your horn.

5 Set not up your horn on high: and speak not with: a stiff neck.

6 For promotion cometh neither from the east, nor from the west: nor yet from the south.

7 And why? God is the judge: he putteth down one, and setteth up another.

8 For in the hand of the Lord there is a cup, and the wine is red: it is full mixed, and he poureth out of the same.

9 As for the dregs thereof: all the ungodly of the earth shall drink them, and suck them out.

10 But I will talk of the God of Jacob: and praise him forever.

11 All the horns of the ungodly also will I break: and the horns of the righteous shall be exalted.

PSALM 76

HOU, even thou, O God, art to be feared: and who may stand in thy sight when thou art angry?

2 Thou didst cause thy judgment to be heard from heaven: the earth trembled, and was still,

3 When God arose to judgment: and to help all the meek upon earth.
4 The fierceness of man shall turn to thy praise: and the remainder of wrath shalt thou restrain.
5 Vow and pay unto the Lord your God, all ye that are round about him: bring presents unto him that ought to be feared.
6 He shall cut off the spirit of princes: and is wonderful among the kings of the earth.

PSALM 77

 WILL cry unto God with my voice: even unto God will I cry with my voice, and he shall hearken unto me.
2 In the time of my trouble I sought the Lord: my sore ran, and ceased not in the night season; my soul refused comfort.
3 When I am in heaviness, I will think upon God: when my heart is vexed, I will complain.
4 Thou boldest mine eyes waking: I am so feeble that I cannot speak.
5 I have considered the days of old: and the years that are past.
6 I call to remembrance my song: and in the night I commune with mine own heart, and search out my spirits.
7 Will the Lord absent himself forever? and will he be no more entreated?
8 Is his mercy clean gone forever? and is his promise come utterly to an end forevermore?
9 Hath God forgotten to be gracious? and will he shut up his lovingkindness in displeasure?
10 And I said, It is mine own infirmity: but I will remember the years of the right hand of the most Highest.
11 I will remember the works of the Lord: and call

to mind thy wonders of old time.
12 I will think also of all thy works: and my talking shall be of thy doings.
13 Thy way, O God, is holy: who is so great a God as our God?
14 Thou art the God that doest wonders: and hast declared thy power among the people.
15 Thou hast mightily delivered thy people: even the sons of Jacob and Joseph.
16 The waters saw thee, O God, the waters saw thee, and were afraid: the depths also were troubled.
17 The clouds poured out water, the air thundered: and thine arrows went abroad.
18 The voice of thy thunder was heard round about: the lightning shone upon the ground; the earth was moved, and shook withal.
19 Thy way is in the sea, and thy paths in the great waters: and thy footsteps are not known.
20 Thou leddest thy people like sheep, by the hand of Moses and Aaron.

PSALM 84

 HOW amiable are thy dwellings: thou Lord of hosts!
2 My soul hath a desire and longing to enter into the courts of the Lord: my heart and my flesh rejoice in the living God.
3 Yea, the sparrow hath found her an house; and the swallow a nest where she may lay her young: even thine altars, O Lord of hosts, my King and my God.
4 Blessed are they that dwell in thy house: they will be always praising thee.
5 Blessed is the man whose strength is in thee: in whose heart are thy ways.
6 Who, going through the vale of misery, use it for

a well: and the pools are filled with water.
7 They will go from strength to strength: and unto the God of gods appeareth every one of them in Sion.
8 O Lord God of hosts, hear my prayer: hearken, O God of Jacob.
9 Behold, O God our defender: and look upon the face of thine Anointed.
10 For one day in thy courts: is better than a thousand.
11 I had rather be a door-keeper in the house of my God: than to dwell in the tents of ungodliness.
12 For the Lord God is a light and defense, the Lord will give grace and glory: and no good thing shall he withhold from them that live a godly life.
13 O Lord God of hosts: blessed is the man that putteth his trust in thee.

PSALM 85

LORD, thou art become gracious unto thy land: thou hast turned away the captivity of Jacob.
2 Thou hast forgiven the offence of thy people: and covered all their sins.
3 Thou hast taken away all thy displeasure: and turned thyself from thy wrathful indignation.
4 Turn us then, O God our Savior: and let thine anger cease from us.
5 Wilt thou be displeased at us forever: and wilt thou stretch out thy wrath from one generation to another?
6 Wilt thou not turn again and quicken us: that thy people may rejoice in thee?
7 Show us thy mercy, O Lord: and grant us thy salvation.
8 I will hearken what the Lord God will say concerning me: for he shall speak peace unto his people,

and to his saints, that they turn not again.
9 For his salvation is nigh them that fear him: that glory may dwell in our land.
10 Mercy and truth have met together: righteousness and peace have kissed each other.
11 Truth shall flourish out of the earth: and righteousness hath looked down from heaven.
12 Yea, the Lord shall show lovingkindness: and our land shall give her increase.
13 Righteousness shall go before him: and shall direct us in the way of his steps.

PSALM 86

BOW down thine ear, O Lord, and hear me: for I am poor and in misery.
2 Preserve thou my soul, for I am holy: my God, save thy servant that putteth his trust in thee.
3 Be merciful unto me, O Lord: for I call daily upon thee.
4 Comfort the soul of thy servant: for unto thee, O Lord, do I lift up my soul.
5 For thou, Lord, art good and gracious: and of great mercy unto them that call upon thee.
6 Give ear, Lord, unto my prayer: and ponder the voice of my humble desires.
7 In the time of my trouble I will call upon thee: for thou hearest me.
8 Among the gods, there is none like unto thee, O Lord: there is none that can do as thou doest.
9 All nations whom thou hast made shall come and worship thee, O Lord: and shall glorify thy Name.
10 For thou art great, and doest wondrous things: thou art God alone.
11 Teach me thy way, O Lord, and I will walk in thy truth: O knit my heart unto thee, that I may fear

thy Name.
12 I will thank thee, O Lord my God, with all my heart: and will praise thy Name forevermore.
13 For great is thy mercy toward me: and thou hast delivered my soul from the nethermost hell.
14 Thou, O Lord God, art full of compassion and mercy: long-suffering, plenteous in goodness and truth.
15 O turn thee unto me, and have mercy upon me: give thy strength unto thy servant, and help the son of thine handmaid.
16 Show some token unto me for good, that they who hate me may see it, and be ashamed: because thou, Lord, hast holpen me, and comforted me.

PSALM 89

Y song shall be always of the lovingkindness of the Lord: with my mouth will I ever be showing thy truth from one generation to another.
2 For I have said, Mercy shall be set up forever: thy truth shalt thou establish in the heavens.
3 I have made a covenant with my chosen: I have sworn unto David my servant;
4 Thy seed will I establish forever: and set up thy throne from one generation to another.
5 O Lord, the very heavens shall praise thy wondrous works: and thy truth in the congregation of thy saints.
6 For who is he among the clouds: that shall be compared unto the Lord?
7 And what is he among the gods: that shall be like unto the Lord?
8 God is very greatly to be feared in the council of the saints: and to be had in reverence of all them that are round about him.
9 O Lord God of hosts, who is like unto thee? thy

truth, most mighty Lord, is on every side.
10 Thou rulest the raging of the sea: thou stillest the waves thereof when they arise.
11 The heavens are thine, the earth is thine: thou hast laid the foundation of the round world, and all that therein is.
12 Thou hast a mighty arm: strong is thy hand, and high is thy right hand.
13 Righteousness and equity are the habitation of thy seat: mercy shall go before thy face.
14 Blessed is the people, O Lord, that can rejoice in thee: they shall walk in the light of thy countenance.
15 Their delight shall be daily in thy Name: and in thy righteousness shall they make their boast.
16 For thou art the glory of their strength: and in thy lovingkindness thou shalt lift up our horns.
17 For the Lord is our defense: the Holy One of Israel is our King.

PSALM 90

ORD, thou hast been our refuge from one generation to another.
2 Before the mountains were brought forth, or ever the earth and the world were made: thou art God from everlasting, and world without end.
3 Thou turnest man to destruction: again thou sayest, Come again, ye children of men.
4 For a thousand years in thy sight are but as yesterday: seeing that is past as a watch in the night.
5 As soon as thou scatterest them, they are even as a sleep: and fade away suddenly like the grass.
6 In the morning it is green, and groweth up: but in the evening it is cut down, dried up, and withered.
7 For we consume away in thy displeasure: and are afraid at thy wrathful indignation.

8 Thou hast set our misdeeds before thee: and our secret sins in the light of thy countenance.
9 For when thou art angry, all our days are gone: we bring our years to an end as it were a tale that is told.
10 The days of our age are threescore years and ten; and though men be so strong, that they come to fourscore years, yet is their strength then but labor and sorrow: so soon passeth it away, and we are gone.
11 But who regardeth the power of thy wrath? for even according to thy fear, so is thy displeasure.
12 So teach us to number our days: that we may apply our hearts unto wisdom.
13 Turn thee again, O Lord, at the last: and be gracious unto thy servants.
14 O satisfy us with thy mercy, and that soon: so shall we rejoice and be glad all the days of our life.
15 Comfort us again now after the time that thou hast plagued us: and for the years wherein we have suffered adversity.
16 Show thy servants thy work: and their children thy glory.
17 And the glorious majesty of the Lord our God be upon us: prosper thou the work of our hands upon us, O prosper thou our handiwork.

PSALM 91

HOSO dwelleth under the defense of the Most High: shall abide under the shadow of the Almighty.
2 I will say unto the Lord, Thou art my hope, and my strong hold: my God, in him will I trust.
3 Surely he shall deliver thee from the snare of the hunter: and from the noisome pestilence.
4 He shall defend thee under his wings, and thou

shalt be safe under his feathers: his faithfulness and truth shall be thy shield and buckler.
5 Thou shalt not be afraid for any terror by night: nor for the arrow that flieth by day;
6 For the pestilence that walketh in darkness: nor for the sickness that destroyeth in the noon-day.
7 A thousand shall fall beside thee, and ten thousand thy right hand: but it shall not come nigh thee.
8 Yea, with thine eyes shalt thou behold: and see the reward of the ungodly.
9 Because thou hast made the Lord, who is my refuge: even the Most High, thy habitation;
10 There shall no evil happen unto thee: neither shall any plague come nigh thy dwelling.
11 For he shall give his angels charge over thee: to keep thee in all thy ways.
12 They shall bear thee in their hands: that thou hurt not thy foot against a stone.
13 Thou shalt go upon the lion and adder: the young lion and the dragon shalt thou tread under thy feet.
14 Because he hath set his love upon me, therefore will I deliver him: I will set him up, because he hath known my Name.
15 He shall call upon me, and I will hear him; yea, I am with him in trouble: I will deliver him, and bring him to honor.
16 With long life will I satisfy him: and show him my salvation.

PSALM 92

T is a good thing to give thanks unto the Lord: and to sing praises unto thy Name, O Most Highest.
2 To tell of thy lovingkindness early in the morning: and of thy truth in the night season.
3 For thou, Lord, hast made me glad through thy

works: and I will rejoice in giving praise for the operations of thy hands.
4 O Lord, how glorious are thy works: thy thought are very deep.
5 An unwise man doth not well consider this: and a fool doth not understand it.
6 When the ungodly are green as the grass, and when all the workers of iniquity do flourish, then they shall be destroyed forever: but thou, Lord, art the Most Highest forevermore.
7 For, lo, thine enemies, O Lord, lo, thine enemies shall perish: and all the workers of wickedness shall be destroyed.
8 The righteous shall flourish like a palm-tree: and shall spread abroad like a cedar of Libanus.
9 Such as are planted in the house of the Lord: shall flourish in the courts of the house of our God.
10 They also shall bring forth more fruit in their old age: and shall be fat and flourishing.
11 That they may show how true the Lord my strength is: and that there is no unrighteousness in him.

PSALM 93

THE Lord is King, and hath put on glorious apparel: the Lord hath put on his apparel, and girded himself with strength.
2 He hath made the round world so sure: that it cannot be moved.
3 Thy throne hath been established of old: thou art from everlasting.
4 The floods have risen, O Lord, the floods have lift up their voice: the floods lift up their waves.
5 The waves of the sea are mighty, and rage horribly: but yet the Lord, who dwelleth on high, is

mightier.
6 Thy testimonies, O Lord, are very sure: holiness becometh thine house forever.

PSALM 95

COME, let us sing unto the Lord: let us heartily rejoice in the strength of our salvation.
2 Let us come before his presence with thanksgiving: and show ourselves glad in him with psalms.
3 For the Lord is a great God: and a great King above all gods.
4 In his hand are all the corners of the earth: and the strength of the hills is his also.
5 The sea is his, and he made it: and his hands prepared the dry land.
6 O come let us worship, and fall down, and kneel before the Lord our Maker.
7 For he is the Lord our God: and we are the people of his pasture, and the sheep of his hand.
8 Today, if ye will hear his voice, harden not your hearts: as in the provocation, and as in the day of temptation in the wilderness;
9 When your fathers tempted me, proved me, and saw my works.
10 Forty years long was I grieved with this generation: and said, It is a people that do err in their hearts; for they have not known my ways.
1 1 Unto whom I sware in my wrath: that they should not enter into my rest.

PSALM 96

SING unto the Lord a new song: sing unto the

Lord, all the whole earth.
2 Sing unto the Lord, and praise his Name: be telling of his salvation from day to day.
3 Declare his honor unto the heathen: and his wonders unto all people.
4 For the Lord is great, and cannot worthily be praised: he is more to be feared than all gods.
5 As for all the gods of the heathen, they are but idols: but it is the Lord that made the heavens.
6 Glory and majesty are before him: strength and beauty are in his sanctuary.
7 Ascribe unto the Lord, O ye kindreds of the people: ascribe unto the Lord glory and power.
8 Ascribe unto the Lord the honor due unto his Name: bring presents, and come into his courts.
9 O worship the Lord in the beauty of holiness: let the whole earth stand in awe of him.
10 Tell it out among the heathen, that the Lord is King: and that it is he who hath made the round world so fast that it cannot be moved; and that he shall judge the people righteously.
11 Let the heavens rejoice, and let the earth be glad: let the sea make a noise, and all that therein is.
12 Let the field be joyful, and all that is in it: then shall all the trees of the wood rejoice before the Lord;
13 For he cometh, for he cometh to judge the earth: and with righteousness to judge the world, and the people with his truth.

PSALM 97

HE Lord is King, the earth may be glad thereof: yea, the multitude of the isles may be glad thereof.
Clouds and darkness are round about him: righteousness and judgment are the habitation of his throne.
3 There shall go a fire before him: and burn up his

enemies on every side.
4 His lightnings enlightened the world: the earth saw it, and was afraid.
5 The hills melted like wax at the presence of the Lord: at the presence of the Lord of the whole earth.
6 The heavens have declared his righteousness: and all the people have seen his glory.
7 Thou, Lord, art higher than all that are in the earth: thou art exalted far above all gods.
8 O ye that love the Lord, see that ye hate the thing which is evil: the Lord preserveth the souls of his saints; he shall deliver them from the hand of the ungodly.
9 There is sprung up a light for the righteous: and joyful gladness for such as are true-hearted.
10 Rejoice in the Lord, ye righteous: and give thanks for a remembrance of his holiness.

PSALM 98

SING unto the Lord a new song: for he hath done marvelous things.
2 With his own right hand, and with his holy arm: hath he gotten himself the victory.
3 The Lord declared his salvation: his righteousness hath he openly showed in the sight of the heathen.
4 He hath remembered his mercy and truth toward the house of Israel: and all the ends of the world have seen the salvation of our God.
5 Show yourselves joyful unto the Lord, all ye lands: sing, rejoice, and give thanks.
6 Let the sea make a noise, and all that therein is: the round world, and they that dwell therein.
7 Let the floods clap their hands, and let the hills be joyful together before the Lord: for he cometh to judge the earth.

8 With righteousness shall he judge the world: and the people with equity.

PSALM 99

 HE Lord is King, be the people never so impatient: he sitteth between the cherubim, be the earth never so unquiet.

2 The Lord is great in Sion: and high above all people.

3 They shall give thanks unto thy Name: which is great, wonderful, and holy.

4 O magnify the Lord our God: and fall down before his footstool, for he is holy.

5 O magnify the Lord our God, and worship him upon his holy hill: for the Lord our God is holy.

PSALM 100

 BE joyful in the Lord, all ye lands: serve the Lord with gladness, and come before his presence with a song.

2 Be ye sure that the Lord he is God; it is he that hath made us, and not we ourselves: we are his people, and the sheep of his pasture.

3 O go your way into his gates with thanksgiving, and into his courts with praise: be thankful unto him, and speak good of his Name.

For the Lord is gracious, his mercy is everlasting: and his truth endureth from generation to generation.

PSALM 102

EAR my prayer, O Lord: and let my cry come unto thee.

2 Hide not thy face from me in the time of my trouble: incline thine ear unto me when I call; O hear me, and that speedily.

3 For my days are consumed away like smoke: and my bones are burnt up as it were a fire-brand.

4 My heart is smitten down, and withered like grass: so that I forget to eat my bread.

5 For the voice of my groaning, my bones will scarce cleave to my flesh.

6 I am become like a pelican in the wilderness: and like an owl that is in the desert.

7 I have watched, and am even as it were a sparrow that sitteth alone upon the house-top.

8 Mine enemies revile me all the day long: and they that are mad upon me are sworn together against me.

9 For I have eaten ashes as it were bread: and mingled my drink with weeping;

10 And that because of thine indignation and wrath: for thou hast taken me up, and cast me down.

11 My days are gone like a shadow: and I am withered like grass.

12 But thou, O Lord, shalt endure forever: and thy remembrance throughout all generations.

13 Thou shalt arise, and have mercy upon Sion: for it is time that thou have mercy upon her, yea, the time is come.

14 And why? thy servants think upon her stones: and it pitieth them to see her in the dust.

1 5 The heathen shall fear thy name, O Lord: and all the kings of the earth thy majesty.

16 When the Lord shall build up Sion: and when his glory shall appear;

17 When he turneth him unto the prayer of the poor destitute: and despiseth not their desire.

18 This shall be written for those that come after: and the people that shall be born shall praise the Lord.
19 For he hath looked down from his sanctuary: out of heaven did the Lord behold the earth;
20 That he might hear the mournings of such as are in captivity: and deliver those that are appointed unto death.
21 That they may declare the name of the Lord in Sion: and his praise in Jerusalem;
22 When the people are gathered together: and the kingdoms also, to serve the Lord.
23 He brought down my strength in my journey: and shortened my days.
24 But I said, O my God, take me not away in the midst of mine age: as for thy years, they endure throughout all generations.
25 Thou, Lord, in the beginning hast laid the foundation of the earth: and the heavens are the work of thy hands.
26 They shall perish, but thou shalt endure: they all shall wax old as doth a garment,
27 And as a vesture shalt thou change them, and they shall be changed: but thou art the same, and thy years shall not fail.
8 The children of thy servants shall continue: and their seed shall stand fast in thy sight.

PSALM 103

RAISE the Lord, O my soul: and all that is within me, praise his holy Name.
2 Praise the Lord, O my soul: and forget not all his benefits.
3 Who forgiveth all thy sins: and healeth all thine infirmities.
4 Who saveth thy life from destruction: and crovvneth

thee with mercy and lovingkindness.
5 Who satisfieth thy mouth with good things: making thee young and lusty as an eagle.
6 The Lord executeth righteousness and judgment for all them that are oppressed.
7 He showed his ways unto Moses: his works unto the children of Israel.
8 The Lord is full of compassion and mercy: long-suffering, and of great goodness.
9 He will not always be chiding: neither keepeth he his anger forever.
10 He hath not dealt with us after our sins: nor rewarded us according to our wickedness.
11 For look how high the heaven is in comparison of the earth: so great is his mercy also toward them that fear him.
12 Look how wide also the east is from the west: so far hath he set our sins from us.
13 Yea, like as a father pitieth his own children: even so is the Lord merciful unto them that fear him.
14 For he knoweth whereof we are made: he remembereth that we are but dust.
1-5 The days of man are but as grass: for he flourisheth as a flower of the field.
16 For as soon as the wind goeth over it, it is gone: and the place thereof shall know it no more.
17 But the merciful goodness of the Lord endureth forever and ever upon them that fear him: and his righteousness upon children's children;
18 Even upon such as keep his covenant: and think upon his commandments to do them.
19 The Lord hath prepared his seat in heaven: and his kingdom ruleth over all.
20 O praise the Lord, ye angels of his, ye that excel in strength: ye that fulfil his commandment, and hearken unto the voice of his words.
21 O praise the Lord, all ye his hosts: ye servants of his that do his pleasure.

22 O speak good of the Lord, all ye works of his, in all places of his dominion: praise thou the Lord, O my soul.

PSALM 104

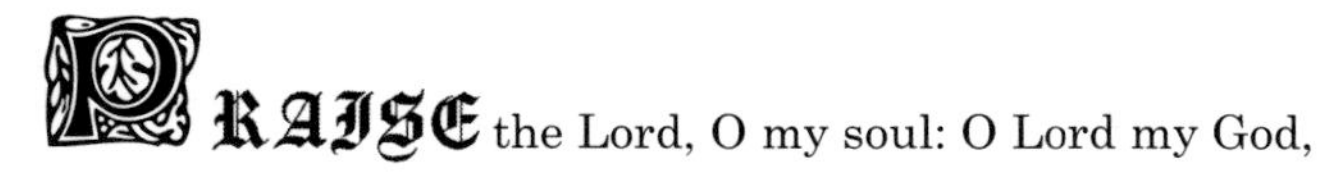
PRAISE the Lord, O my soul: O Lord my God, thou art become exceeding glorious, thou art clothed with majesty and honor.

2 Thou deckest thyself with light as it were with a garment: and spreadest out the heavens like a curtain.

3 Who layeth the beams of his chambers in the waters: and maketh the clouds his chariot, and walketh upon the wings of the wind.

4 He maketh his angels spirits: and his ministers a flaming fire.

5 He laid the foundations of the earth: that it never should move at any time.

6 Thou coveredst it with the deep like as with a garment: the waters stood above the mountains.

7 At thy rebuke they fled: at the voice of thy thunder they hasted away.

8 They go up as high as the hills, and down to the valleys beneath: even unto the place which thou hast appointed for them.

9 Thou hast set them their bounds which they shall not pass: neither turn again to cover the earth.

10 He sendeth the springs into the valleys which run among the hills.

1 1 All beasts of the field drink thereof: and the wild asses quench their thirst.

12 Beside them shall the fowls of the air have their habitation: and sing among the branches.

13 He watereth the hills from above: the earth is filled with the fruit of thy works.

14 He bringeth forth grass for the cattle: and green

herb for the service of men.
15 That he may bring food out of the earth, and wine that maketh glad the heart of man: and oil to make him a cheerful countenance, and bread to strengthen man's heart.
16 The trees of the Lord also are full of sap: even the cedars of Libanus which he hath planted.
17 Wherein the birds make their nests: and the fir-trees are a dwelling for the stork.
18 The high hills are a refuge for the wild goats: and so are the stony rocks for the conies.
19 He appointed the moon for certain seasons: and the sun knoweth his going down.
20 Thou makest darkness, and it is night: wherein all the beasts ot tne forest do move.
2 1 The lions roaring after their prey: do seek their meat from God.
22 The sun ariseth, and they get them away together: and lay them down in their dens.
23 Man goeth forth to his work, and to his labor: until the evening.
24 O Lord, how manifold are thy works: in wisdom hast thou made them all; the earth is full of thy riches.
25 So is the great and wide sea also: wherein are things creeping innumerable, both small and great beasts.
26 There go the ships, and there is that leviathan: whom theu hast made to take his pastime therein.
27 These wait all upon thee: that thou mayest give them meat in due season.
28 When thou givest it them, they gather it: and when thou openest thine hand, they are filled with good.
29 When thou hidest thy face, they are troubled: when thou takest away their breath, they die, and are turned again to their dust.
30 Thou sendest forth thy Spirit, they are created:

and thou renewest the face of the earth.
31 The glorious Majesty of the Lord shall endure forever: the Lord shall rejoice in his works.
32 The earth shall tremble at the look of him: if he do but touch the hills, they shall smoke.
33 I will sing unto the Lord as long as I live: I will praise my God while I have my being.
34 And so shall my words please him: my joy shall be in the Lord.
35 As for sinners, they shall be consumed out of the earth, and the ungodly shall come to an end: praise thou the Lord, O my soul, praise the Lord.

PSALM 107. PART 1.

 GIVE thanks unto the Lord, for he is gracious: and his mercy endureth forever.
2 Let them give thanks whom the Lord hath redeemed: and delivered from the hand of the enemy;
3 And gathered them out of the lands, from the east, and from the west: from the north, and from the south.
4 They went astray in the wilderness out of the way: and found no city to dwell in.
5 Hungry and thirsty: their soul fainted in them.
6 So they cried unto the Lord in their trouble: and he delivered them from their distress.
7 He led them forth by the right way: that they might go to a city of habitation.
8 O that men would therefore praise the Lord for his goodness: and declare the wonders that he doeth for the children of men!
9 For he satisfieth the longing soul: and filleth the hungry soul with goodness;
10 Such as sit in darkness and in the shadow of death: being fast bound in misery and iron.

11 Because they rebelled against the words of the Lord: and lightly regarded the counsel of the Most Highest;
12 He also brought down their heart through heaviness: they fell down, and there was none to help them.
13 Then they cried unto the Lord in their trouble: and he delivered them out of their distress.
14 For he brought them out of darkness, and out of the shadow of death: and brake their bonds in sunder.
15 O that men would therefore praise the Lord for his goodness: and declare the wonders that he doeth for the children of men!
16 For he hath broken the gates of brass: and smitten the bars of iron in sunder.
17 Foolish men are plagued for their offence: and because of their wickedness.
18 Their soul abhorreth all manner of meat: and they draw near unto the gates of death.
19 Then they cry unto the Lord in their trouble: and he delivereth them out of their distress.
20 He sent his word, and healed them: and they were saved from their destruction.
21 O that men would therefore praise the Lord for his goodness: and declare the wonders that he doeth for the children of men!
22 That they would offer unto him the sacrifice of thanksgiving: and tell out his works with gladness!

PSALM 107. PART 2.

HEY that go down to the sea in ships: and occupy their business in great waters;
2 These men see the works of the Lord: and his wonders in the deep.
3 For at his word the stormy wind ariseth: which lifteth up the waves thereof.

4 They are carried up to the heaven, and down again to the deep: their soul melteth away because of the trouble.
5 They reel to and fro, and stagger like a drunken man: and are at their wit's end.
6 Then they cry unto the Lord in their trouble: and he delivereth them out of their distress.
7 For he maketh the storm a calm: so that the waves thereof are still.
8 Then they are glad, because they are at rest: so he bringeth them unto the haven where they would be.
9 O that men would therefore praise the Lord for his goodness: and declare the wonders that he doeth for the children of men!
10 That they would exalt him also in the congregation of the people: and praise him in the assembly of the elders.
11 Who turneth the floods into a wilderness: and the water-springs into dry ground.
12 A fruitful land maketh he barren: for the wickedness of them that dwell therein.
13 Again, he maketh the wilderness a standing water: and water-springs of a dry ground.
14 And there he setteth the hungry: that they may build them a city to dwell in;
15 That they may sow their land, and plant vineyards: to yield them fruits of increase.
16 He blesseth them so that they multiply exceedingly: and suffereth not their cattle to decrease.
17 Again, when they are diminished, and brought low: through oppression, through any plague or trouble;
18 Though he suffer them to be evil entreated through tyrants: and let them wander out of the way in the wilderness;
19 Yet helpeth he the poor out of misery: and maketh him households like a flock of sheep.
20 The righteous will consider this, and rejoice:

and the mouth of all wickedness shall be stopped.
21 Whoso is wise will ponder these things: and they shall understand the lovingkindness of the Lord.

PSALM 111

WILL give thanks unto the Lord with my whole heart: secretly among the faithful, and in the congregation.
2 The works of the Lord are great: sought out of all them that have pleasure therein.
3 His work is worthy to be praised, and had in honor: and his righteousness endureth forever.
4 The merciful and gracious Lord hath so done his marvelous works: that they ought to be had in remebrance.
5 He hath given meat unto them that fear him: he will be ever mindful of his covenant.
6 The works of his hands are verity and judgment: and all his commandments are true.
7 They stand fast forever and ever: and are done in truth and equity.
8 He sent redemption unto his people: he hath commanded his covenant forever; holy and reverend is his Name.
9 The fear of the Lord is the beginning of wisdom: a good understanding have all they that do thereafter: the praise of it endureth forever.

PSALM 112

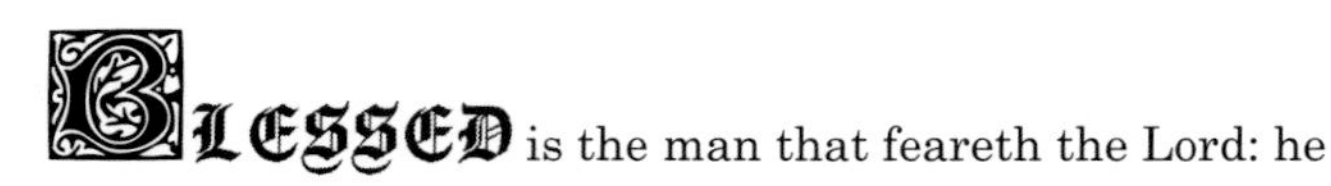
BLESSED is the man that feareth the Lord: he hath great delight in his commandments.
2 His seed shall be mighty upon earth: the generation of the faithful shall be blessed.
3 Riches and plenteousness shall be in his house:

and his righteousness endureth forever.
4 Unto the godly there ariseth up light in the darkness: he is merciful, loving, and righteous.
5 A good man is merciful, and lendeth: and will guide his words with discretion.
6 Surely he shall not be moved: and the righteous shall be had in everlasting remembrance.
7 He will not be afraid of any evil tidings: for his heart standeth fast, and believeth in the Lord.
8 He hath dispersed abroad, and given to the poor: and his righteousness remaineth forever; his horn shall be exalted with honor.
9 The ungodly shall see it, and it shall grieve him: he shall gnash with his teeth, and consume away; the desire of the ungodly shall perish.

PSALM 113

 RAISE the Lord, ye servants of his: O praise the Name of the Lord.
2 Blessed be the Name of the Lord: from this time forth forevermore.
3 The Lord's Name is praised: from the rising up of the sun unto the going down of the same.

4 The Lord is high above all heathen: and his glory above the heavens.
5 Who is like unto the Lord our God, who hath his dwelling so high: and yet humbleth himself to behold the things that are in heaven and earth?
6 He taketh up the simple out of the dust: and lifteth the poor out of the mire;
7 That he may set him with the princes: even with the princes of his people.
8 He maketh the barren woman to keep house: and to be a joyful mother of children.

PSALM 114

WHEN Israel came out of Egypt, and the house of Jacob from among the strange people;
2 Judah was his sanctuary: and Israel his dominion.
3 The sea saw that, and fled: Jordan was driven back.
4 The mountains skipped like rams: and the little hills like young sheep.
5 What aileth thee, O thou sea, that thou fleddest: and thou Jordan, that thou wast driven back?
6 Ye mountains, that ye skipped like rams: and ye little hills, like young sheep?
7 Tremble, thou earth, at the presence of the Lord: at the presence of the God of Jacob;
8 Who turned the hard rock into a standing water and the flint-stone into a springing well.

PSALM 115

NOT unto us, O Lord, not unto us, but unto thy Name give the praise: for thy loving mercy, and for thy truth's sake
2 Wherefore shall the heathen say: Where is now their God?
3 As for our God, he is in heaven: he hath done whatsoever pleased him.
4 O Israel, trust thou in the Lord: he is their succor and defense.
5 Ye house of Aaron, put your trust in the Lord: he is their helper and defender.
6 Ye that fear the Lord, put your trust in the Lord: he is their helper and defender.
7 The Lord hath been mindful of us, and he shall

bless us: even he shall bless the house of Israel; he shall bless the house of Aaron.

8 He shall bless them that fear the Lord, both small and great.

9 The Lord shall increase you more and more: you and your children.

10 Ye are the blessed of the Lord: who made heaven and earth.

1 1 All the whole heavens are the Lord's: the earth hath he given to the children of men.

12 The dead praise not thee, O Lord: neither any that go down into silence.

13 But we will praise the Lord: from this time forth forevermore. Praise the Lord.

PSALM 116

 AM well pleased that the Lord hath heard the voice of my prayer;

2 That he hath inclined his ear unto me: therefore will I call upon him as long as I live.

3 The snares of death compassed me round about: and the pains of hell gat hold upon me.

4 I found trouble and heaviness, and I called upon the name of the Lord: O Lord, I beseech thee, deliver my soul.

5 Gracious is the Lord, and righteous: yea, our God is merciful.

6 The Lord preserveth the simple: I was in misery, and he helped me.

7 Turn again then unto thy rest, O my soul: for the Lord hath rewarded thee.

8 And why? thou hast delivered my soul from death: mine eyes from tears, and my feet from falling.

9 I will walk before the Lord: in the land of the living.

10 I believed, and therefore have I spoken; but I was sore troubled: I said in my haste, All men are liars.
1 1 What reward shall I give unto the Lord: for all the benefits which he hath done unto me?
121 will receive the cup of salvation: and call upon the Name of the Lord.
131 will pay my vows now in the presence of all his people: right dear in the sight of the Lord is the death of his saints.
14 Behold, O Lord, how that I am thy servant: I am thy servant, and the son of thine handmaid; thou hast broken my bonds in sunder.
15 I will offer to thee the sacrifice of thanksgiving: and will call upon the Name of the Lord.
16 I will pay my vows unto the Lord, in the sight of all his people: in the courts of the Lord's house, even in the midst of thee, O Jerusalem. Praise the Lord.

PSALM 117

 RAISE the Lord, all ye heathen: praise him, all ye nations.
2 For his merciful kindness is ever more and more towards us: and the truth of the Lord endureth for ever. Praise the Lord.

PSALM 118

 GIVE thanks unto the Lord, for he is gracious: because his mercy endureth forever.
2 Let Israel now confess, that he is gracious: and that his mercy endureth forever.
3 Let the house of Aaron now confess: that his mercy endureth forever.

4 Yea, let them now that fear the Lord confess: that his mercy endureth forever.
5 I called upon the Lord in trouble: and the Lord heard me at large.
6 The Lord is on my side: I will not fear what man doeth unto me.
7 The Lord taketh my part with them that help me: therefore shall I see my desire upon mine enemies.
8 It is better to trust in the Lord: than to put any confidence in man.
9 It is better to trust in the Lord: than to put any confidence in princes.
10 All nations compassed me round about: but in the Name of the Lord will I destroy them.
1 1 They kept me in on every side, they kept me in, I say, on every side: but in the Name of the Lord will I destroy them.
12 They came about me like bees, and are extinct even as the fire among the thorns: for in the Name of the Lord I will destroy them.
1 3 Thou hast thrust sore at me, that I might fall: but the Lord was my help.
14 The Lord is my strength and my song: and is become my salvation.
15 The voice of joy and health is in the dwelling of the righteous: the right hand of the Lord bringeth mighty things to pass.
16 The right hand of the Lord hath the pre-eminence: the right hand of the Lord bringeth mighty things to pass.
17 I shall not die, but live: and declare the works of the Lord.
18 The Lord hath chastened and corrected me: but he hath not given me over unto death.
19 Open me the gates of righteousness: that I may go into them, and give thanks unto the Lord.
20 This is the gate of the Lord: the righteous shall enter into it.

21 I will thank thee: for thou hast heard me, and art become my salvation.
22 The same stone which the builders refused: is become the head-stone of the corner.
23 This is the Lord's doing: and it is marvelous in our eyes.
24 This is the day which the Lord hath made: we will rejoice and be glad in it.
25 Help me now, O Lord: O Lord, send us now prosperity.
26 Blessed be he that cometh in the Name of the Lord: we have wished you good luck, ye that are of the house of the Lord.
27 God is the Lord, who hath showed us light: bind the sacrifice with cords, yea, even unto the horns of the altar.
28 Thou art my God, and I will thank thee: thou art my God, and I will praise thee.
29 O give thanks unto the Lord, for he is gracious: and his mercy endureth forever.

PSALM 119

BLESSED are those that are undefiled in the way: and walk in the law of the Lord.
Blessed are they that keep his testimonies: and seek him with their whole heart.
3 For they who do no wickedness: walk in his ways.
4 Thou hast charged: that we should diligently keep thy commandments.
5 O that my ways were made so direct: that I might keep thy statutes!
6 So shall I not be confounded: while I have respect unto all thy commandments.
7 I will thank thee with an unfeigned heart: when I shall have learned the judgments of thy righteousness.

8 I will keep thy statutes: O forsake me not utterly.

WHEREWITHAL shall a young man cleanse his way? Even by ruling himself after thy word.

2 With my whole heart have I sought thee: O let me not go wrong out of thy commandments.

3 Thy words have I hid within my heart: that I might not sin against thee.

4 Blessed art thou, O Lord: O teach me thy statutes.

5 With my lips have I been telling: of the judgments of thy mouth.

6 I have had as great delight in the way of thy testimonies: as in all manner of riches.

7 I will talk of thy commandments: and have respect unto thy ways.

8 My delight shall be in thy statutes: and I will not forget thy word.

O DO well unto thy servant: that I may live, and keep thy word.

2 Open thou mine eyes: that I may see the wondrous things of thy law.

3 I am a stranger upon earth: O hide not thy commandments from me.

4 My soul breaketh out for the very fervent desire: that it hath always unto thy judgments.

5 Thou hast rebuked the proud: and cursed are they that do err from thy commandments.

6 O turn from me shame and rebuke: for I have kept thy testimonies.

7 Princes also did sit and speak against me: but thy servant is occupied in thy statutes.

For thy testimonies are my delight: and my counsellors.

MY soul cleaveth to the dust: O quicken thou me, according to thy word.

I have acknowledged my ways, and thou heardest me: O teach me thy statutes.

3 Make me to understand the way of thy commandments: and so shall I talk of thy wondrous works.
4 My soul melteth away for very heaviness: comfort thou me according to thy word.
5 Take from me the way of lying: and cause thou me to make much of thy laws.
6 I have chosen the way of truth: and thy judgments have I laid before me.
7 I have stuck unto thy testimonies: O Lord, confound me not.
8 I will run the way of thy commandments: when thou hast set my heart at liberty.

TEACH me, O Lord, the way of thy statutes: and I shall keep it unto the end.
2 Give me understanding, and I shall keep thy law: yea, I shall keep it with my whole heart.
3 Make me to go in the path of thy commandments: for therein is my desire.
4 Incline my heart unto thy testimonies: and not to covetousness.
5 O turn away mine eyes, lest they behold vanity: and quicken thou me in thy way.
6 O stablish thy word in thy servant: that I may fear thee.
7 Take away the rebuke that I am afraid of: for thy judgments are good.
Behold, my delight is in thy commandments: O quicken me in thy righteousness.

LET thy loving mercy also come unto me, O Lord: even thy salvation, according unto thy word.
2 So shall I make answer unto him that reproacheth me: for my trust is in thy word.
3 O take not the word of thy truth utterly out of my mouth: for my hope is in thy judgments.
4 So shall I always keep thy law: yea, forever and ever.

5 And I will walk at liberty: for I seek thy commandments.

6 I will speak of thy testimonies also even before kings: and will not be ashamed.

7 And my delight shall be in thy commandments: which I have loved.

8 My hands also will I lift up unto thy commandments, which I have loved: and my study shall be in thy statutes.

O THINK upon thy servant, as concerning thy word: wherein thou hast caused me to put my trust.

2 The same is my comfort in my trouble: for thy word hath quickened me.

The proud have had me exceedingly in derision: yet have I not shrunk from thy law.

4 For I remembered thine everlasting judgments, O Lord: and received comfort.

5 I am horribly afraid for the ungodly: that forsake thy law.

6 Thy statutes have been my songs: in the house of my pilgrimage.

7 I have thought upon thy Name, O Lord, in the night-season: and have kept thy law.

8 This I had: because I kept thy commandments.

THOU art my portion, O Lord: I have promised to keep thy law.

2 I made my humble petition in thy presence with my whole heart: O be merciful unto me, according to thy word.

3 I called mine own ways to remembrance: and turned my feet unto thy testimonies.

4 I made haste, and prolonged not the time: to keep thy commandments.

5 The congregations of the ungodly have robbed me: but I have not forgotten thy law.

6 At midnight I will rise to give thanks unto thee: because of thy righteous judgments.
7 I am a companion of all them that fear thee: and keep thy commandments.
8 The earth, O Lord, is full of thy mercy: O teach me thy statutes.

O LORD, thou hast dealt graciously with thy servant: according unto thy word.
2 O teach me true understanding and knowledge: for I have believed thy commandments.
3 Before I was troubled I went wrong: but now I have kept thy word.
4 Thou art good and gracious: O teach me thy statutes.
The proud have imagined a lie against me: but I will keep thy commandments with my whole heart.
6 Their heart is fat as brawn: but my delight hath been in thy law.
7 It is good for me that I have been in trouble: that I may learn thy statutes.
8 The law of thy mouth is dearer unto me: than thousands of gold and silver.

THY hands have made me and fashioned me: O give me understanding, that I may learn thy commandments.
2 They that fear thee will be glad when they see me: because I have put my trust in thy word.
3 I know, O Lord, that thy judgments are right: and that thou, of very faithfulness, hast caused me to be troubled.
4 O let thy merciful kindness be my comfort: according to thy word unto thy servant.
5 O let thy loving mercies come unto me, that I may live: for thy law is my delight.
6 Let the proud be ashamed, for they go wickedly about to destroy me: but I will be occupied in thy commandments.

7 Let such as fear thee, and have known thy testimonies: be turned unto me.
8 O let my heart be sound in thy statutes: that I be not ashamed.

MY soul hath longed for thy salvation: and I have a good hope because of thy word.
2 Mine eyes long for thy word: saying, O when wilt thou comfort me?
For I am become like a bottle in the smoke: yet do I not forget thy statutes.
4 How many are the days of thy servant: when wilt thou be avenged of them that persecute me?
5 The proud have digged pits for me: which are not after thy law.
6 All thy commandments are true: they persecute me falsely; O be thou my help.
7 They had almost made an end of me upon earth: but I forsook not thy commandments.
8 O quicken me after thy lovingkindness: and so shall I keep the testimonies of thy mouth.

O LORD, thy word: endureth forever in heaven.

2 Thy truth also remaineth from one generation to another: thou hast laid the foundation of the earth, and it abideth.
3 They continue this day according to thine ordinance: for all things serve thee.
4 If my delight had not been in thy law: I should have perished in my trouble.
5 I will never forget thy commandments: for with them thou hast quickened me.
6 I am thine, save me: for I have sought thy commandments.
7 The ungodly laid wait for me, to destroy me: but I will consider thy testimonies.
8 I see that all things come to an end: but thy commandment is exceeding broad.

LORD, what love have I unto thy law: all the day long is my study in it.
2 Thou through thy commandments hast made me wiser than mine enemies: for they are ever with me.
3 I have more understanding than my teachers: for thy testimonies are my study.
4 I am wiser than the aged: because I keep thy commandments.
5 I have refrained my feet from every evil way: that I may keep thy word.
6 I have not shrunk from thy judgments: for thou teachest me.
7 O how sweet are thy words unto my taste: yea, sweeter than honey unto my mouth.
8 Through thy commandments I get understanding: therefore I hate all evil ways.

THY word is a lantern unto my feet: and a light unto my path.
2 I have sworn, and am steadfastly purposed: to keep thy righteous judgments.
3 I am troubled above measure: quicken me, O Lord, according to thy word.
4 Let the free-will offerings of my mouth please thee, O Lord: and teach me thy judgments.
5 My soul is always in my hand: yet do I not forget thy law.
6 The ungodly have laid a snare for me: but yet I swerved not from thy commandments.
7 Thy testimonies have I claimed as mine heritage forever: and why? they are the very joy of my heart.
8 I have applied my heart to fulfil thy statutes always: even unto the end.

I HATE them that imagine evil things: but thy law do I love.
2 Thou art my defense and shield: and my trust is

in thy word.

3 Away from me, ye wicked: I will keep the commandments of my God.

4 O establish me according to thy word, that I may live: and let me not be disappointed of my hope.

5 Hold thou me up, and I shall be safe: yea, my delight shall be ever in thy statutes.

6 Thou hast trodden down all them that depart from thy statutes: for they imagine but deceit.

Thou puttest away all the ungodly of the earth like dross: therefore I love thy testimonies.

8 My flesh trembleth for fear of thee: and I am afraid of thy judgments.

I DEAL with the thing that is lawful and right: O give me not over unto mine oppressors.

2 Make thou thy servant to delight in that which is good: let not the proud oppress me.

3 Mine eyes are wasted away with looking for thy health: and for the word of thy righteousness.

4 O deal with thy servant according unto thy loving mercy: and teach me thy statutes.

5 I am thy servant: O grant me understanding, that I may know thy testimonies.

6 It is time for thee, Lord, to lay to thine hand: for they have destroyed thy law.

7 For I love thy commandments: above gold and precious stones.

8 Therefore I esteem all thy precepts concerning all things to be right: and all false ways I utterly abhor.

THY testimonies are wonderful: therefore doth my soul keep them.

2 When thy word goeth forth: it giveth light and understanding unto the simple.

3 I opened my mouth, and drew in my breath: for my delight was in thy commandments.

4 O look thou upon me, and be merciful unto me:

as thou usest to do unto those that love thy Name.
5 Order my steps in thy word: and so shall no wickedness have dominion over me.
6 O deliver me from the wrongful dealings of men: and so shall I keep thy commandments.
7 Show the light of thy countenance upon thy servant: and teach me thy statutes.
8 Mine eyes gush out with water: because men keep not thy law.

RIGHTEOUS art thou, O Lord: and true are thy judgments.
2 The testimonies that thou hast commanded: are exceeding righteous and true.
3 My zeal hath even consumed me: because mine enemies have forgotten thy words.
4 Thy word is tried to the uttermost: and thy servant loveth it.
5 I am small, and of no reputation: yet do I not forget thy commandments.
6 Thy righteousness is an everlasting righteousness: and thy law is the truth.
7 Trouble and heaviness have taken hold upon me yet is my delight in thy commandments.
8 The righteousness of thy testimonies is everlasting: O grant me understanding, and I shall live.

I CALL with my whole heart: hear me, O Lord, I will keep thy statutes.
2 Yea, even unto thee do I call: help me, and I shall keep thy testimonies.
3 Early in the morning do I cry unto thee: for in thy word is my trust.
4 Mine eyes prevent the night-watches: that I may be occupied in thy words.
5 Hear my voice, O Lord, according unto thy loving-kindness: quicken me, according as thou art wont.
6 They draw nigh that of malice persecute me: and

are afar from thy law.

7 Be thou nigh at hand, O Lord: for all thy commandments are true.

8 As concerning thy testimonies, I have known long since: that thou hast founded them forever.

O CONSIDER mine adversity, and deliver me: for I do not forget thy law.

2 Avenge thou my cause, and deliver me: quicken me, according to thy word.

3 Health is far from the ungodly: for they regard not thy statutes.

4 Great is thy mercy, O Lord: quicken me, as thou art wont.

5 Many there are that trouble me, and persecute me: yet do I not swerve from thy testimonies.

6 It grieveth me when I see the transgressors: because they keep not thy law.

7 Consider, O Lord, how I love thy commandments: O quicken me, according to thy lovingkindness.

8 Thy word is true from everlasting: all the judgments of thy righteousness endure forevermore.

PRINCES have persecuted me without a cause: but my heart standeth in awe of thy word.

2 I am as glad of thy word: as one that findeth great spoils.

3 As for lies, I hate and abhor them: but thy law do I love.

4 Seven times a day do I praise thee: because of thy righteous judgments.

5 Great is the peace that they have who love thy law: and they are not offended at it.

6 Lord, I have looked for thy saving health: and done after thy commandments.

7 My soul hath kept thy testimonies: and loved them exceedingly.

8 I have kept thy commandments and testimonies: for all my ways are before thee.

LET my complaint come before thee, O Lord: give me understanding, according to thy word.

2 Let my supplication come before thee: deliver me, according to thy word.

3 My lips shall speak of thy praise: when thou hast taught me thy statutes.

4 Yea, my tongue shall sing of thy word: for all thy commandments are righteous.

5 Let thine hand help me: for I have chosen thy commandments.

6 I have longed for thy saving health, O Lord: and in thy law is my delight.

7 O let my soul live, and it shall praise thee: and thy judgments shall help me.

8 I have gone astray like a sheep that is lost: O seek thy servant, for I do not forget thy commandments.

PSALM 121

WILL lift up mine eyes unto the hills: from whence cometh my help.

2 My help cometh even from the Lord: who hath made heaven and earth.

3 He will not suffer thy foot to be moved: and he that keepeth thee will not sleep.

4 Behold, he that keepeth Israel: shall neither slumber nor sleep.

5 The Lord himself is thy keeper: the Lord is thy defense upon thy right hand.

6 So that the sun shall not smite thee by day: neither the moon by night.

7 The Lord shall preserve thee from all evil: yea, it is even he that shall keep thy soul.

8 The Lord shall preserve thy going out and thy coming in: from this time forth forevermore.

PSALM 123

NTO thee I lift up mine eyes: O thou that dwellest in the heavens.

2 Behold, even as the eyes of servants look unto the hand of their masters, and as the eyes of a maiden unto the hand of her mistress: even so our eyes wait upon the Lord our God, until he have mercy upon us.

3 Have mercy upon us, O Lord, have mercy upon us: for we are utterly despised.

4 Our soul is filled with the scornful reproof of the wealthy: and with the despitefulness of the proud.

PSALM 124

IF the Lord himself had not been on our side, now may Israel say: if the Lord himself had not been on our side, when men rose up against us;

2 They had swallowed us up quick: when they were so wrathfully displeased at us.

3 Yea, the waters had drowned us: and the stream had gone over our soul.

4 The deep waters of the proud: had gone over our soul.

5 But praised be the Lord: who hath not given us over for a prey unto their teeth..

6 Our soul is escaped, even as a bird out of the snare of the fowler: the snare is broken, and we are delivered.

7 Our help standeth in the name of the Lord: who hath made heaven and earth.

PSALM 125

THEY that put their trust in the Lord shall be even as the mount Sion: which cannot be removed, but standeth fast forever.

2 The hills stand about Jerusalem: even so standeth the Lord round about his people, from this time forth forevermore.

3 For the rod of the ungodly shall not rest upon the lot of the righteous: lest the righteous put their hand unto wickedness.

4 Do well, O Lord: unto those that are good and true of heart.

5 As for such as turn back unto their own wickedness: the Lord shall lead them forth with the evil-doers; but peace shall be upon Israel.

PSALM 126

HEN the Lord turned again the captivity of Sion: then were we like unto them that dream.

2 Then was our mouth filled with laughter: and our tongue with joy.

3 Then said they among the heathen: The Lord hath done great things for them.

4 Yea, the Lord hath done great things for us: whereof we rejoice.

5 Turn our captivity, O Lord: as the rivers in the south.

6 They that sow in tears: shall reap in joy.

7 He that now goeth on his way weeping, and beareth forth good seed: shall doubtless come again with joy, and bring his sheaves with him.

PSALM 127

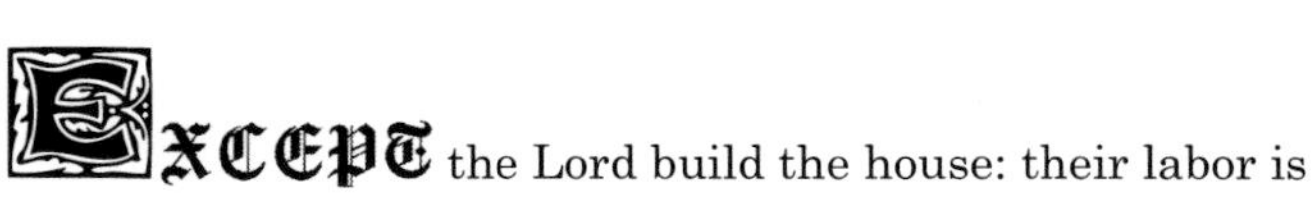

Except the Lord build the house: their labor is but lost that build it.

2 Except the Lord keep the city: the watchman waketh but in vain.

3 It is but lost labor that ye haste to rise up early, and so late take rest, and eat the bread of carefulness: for so he giveth his beloved sleep.

4 Lo, children and the fruit of the womb: are an heritage and gift that cometh of the Lord.

5 Like as the arrows in the hands of the giant: even so are the young children.

6 Happy is the man that hath his quiver full of them: they shall not be ashamed when they speak with their enemies in the gate.

PSALM 128

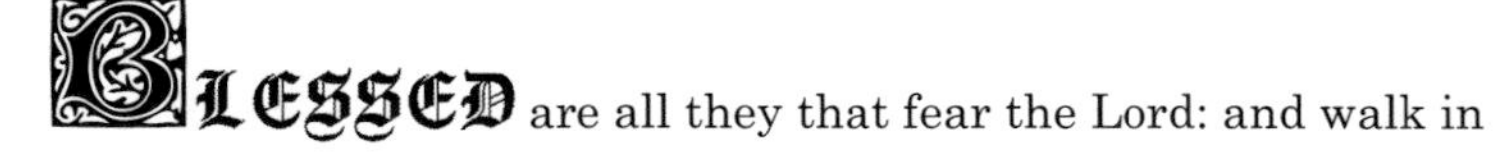

Blessed are all they that fear the Lord: and walk in his ways.

2 For thou shalt eat the labors of thine hands: O well shall it be with thee, and happy shalt thou be.

3 Thy wife shall be as the fruitful vine: upon the walls of thine house;

4 Thy children like olive-branches: round about thy table.

5 Lo, thus shall the man be blessed: that feareth the Lord.

6 The Lord from out of Sion shall so bless thee: that thou shalt see Jerusalem in prosperity all thy life long;

7 Yea, that thou shalt see thy children's children: and peace upon Israel.

PSALM 130

UT of the deep have I called unto thee, O Lord:

Lord, hear my voice.
2 O let thine ears consider well: the voice of my complaint.
3 If thou, Lord, wilt be extreme to mark what is done amiss: O Lord, who may abide it?
4 But there is mercy with thee: therefore shalt thou be feared.
5 I look for the Lord; my soul doth wait for him: in his word is my trust.
6 My soul fleeth unto the Lord before the morning watch: I say, before the morning watch.
7 O Israel, trust in the Lord: for with the Lord there is mercy, and with him is plenteous redemption.
8 And he shall redeem Israel: from all his sins.

PSALM 131

ORD, I am not high-minded: I have no proud looks.

2 I do not exercise myself in great matters: which are too high for me.
3 But I refrain my soul, and keep it low, like as a child that is weaned from his mother: yea, my soul is even as a weaned child.
4 O Israel, trust in the Lord: from this time forth forevermore.

PSALM 133

EHOLD, how good and joyful a thing it is: brethren, to dwell together in unity.
2 It is like the precious ointment upon the head, that ran down unto the beard: even unto Aaron's beard, and went down to the skirts of his clothing.
3 Like as the dew of Hermon: which fell upon the hill of Sion.
4 For there the Lord promised his blessing: and life forevermore.

PSALM 135

RAISE the Lord, laud ye the Name of the Lord: O ye servants of the Lord;
2 Ye that stand in the house of the Lord: in the courts of the house of our God.
3 O praise the Lord, for the Lord is gracious: O sing praises unto his Name, for it is lovely.
4 For why? the Lord hath chosen Jacob unto himself: and Israel for his own possession.
5 For I know that the Lord is great: and that our Lord is above all gods.
6 Whatsoever the Lord pleased, that he did in heaven, and in earth: and in the sea, and in all deep places.
7 He bringeth forth the clouds from the ends of the world: and sendeth forth lightnings with the rain, bringing the winds out of his treasures.
8 Thy Name, O Lord, endureth forever: so doth thy memorial, O Lord, from one generation to another.
9 For the Lord will avenge his people: and be gracious unto his servants.
10 Praise the Lord, ye house of Israel: praise the

Lord, ye house of Aaron.
11 Praise the Lord, ye house of Levi: ye that fear the Lord, praise the Lord.
12 Praised be the Lord out of Sion: who dwelleth at Jerusalem.

PSALM 138

 WILL give thanks unto thee, O Lord, with my whole heart: even before the gods will I sing praises unto thee.
2 I will worship toward thy holy temple, and praise thy Name, because of thy lovingkindness and truth: for thou hast magnified thy Name, and thy word, above all things.
3 When I called upon thee, thou heardest me: and enduedst my soul with much strength.
4 All the kings of the earth shall praise thee, O Lord: when they hear the words of thy mouth.
5 Yea,, they shall sing in the ways of the Lord: that great is the glory of the Lord.
6 For though the Lord be high, yet hath he respect unto the lowly: as for the proud, he beholdeth them afar off.
7 Though I walk in the midst of trouble, yet shalt thou refresh me: thou shalt stretch forth thy hand upon the furiousness of mine enemies, and thy right hand shall save me.
8 The Lord shall make good his lovingkindness toward me: yea, thy 'mercy, O Lord, endureth forever; forsake not then the works of thine own hands.

PSALM 139

 LORD, thou hast searched me out, and known me: thou knowest my down-sitting and mine up-rising; thou understandest my thoughts long before.

2 Thou art about my path, and about my bed: and spiest out all my ways.

3 For lo, there is not a word in my tongue: but thou, O Lord, knowest it altogether.

4 Thou hast fashioned me behind and before: and laid thine hand upon me.

5 Such knowledge is too wonderful and excellent for me: I cannot attain unto it.

6 Whither shall I go then from thy Spirit: or whither shall I go then from thy presence?

7 If I climb up into heaven, thou art there: if I go down to hell, thou art there also.

8 If I take the wings of the morning: and remain in the uttermost parts of the sea;

9 Even there also shall thy hand lead me: and thy right hand shall hold me.

10 If I say, Peradventure the darkness shall cover me: then shall my night be turned into day.

11 Yea, the darkness is no darkness with thee, but the night is as clear as the day: the darkness and light to thee are both alike.

12 For my reins are thine: thou hast covered me in my mother's womb.

13 I will give thanks unto thee, for I am fearfully and wonderfully made: marvelous are thy works; and that my soul knoweth right well.

14 My substance was not hid from thee when I was made in secret: and curiously wrought in the lowest parts of the earth.

15 Thine eyes did see my substance yet being imperfect: and in thy book were all my members written;

16 Which day by day were fashioned: when as yet there was none of them.

17 How dear are thy counsels unto me, O God: O how great is the sum of them!
18 If I should count them, they are more in number than the sand: when I awake, I am present with thee.
19 Try me, O God, and seek the ground of my heart: prove me, and examine my thoughts.
20 Look well if there be any way of wickedness in me: and lead me in the way everlasting.

PSALM 141

LORD, I call upon thee, haste thee unto me: and consider my voice when I cry unto thee.
2 Let my prayer be set forth in thy sight as the incense: and the lifting up of my hands as the evening sacrifice.
3 Set a watch, O Lord, before my mouth: and keep the door of my lips.
4 O let not mine heart be inclined to any evil thing: let me not be occupied in ungodly works with the men that work wickedness; and let me not eat of their dainties.
5 Let the righteous rather smite me friendly: and reprove me.
6 Mine eyes look unto thee, O Lord God: in thee is- my trust; O cast not out my soul.
7 Keep me from the snare that they have laid for me: and from the traps of the wicked doers.

PSALM 142

 CRIED unto the Lord with my voice: yea, even unto the Lord did I make my supplication.
2 I poured out my complaints before him: and

showed him of my trouble.
3 When my spirit was in heaviness, thou knewest my path: in the way wherein I walked have they secretly laid a snare for me.
4 I looked also upon my right hand: and saw there was no man that would know me.
5 I had no place to flee unto: and no man cared for my soul.
6 I cried unto thee, O Lord, and said: Thou art my hope and my portion in the land of the living.
7 Consider my complaint: for I am brought very low.
8 O deliver me from my persecutors: for they are too strong for me.
9 Bring my soul out of prison, that I may give thanks unto thy Name: which thing if thou wilt grant me, then shall the righteous resort unto my company.

PSALM 143

EAR my prayer, O Lord, and consider my desire: hearken unto me, for thy truth and righteousness' sake.
2 And enter not into judgment with thy servant: for in thy sight shall no man living be justified.
3 My spirit is vexed within me: and my heart within me is desolate.
4 Yet do I remember the time past; I muse upon all thy works: yea, I exercise myself in the works of thy hands.
5 I stretch forth my hands unto thee: my soul gaspeth unto thee as a thirsty land.
6 Hear me, O Lord, and that soon, for my spirit waxeth faint: hide not thy face from me, lest I be like unto them that go down into the pit.
7 O let me hear thy lovingkindness betimes in the

morning; for in thee is my trust: show thou me the way that I should walk in; for I lift up my soul unto thee.

8 Deliver me, O Lord, from mine enemies: for I flee unto thee to hide me.

9 Teach me to do the thing that pleaseth thee; for thou art my God: let thy loving Spirit lead me forth into the land of righteousness.

10 Quicken me, O Lord, for thy Name's sake: and for thy righteousness' sake bring my soul out of trouble.

PSALM 144

BLESSED be the Lord my strength: who teacheth my hands to war, and my fingers to fight;

2 My hope and my fortress, my castle and deliverer, my defender, in whom I trust: who subdueth my people that is under me.

3 Lord, what is man, that thou hast such respect unto him: or the son of man, that thou so regardest him?

4 Man is like a thing of nought: his time passeth away like a shadow.

5 Bow thy heavens, O Lord, and come down: touch the mountains, and they shall smoke.

6 Cast forth thy lightning, and tear them: shoot out thine arrows, and consume them.

7 Send down thine hand from above: deliver me, and take me out of the great waters, from the hand of strange children;

8 Whose mouth talketh of vanity: and their right hand is a right hand of wickedness.

9 I will sing a new song unto thee, O God: thou dost give victory unto kings, and hast delivered David thy servant from the peril of the sword.

10 Save me, and deliver me from the hand of strange children: whose mouth talketh of vanity, and their right hand is a right hand of iniquity;
11 That our sons may grow up as the young plants: and our daughters may be as the polished corners of the temple;
12 That our garners may be full and plenteous with all manner of store: that our sheep may bring forth thousands and ten thousands in our streets;
13 That our oxen may be strong to labor, that there may be no decay: no leading into captivity, and no complaining in our streets.
14 Happy are the people that are in such a case: yea, blessed are the people who have the Lord for their God.

PSALM 145

 WILL magnify thee, O God, my King: and I will praise thy Name forever and ever.
2 Every day will I give thanks unto thee: and praise thy Name forever and ever.
3 Great is the Lord and marvelous, worthy to be praised: there is no end of his greatness.
4 One generation shall praise thy works unto another: and declare thy power.
5 As for me, I will be talking of thy worship: thy glory, thy praise, and thy wondrous works.
6 So that men shall speak of the might of thy marvellous acts: and I will also tell of thy greatness.
7 The memorial of thine abundant kindness shall be showed: and men shall sing of thy righteousness.
8 The Lord is gracious and merciful: long-suffering, and of great goodness.
9 The Lord is loving unto every man: and his mercy is over all his works.

10 All thy works praise thee, O Lord: and thy saints give thanks unto thee.
1 1 They show the glory of thy kingdom: and talk of thy power.
12 That thy power, thy glory, and the mightiness of thy kingdom: might be known unto men.
1 3 Thy kingdom is an everlasting kingdom: and thy dominion endureth throughout all ages.
14 The Lord upholdeth all such as fall: and lifteth up all those that are bowed down.
15 The eyes of all wait upon thee, O Lord: and thou givest them their meat in due season.
16 Thou openest thine hand: and fillest all things living with plenteousness.
17 The Lord is righteous in all his ways: and holy in all his works.
18 The Lord is nigh unto all them that call upon him: yea, all such as call upon him faithfully.
19 He will fulfil the desire of them that fear him: he also will hear their cry, and will help them.
20 The Lord preserveth all them that love him: but all the ungodly will he destroy.
21 My mouth shall speak the praise of the Lord: and let all flesh give thanks unto his holy Name for ever and ever.

PSALM 146

PRAISE the Lord, O my soul; while I live will I praise the Lord: yea, as long as I have any being, I will sing praises unto my God.
2 O put not your trust in princes, nor in any child of man: for there is no help in them.
3 For when the breath of man goeth forth, he re-turneth to his earth: and then all his thoughts perish.
4 Blessed is he that hath the God of Jacob for his

help: and whose hope is in the Lord his God;
5 Who made heaven and earth, the sea, and all that therein is: who keepeth his promise forever;
6 Who helpeth them to right that suffer wrong: who feedeth the hungry.
7 The Lord looseth men out of prison: the Lord giveth sight to the blind.
8 The Lord helpeth them that are fallen: the Lord careth for the righteous.
9 The Lord careth for the strangers; he defendeth the fatherless and widow: as for the way of the ungodly, he turneth it upside down.
10 The Lord thy God, O Sion, shall be King for evermore: and throughout all generations.

PSALM 147

 PRAISE the Lord, for it is a good thing to sing praises unto our God: yea, a joyful and a pleasant thing it is to be thankful.
2 The Lord doth build up Jerusalem: and gather together the outcasts of Israel.
3 He healeth those that are broken in heart: and giveth medicine to heal their sickness.
4 He telleth the number of the stars; and calleth them all by their names.
5 Great is our Lord, and great is his power: yea, and his wisdom is infinite.
6 The Lord setteth up the meek: and bringeth the ungodly down to the ground.
7 O sing unto the Lord with thanksgiving: sing praises unto our God;
8 Who covereth the heaven with clouds, and prepareth rain for the earth: and maketh the grass to grow upon the mountains, and herb for the use of men.
9 Who giveth fodder unto the cattle: and feedeth

the young ravens that call upon him.
10 He hath no pleasure in the strength of a horse: neither delighteth he in any man's legs.
11 But the Lord's delight is in them that fear him: and put their trust in his mercy.
12 Praise the Lord, O Jerusalem: praise thy God, O Sion.
13 For he hath made fast the bars of thy gates: and hath blessed thy children within thee.
14 He maketh peace in thy borders: and filleth thee with the flour of wheat.
15 He sendeth forth his commandment upon the earth: and his word runneth very swiftly.
16 He giveth snow like wool: and scattereth the hoar-frost like ashes.
17 He casteth forth his ice like morsels: who is able to abide his frost?
18 He sendeth out his word, and melteth them: he bloweth with his wind, and the waters flow.
19 He showeth his word unto Jacob: his statutes and ordinances unto Israel.
20 He hath not dealt so with any nation: neither have the heathen knowledge of his laws.

PSALM 148

 PRAISE the Lord of heaven: praise him in the height.
2 Praise him, all ye angels of his: praise him, all his host.
3 Praise him, sun and moon: praise him, all ye stars and light.
4 Praise him, all ye heavens: and ye waters that are above the heavens.
5 Let them praise the Name of the Lord: for he spake the word, and they were made; he commanded,

and they were created.
6 He hath established them forever and ever: he hath given them a law which shall not be broken.
7 Praise the Lord upon earth: ye dragons, and all deeps;
8 Fire and hail, snow and vapors: wind and storm, fulfilling his word;
9 Mountains and hills: fruitful trees and all cedars;
10 Beasts and all cattle: creeping things and feathered fowls;
1 1 Kings of the earth and all people: princes and all judges of the world;
12 Young men and maidens, old men and children, praise the Name of the Lord: for his Name only is excellent, and his praise above heaven and earth.
13 He shall exalt the horn of his people, all his saints shall praise him: even the children of Israel, even the people that serveth him.

PSALM 150

 PRAISE God in his holiness: praise him in the firmament of his power.
2 Praise him in his noble acts: praise him according to his excellent greatness.
3 Let everything that hath breath: praise the Lord.

About the Author

John Wesley, the founder of Methodism, was born on June 28, 1703. He was an ordained priest in the Church of England and he sought religious renewal within the Church. The religious societies he founded, originally called "Methodist" by his detractors due to Wesley's methodical approach to Christian living, sparked a worldwide movement. Wesley was responsible for the resurgence of conservative Arminian theology in 18th century England. Wesley's theology not only had an immense impact on the Methodist movement, but his influence also helped mold the Holiness and Pentecostal movements.

List of Illustrations

Made in United States
North Haven, CT
29 April 2023

36038358R00286